Level 1 • Part 2
Integrated Chinese
中文听说读写

TEXTBOOK Simplified Characters

Third Edition

THIRD EDITION BY

Yuehua Liu and Tao-chung Yao
Nyan-Ping Bi, Liangyan Ge, Yaohua Shi

ORIGINAL EDITION BY

Tao-chung Yao and Yuehua Liu
Liangyan Ge, Yea-fen Chen, Nyan-Ping Bi,
Xiaojun Wang, Yaohua Shi

CHENG & TSUI COMPANY

Boston

Third Edition / seventh printing July 2015

20 19 18 17 16 15   7 8 9 10 11 12

Published by
Cheng & Tsui Company, Inc.
25 West Street
Boston, MA 02111-1213 USA
Fax (617) 426-3669
www.cheng-tsui.com
"Bringing Asia to the World"™
ISBN 978-0-88727-671-2— ISBN 978-0-88727-670-5 (pbk.)

Cover Design: studioradia.com

Cover Photographs: Man with map © Getty Images; Shanghai skyline © David Pedre/iStockphoto; Building with masks © Wu Jie; Night market © Andrew Buko. Used by permission.

Interior Design: Wanda España, Wee Design

Illustrations: 洋洋兔动漫

Tai Chi photo, p. 252: Jgremillot

Great Wall photo (left), p. 261: Marianna Natale

Great Wall photo (right), p. 261: Brian Snelson

Library of Congress Cataloging-in-Publication Data

Integrated Chinese: textbook traditional characters = [Zhong wen ting shuo du xie]. Level 1. Part 2 / Yuehua Liu ... [et al.] — 3rd ed.
    p. cm.
  Includes indexes.
  ISBN 978-0-88727-673-6 (trad. hbk.) — ISBN 978-0-88727-672-9 (trad. pbk.) — ISBN 978-0-88727-671-2 (simp. hbk.) — ISBN 978-0-88727-670-5 (simp. pbk.)
  1. Chinese language—Textbooks for foreign speakers—English. I. Liu, Yuehua. II. Title: Zhong wen ting shuo du xie.

  PL1129.E5I683 2008
    495.1'82421—dc22

                    2008062321

The *Integrated Chinese* series includes books, workbooks, character workbooks, audio products, multimedia products, teacher's resources, and more. Visit **www.cheng-tsui.com** for more information on the other components of *Integrated Chinese*.

Printed in Canada

Expand your *Integrated Chinese* Study

with support for the whole series

Textbooks, Workbooks, Character Workbooks, Teacher's Handbooks, and **Audio CDs** work together as a comprehensive curriculum.

Online Workbooks, eTextbooks, BuilderCards, and **Textbook DVDs for all levels** take study further and add flexibility to the classroom.

INTEGRATED CHINESE COMPANION WEBSITE

More supplements for students, more support for teachers!

www.cheng-tsui.com/integratedchinese

Kù Chinese

eFlashcards

STUDENTS Sharpen your vocabulary recognition and pronunciation with new *eFlashcards* and learn fun idioms and slang with the video series *Kù Chinese*.

TEACHERS Enhance your classroom instruction with *Video Activity Worksheets* (available for all *Integrated Chinese* DVDs), sentence pattern drills, teacher-generated PowerPoints®, and additional tools for testing and assessment.

Visit www.cheng-tsui.com or call 1-800-554-1963 for more information about other supplementary materials, such as graded readers, listening comprehension workbooks, character guides, and reference materials.

Lesson 11: Talking about the Weather   1

Lesson 12: Dining   31

Learning Objectives

Relate and Get Ready

Lesson 13: Asking Directions   63

Lesson 14: Birthday Party   101

Lesson 15: Seeing a Doctor   133

That's How the Chinese Say It! (Lesson 11–Lesson 15)   **165**

Lesson 16: Dating   **169**

Lesson 17: Renting an Apartment   199

Lesson 18: Sports   227

Lesson 19: Travel   257

More Companions for Integrated Chinese

The Way of Chinese Characters
The Origins of 450 Essential Words

By Jianhsin Wu, Illustrated by Chen Zheng, Chen Tian

Learn characters through a holistic approach.

Making Connections
Enhance Your Listening Comprehension in Chinese

By Madeline K. Spring

Improve listening skills using everyday conversations.

Tales and Traditions
Readings in Chinese Literature Series

Compiled by Yun Xiao, et al.

Read level-appropriate excerpts from the Chinese folk and literary canon.

Readings in Chinese Culture Series

By Qun Ao, Weijia Huang

Increase reading and cultural proficiency with level-appropriate essays about Chinese culture.

Integrated Chinese BuilderCards
Much More than Vocabulary Flashcards

By Song Jiang, Haidan Wang

Reinforce and build vocabulary with flashcards.

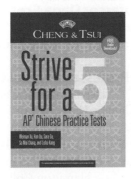

Strive for a 5
AP* Chinese Practice Tests

By Weiman Xu, Han Qu, Sara Gu, So Mui Chang, Lisha Kang

Prepare for the AP exam with eight practice tests, tips, and more.

Cheng & Tsui Chinese Character Dictionary
A Guide to the 2000 Most Frequently Used Characters

Edited by Wang Huidi

Master the 2,000 most-used characters.

Cheng & Tsui Chinese Measure Word Dictionary
A Chinese-English English-Chinese Usage Guide

Compiled by Jiqing Fang, Michael Connelly

Speak and write polished Chinese using this must-have reference.

Visit **www.cheng-tsui.com** to view samples, place orders, and browse other language-learning materials.

*Advanced Placement and AP are registered trademarks of the College Board, which was not involved in the production of, and does not endorse, this product.

Publisher's Note

When *Integrated Chinese* was first published in 1997, it set a new standard with its focus on the development and integration of the four language skills (listening, speaking, reading, and writing). Today, to further enrich the learning experience of the many users of *Integrated Chinese* worldwide, Cheng & Tsui is pleased to offer this revised and updated third edition of *Integrated Chinese*. We would like to thank the many teachers and students who, by offering their valuable insights and suggestions, have helped *Integrated Chinese* evolve and keep pace with the many positive changes in the field of Chinese language instruction. *Integrated Chinese* continues to offer comprehensive language instruction, with many new features and useful shared resources available on our website at **www.cheng-tsui.com**.

The Cheng & Tsui Chinese Language Series is designed to publish and widely distribute quality language learning materials created by leading instructors from around the world. We welcome readers' comments and suggestions concerning the publications in this series. Please contact the following members of our Editorial Board, in care of our Editorial Department (e-mail: editor@cheng-tsui.com).

Preface to the Third Edition

It has been over ten years since *Integrated Chinese* (IC) came into existence in 1997. During these years, amid all the historical changes that took place in China and the rest of the world, the demand for Chinese language teaching-learning materials has been growing dramatically. We are greatly encouraged by the fact that *IC* not only has been a widely used textbook at the college level all over the United States and beyond, but also has become increasingly popular with advanced language students at high schools. Over the years, regular feedback from the users of *IC*, both students and teachers, has greatly facilitated our repeated revisions of the series. Following its second edition published in 2005 that featured relatively minor changes and adjustments, the third edition is the result of a much more extensive revision.

Changes in the Third Edition

Manageable Number of Lessons

Level 1 now contains 10 lessons in Part 1 and 10 lessons in Part 2 for maximum flexibility. Based on the reports from many teachers that they could not finish all the lessons in the Level 1 volumes within one academic year, we have, for the third edition, eliminated the chapters "At the Library" and "At the Post Office," as the language contents in these chapters have become somewhat obsolete. The chapter "Hometown" has also been removed, but part of its content has been incorporated into other chapters.

Revised Storyline

In the present edition, a new, connected storyline about a diverse group of students strings together all the dialogues and narratives in the lessons throughout Level 1. The relationships among the main characters are more carefully scripted. We want the students to get to know the characters well and to find out how things develop among them. We hope that, by getting to know more about each cast member, the students will be more involved in the process of learning the language.

Current Vocabulary

As in the earlier editions, the third edition makes a special effort to reflect students' life. Additionally, we have updated some of the vocabulary items and expressions in the hope of keeping pace with the evolution of contemporary Chinese and enhancing students' ability to communicate. In the meantime, we have deleted some words and expressions that are of relatively lower frequencies of usage. As a result, the total number of vocabulary items for the series is moderately reduced. The grammar sequence, however, remains fundamentally unchanged.

Clear Learning Objectives and Engaging Learner-Centered Approach

Ever since its inception in 1997, *IC* has been a communication-oriented language textbook which also aims at laying a solid foundation in language form and accuracy for students. The third edition holds fast to that pedagogic philosophy. On top of that, it has adopted a task-based teaching approach, which is intended to intensify students' motivation and heighten their awareness of the learning objectives in each chapter. Each lesson includes Learning Objectives and Relate and Get Ready questions at the beginning to focus students' study. At the end of each lesson, there is a Progress Checklist to be used by students in self-testing their fulfillment of the learning objectives.

It is our hope that these changes will enable students to learn Chinese in a more efficient and pragmatic way and develop their language proficiency and problem-solving abilities in real-life situations. In their feedback to us, many users of previous editions of *IC* noted that, more than many other Chinese language textbooks, *IC* was effective in developing students' abilities to use the language. While making all the efforts to retain that merit in the new edition, we have endeavored to place language acquisition in a real-world context and make *IC* all the more conducive to active use of the language in the classroom and, more importantly, beyond it.

Contextualized Grammar and Interactive Language Practice

The somewhat mechanical drills on sentence patterns in the earlier editions are now replaced by Language Practice exercises based on simulated real-life situations. In particular, we have increased the number of interactive exercises and exercises that serve the purpose of training students' abilities in oral communication and discourse formation. Similar changes are also to be seen in the *Integrated Chinese* workbook, which offers new exercises that are more distinctly communication-oriented and more closely aligned with the learning objectives of each chapter. The exercises in the workbook cover the three modes of communication as explained in the "Standards for Foreign Language Learning in the 21st Century": interpretive, interpersonal and presentational. To help the user locate different types of exercises, we have labeled the workbook exercises in terms of the three communication modes.

Linguistically and Thematically Appropriate Cultural Information and Authentic Materials

In comparison with the earlier editions, there is more cultural information in the third edition. The revised texts provide a broader perspective on Chinese culture, and important cultural features and topics are discussed in the "Culture Highlights." In the meantime, more up-to-date language ingredients, such as authentic linguistic materials, new realia, and new illustrations, are introduced with a view towards reflecting cultural life in the dynamic and rapidly changing contemporary China. We believe that language is a carrier of culture and a second/foreign language is acquired most efficiently in its native cultural setting. Based on that conviction, we have attempted to offer both linguistic and cultural information in a coherent, consistent manner and simulate a Chinese cultural environment in our texts, especially those that are set in China.

All-New, Colorful, and User-Friendly Design

Where design and layout are concerned, the third edition represents a significant improvement. We have taken full advantage of colors to highlight different components of each chapter, and have brought in brand-new illustrations and photos to complement the content of the text. The book has also been thoroughly redesigned for optimal ease of use.

Updated Audio Recordings

Throughout this book, an audio CD icon 💿 appears next to the main texts, vocabulary, and pronunciation exercises. This symbol indicates the presence of audio recordings, which are available on the companion audio CD set.

Acknowledgments

During the course of preparing for the third edition, we accumulated more academic and intellectual debts than any acknowledgment can possibly repay. We wish to express our deep gratitude to all those who helped us in so many different ways. In particular, our heartfelt thanks go to the editor, Professor Zheng-sheng Zhang of San Diego State University; colleagues and friends at Beijing Language and Culture University; and Ms. Laurel Damashek at Cheng & Tsui.

As authors, we take great pleasure in the contributions that *IC* has made to Chinese teaching and learning over the past ten years, and we also feel the weight of responsibility. In retrospect, *IC* has traversed a long way since its earliest incarnation, yet we know its improvement will not end with the present edition. We promise to renew our efforts in the future, and we expect to continue to benefit from the invaluable comments and suggestions we receive from the users.

An Overview of the New Features of the Third Edition

Chapter Opener

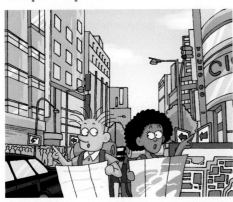

Each lesson opens with an illustration that highlights the theme for the lesson.

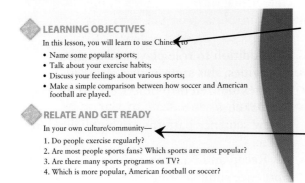

LEARNING OBJECTIVES

In this lesson, you will learn to use Chinese to

- Name some popular sports;
- Talk about your exercise habits;
- Discuss your feelings about various sports;
- Make a simple comparison between how soccer and American football are played.

RELATE AND GET READY

In your own culture/community—

1. Do people exercise regularly?
2. Are most people sports fans? Which sports are most popular?
3. Are there many sports programs on TV?
4. Which is more popular, American football or soccer?

Learning Objectives for every lesson help students focus their study and envision what they will have accomplished at the end of the lesson.
The self-reflective questions in **Relate and Get Ready** help students to reflect on similarities and differences between their native language and culture and Chinese language and culture.

Dialogue Design

Each dialogue or narrative begins with an illustration depicting the scene. For the main characters, instead of the characters' names, their avatar icons appear in the dialogue. This helps the students get acquainted with the characters more quickly.

Dialogue II: Eating in a Cafeteria

（今天是星期四，学生餐厅有中国菜，师傅是上海人。）

Language Notes and Grammar Callouts

（李友给王朋打电话。）

王朋，你做什么呢①？

我看书呢。

今天高小音过生日①，晚上我们在她家开舞会，你能去吗？

能去。几点？

LANGUAGE NOTES

❶ Apart from 过生日 (guò shēngrì, to celebrate one's birthday), the verb 过 (guò, to live [a life]; to observe [a holiday]; to celebrate [a festival]) appears in many other expressions such as 过年 (guò nián, to celebrate the New Year), 过节 (guò jié, to celebrate a festival), and 过日子 (guò rìzi, to live one's life; to live from day to day).

The **Language Notes** are clearly marked and numbered in green circles, and placed next to the dialogue for ease of reference. The **grammar points** are highlighted and numbered in red to draw the students' attention to the language forms covered in the Grammar section of each lesson.

Vocabulary Section

VOCABULARY

11.	狗	gǒu	n	dog
12.	脸	liǎn	n	face
13.	圆	yuán	adj	round
14.	眼睛	yǎnjing	n	eye
15.	鼻子	bízi	n	nose
16.	嘴	zuǐ	n	mouth
17.	像	xiàng	v	to be like; to look like; to take after
18.	长大	zhǎng dà	vc	to grow up
19.	一定	yídìng	adj/adv	certain(ly); definite(ly)
20.	蛋糕	dàngāo	n	cake
21.	最	zuì	adv	most, (of superlative degree) -est

Proper Nouns

| 22. | 海伦 | Hǎilún | | Helen |
| 23. | 汤姆 | Tāngmǔ | | Tom |

A low-frequency character that the teacher may decide not to have the students practice writing is shown in a shaded gray color.

Language Practice

A. Rules Are Rules

Parents and teachers always seem to have more rules for their children and students. Work with a partner and figure out what the rules are, based on the visuals.

EXAMPLE:

做功课的时候，
不准/不能看电视。

Zuò gōngkè de shíhou,
bù zhǔn/bù néng kàn diànshì.

1.

In addition to role plays and partner activities, this section also includes contextualized drill practice with the help of visual cues.
New sentence patterns are highlighted in blue.
A **Recap and Narrate** activity lets students practice summarizing the dialogues in their own words.

Customized Learning: How About You?

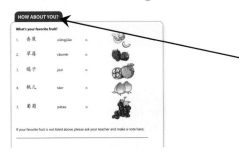

Beginning students need not be overwhelmed by additional vocabulary items that do not seem to be very useful or relevant to them. However, they should be given opportunities to select and learn words and phrases that relate to their own interests and experiences. **How About You?** provides this personalized vocabulary space.

Culture Highlights

A theatrical scene from Beijing Opera

Photos or other authentic materials accompany the culture notes.

Self-Reflection: Progress Checklist

It's important for students to feel engaged and responsible for their own learning. At the end of each lesson, students are asked to check on their learning progress and evaluate whether they have achieved the learning objectives.

Functional Expressions: That's How the Chinese Say It!

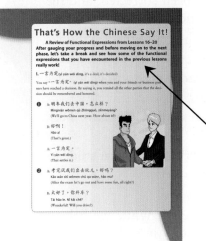

After every five lessons, **That's How the Chinese Say It** provides a review of the functional expressions that have appeared in the texts. It includes additional linguistic and cultural contexts to demonstrate the use of these expressions.

Preface to the Second Edition

The *Integrated Chinese* series is an acclaimed, best-selling introductory course in Mandarin Chinese. With its holistic, integrated focus on the four language skills of listening, speaking, reading, and writing, it teaches all the basics beginning and intermediate students need to function in Chinese. *Integrated Chinese* helps students understand how the Chinese language works grammatically, and how to use Chinese in real life.

The Chinese title of *Integrated Chinese*, which is simply 中文听说读写 (*Zhōngwén Tīng Shuō Dú Xiě*), reflects our belief that a healthy language program should be a well-balanced one. To ensure that students will be strong in all skills, and because we believe that each of the four skills needs special training, the exercises in the *Integrated Chinese* Workbooks are divided into four sections of listening, speaking, reading, and writing. Within each section, there are two types of exercises, namely, traditional exercises (such as fill-in-the-blank, sentence completion, translation, etc.) to help students build a solid foundation, and communication-oriented exercises to prepare students to face the real world.

How *Integrated Chinese* Has Evolved

Integrated Chinese (IC) began in 1993 as a set of course materials for beginning and intermediate Chinese courses taught at the East Asian Summer Language Institute's Chinese School at Indiana University. Since that time, it has become a widely used series of Chinese language textbooks in the United States and beyond. Teachers and students appreciate the fact that *IC*, with its focus on practical, everyday topics and its numerous and varied exercises, helps learners build a solid foundation in the Chinese language.

What's New in the Second Edition

Thanks to all those who have used *Integrated Chinese* and given us the benefit of their suggestions and comments, we have been able to produce a second edition that includes the following improvements:

▲ Typographical errors present in the first edition have been corrected, and the content has been carefully edited to ensure accuracy and minimize errors.

▲ The design has been revised and improved for easier use, and the Textbooks feature two colors.

▲ **Revised illustrations** and **new photos** provide the reader with visual images and relevant cultural information.

▲ Many **new culture notes** and examples of **functional expressions** have been added.

▲ **Grammar and phonetics explanations** have been rewritten in more student-friendly language.

▲ **Workbook listening and reading sections** have been revised.

▲ **A new flexibility for the teaching of characters** is offered. While we believe that students should learn to read all of the characters introduced in the lessons, we are aware that different Chinese programs have different needs. Some teachers may wish to limit the number of characters for which students have responsibility, especially in regards to writing requirements. To help such teachers, we have identified a number of lower-frequency Chinese characters and marked them with a pound sign (#) in the vocabulary lists. Teachers might choose to accept *pinyin* in place of these characters in homework and tests. The new edition adds flexibility in this regard.

▲ **The Level 1 Workbooks** have been reorganized. The Workbook exercises have been divided into two parts, with each part corresponding to one of the dialogues in each lesson. This arrangement will allow teachers to more easily teach the dialogues separately. They may wish to use the first two or three days of each lesson to focus on the first dialogue, and have students complete the exercises for the first dialogue. Then, they can proceed with the second dialogue, and have students complete the exercises for the second dialogue. Teachers may also wish to give separate quizzes on the vocabulary associated with each dialogue, thus reducing the number of new words students need to memorize at any one time.

▲ **Level 2 offers full text in simplified and traditional characters.** The original Level 2 Textbook and Workbook, which were intended to be used by both traditional- and simplified-character learners, contained sections in which only the traditional characters were given. This was of course problematic for students who were principally interested in learning simplified characters. This difficulty has been resolved in the new edition, as we now provide both traditional and simplified characters for every Chinese sentence in both the Textbook and the Workbook.

Basic Organizational Principles

In recent years, a very important fact has been recognized by the field of language teaching: the ultimate goal of learning a language is to communicate in that language.

Integrated Chinese is a set of materials that gives students grammatical tools and also prepares them to function in a Chinese language environment. The materials cover two years of instruction, with smooth transitions from one level to the next. They first cover everyday life topics and gradually move to more abstract subject matter. The materials are not limited to one method or one approach, but instead they blend several teaching approaches that can produce good results. Here are some of the features of *Integrated Chinese* which make it different from other Chinese language textbooks:

Integrating Pedagogical and Authentic Materials

All of the materials are graded in *Integrated Chinese*. We believe that students can grasp the materials better if they learn simple and easy-to-control language items before the more difficult or complicated ones. We also believe that students should be taught some authentic materials even in the first year of language instruction. Therefore, most of the pedagogical materials are actually simulated authentic materials. Real authentic materials (written by native Chinese speakers for native Chinese speakers) are incorporated in the lessons when appropriate.

Integrating Written Style and Spoken Style

One way to measure a person's Chinese proficiency is to see if s/he can handle the "written style" (书面语, shūmiànyǔ) with ease. The "written style" language is more formal and literal than the "spoken style" (口语, kǒuyǔ); however, it is also widely used in news broadcasts and formal speeches. Inaddition to "spoken style" Chinese, basic "written style" expressions are gradually introduced in *Integrated Chinese*.

Integrating Traditional and Simplified Characters

We believe that students should learn to handle Chinese language materials in both the traditional and the simplified forms. However, we also realize that it could be rather confusing and overwhelming to teach students both the traditional and the simplified forms from day one. A reasonable solution to this problem is for the student to concentrate on one form, either traditional or simplified, at the first level, and to acquire the other form during the second level. Therefore, for Level 1, *Integrated Chinese* offers two editions of the Textbooks and the Workbooks, one using traditional characters and one using simplified characters, to meet different needs.

We believe that by the second year of studying Chinese, all students should be taught to read both traditional and simplified characters. Therefore, the text of each lesson in Level 2 is shown in both forms, and the vocabulary list in each lesson also contains both forms. Considering that students in a second-year Chinese language class might come from different backgrounds and that some of them may have learned the traditional form and others the simplified form, students should be allowed to write in either traditional or simplified form. It is important that the learner write in one form only, and not a hybrid of both forms.

Integrating Teaching Approaches

Realizing that there is no one single teaching method which is adequate in training a student to be proficient in all four language skills, we employ a variety of teaching methods and approaches in *Integrated Chinese* to maximize the teaching results. In addition to the communicative approach, we also use traditional methods such as grammar-translation and direct method.

Online Supplements to Integrated Chinese

Integrated Chinese is not a set of course materials that employs printed volumes only. It is, rather, a network of teaching materials that exist in many forms. Teacher keys, software, and more are available from www.cheng-tsui.com, Cheng & Tsui Company's online site for downloadable and web-based resources. Please visit this site often for new offerings.

Other materials are available at the IC website, http://eall.hawaii.edu/yao/icusers/, which was set up by Ted Yao, one of the principal *Integrated Chinese* authors, when the original edition of *Integrated Chinese* was published. Thanks to the generosity of teachers and students who are willing to share their materials with other *Integrated Chinese* users, this website is constantly growing, and has many useful links and resources. The following are some of the materials created by the community of *Integrated Chinese* users that are available at the *Integrated Chinese* website.

Links to resources that show how to write Chinese characters, provide vocabulary practice, and more.

Pinyin supplements for all *Integrated Chinese* books. Especially useful for Chinese programs that do not teach Chinese characters.

Teacher's resources.

About the Format

Considering that many teachers might want to teach their students how to speak the language before teaching them how to read Chinese characters, we decided to place the *pinyin* text before the Chinese-character text in each of the eleven lessons of the Level 1 Part 1 Textbook.

Since *pinyin* is only a vehicle to help students learn the pronunciation of the Chinese language and is not a replacement for the Chinese writing system, it is important that students can read out loud in Chinese by looking at the Chinese text and not just the *pinyin* text. To train students to deal with the Chinese text directly without relying on *pinyin*, we moved the *pinyin* text to the end of each lesson in the Level 1 Part 2 Textbook. Students can refer to the *pinyin* text to verify a sound when necessary.

We are fully aware of the fact that no two Chinese language programs are identical and that each program has its own requirements. Some schools will cover a lot of material in one year while some others will cover considerably less. Trying to meet the needs of as many schools as possible, we decided to cover a wide range of material, both in terms of vocabulary and grammar, in *Integrated Chinese*. To facilitate oral practice and to allow students to communicate in real-life situations, many supplementary vocabulary items are added to each lesson. However, the characters in the supplementary vocabulary sections are not included in the Character Workbooks. In the Character Workbooks, each of the characters is given a frequency indicator based on the *Hànyǔ Pínlǜ Dà Cídiǎn* (汉语频率大辞典). Teachers can decide for themselves which characters must be learned.

Acknowledgments

Since publication of the first edition of *Integrated Chinese*, in 1997, many teachers and students have given us helpful comments and suggestions. We cannot list all of these individuals here, but we would like to reiterate our genuine appreciation for their help. We do wish to recognize the following individuals who have made recent contributions to the *Integrated Chinese* revision. We are indebted to Tim Richardson, Jeffrey Hayden, Ying Wang and Xianmin Liu for field-testing the new edition and sending us their comments and corrections. We would also like to thank Chengzhi Chu for letting us try out his "Chinese TA," a computer program designed for Chinese teachers to create and edit teaching materials. This software saved us many hours of work during the revision. Last, but not least, we want to thank Jim Dew for his superb professional editorial job, which enhanced both the content and the style of the new edition.

As much as we would like to eradicate all errors in the new edition, some will undoubtedly remain, so please continue to send your comments and corrections to editor@cheng-tsui.com, and accept our sincere thanks for your help.

Scope and Sequence

Lessons	Topics & Themes	Sections & Contexts	Learning Objectives & Functions
11	Talking about the Weather	1. Tomorrow's Weather Will Be Even Better! 2. The Weather Here Is Awful!	1. Employ basic terms for weather patterns and phenomena 2. Describe simple weather changes 3. Compare the weather of two places 4. Talk about what you may do in nice or bad weather 5. Present a simple weather forecast
12	Dining	1. Dining Out 2. Eating in a Cafeteria	1. Ask if there are seats available in a restaurant 2. Order Chinese dishes 3. Tell the waiter your dietary preferences and restrictions 4. Ask the restaurant to recommend dishes 5. Rush your order 6. Pay for your meal 7. Get the correct change after your payment
13	Asking Directions	1. Where Are You Off To? 2. Going to Chinatown	1. Ask for and give directions 2. Identify locations by using landmarks as references 3. Describe whether two places are close to or far away from one another 4. State where you are heading and the purpose of going there
14	Birthday Party	1. Let's Go to a Party! 2. Attending a Birthday Party	1. Ask a friend to go to a party with you 2. Suggest things to take to a get-together 3. Offer someone a ride and arrange a time and place to meet 4. Thank people for their gifts 5. Describe a duration of time 6. Talk about the year of your birth and your Chinese zodiac sign 7. Give a simple description of someone's facial features
15	Seeing a Doctor	1. My Stomachache Is Killing Me! 2. Allergies	1. Talk about basic symptoms of a cold 2. Describe common symptoms of allergies 3. Understand and repeat instructions on when and how often to take medications 4. Talk about why you do or don't want to see the doctor 5. Urge others to see a doctor when they are not feeling well
That's How the Chinese Say It!			Review functional expressions from Lessons 11–15

Forms & Accuracy	Culture Highlights
1. Comparative Sentences with 比 (bǐ) (I) 2. The Particle 了 (le) (III) 3. The Modal Verb 会 (huì, will) (II) 4. Adj+(一)点儿 ({yì} diǎnr) 5. The Adverb 又 (yòu, again) 6. Adj/V + 是 (shì) + Adj/V, + 可是/但是… (kěshì/dànshì…)	Temperature scale in China Climate conditions in China Western place names in Chinese Internet bars in China
1. 一…也/都…不/没… (yì…yě/dōu…bù/méi) 2. Adverb 多/少 (duō/shǎo) + V 3. 刚 (gāng) vs 刚才 (gāngcái) 4. Resultative Complements (I) 5. 好 (hǎo) as a Resultative Complement 6. Reduplication of Adjectives 7. The Verb 来 (lái)	Principal cuisines in China Staple foods on the Chinese menu Food culture in China Western fast food in China
1. Direction and Location Words 2. Comparative Sentences with 没(有) (méi{yǒu}) 3. 那么 (nàme) Indicating Degree 4. 到 (dào) + Place + 去 (qù) + Action 5. The Dynamic Particle 过 (guo) 6. Reduplication of Verbs 7. Resultative Complements (II) 8. 一…就… (yī…jiù…, as soon as…then…)	Greetings in Chinese Traffic lights in China Terms for spoken and written Chinese
1. 呢 (ne) Indicating an Action in Progress 2. Verbal Phrases and Subject-Predicate Phrases Used as Attributives 3. Time Duration 4. Sentences with 是…的 (shì…de) 5. 还 (hái, still) 6. 又…又… (yòu…yòu…, both…and…)	Dinner parties in China Singing karaoke in China Gift giving in China Chinese zodiac signs
1. 死 (sǐ) Indicating an Extreme Degree 2. Times of Actions 3. 起来 (qi lai) indicating the Beginning of an Action 4. 把 (bǎ) Construction (I) 5. The Preposition 对 (duì) 6. 越来越… (yuè lái yuè…) 7. 再说 (zàishuō)	Medicine in China Outpatient visits in China Medical insurance in China
1. 在 (zài, to exist) 2. Complimentary Expressions 3. 怎么了 (Zěnme le? What's the matter? What's wrong?) 4. 糟糕 (zāogāo, [It's] awful/What a mess)	

Lessons	Topics & Themes	Sections & Contexts	Learning Objectives & Functions
16	Dating	1. Seeing a Movie 2. Turning Down an Invitation	1. Describe how long you've known someone 2. Invite someone to go on a date 3. Make the necessary arrangements to go out with friends 4. Accept a date courteously 5. Decline a date politely 6. End a phone conversation without hurting the other person's feelings
17	Renting an Apartment	1. Finding a Better Place 2. Calling about an Apartment for Rent	1. Describe your current and ideal living quarters 2. Name common pieces of furniture 3. State how long you have been living at your current residence 4. Comment briefly on why a place is or isn't good for someone 5. Discuss and negotiate rent, utilities, and security deposits
18	Sports	1. My Gut Keeps Getting Bigger and Bigger! 2. Watching American Football	1. Name some popular sports 2. Talk about your exercise habits 3. Discuss your feelings about various sports 4. Make a simple comparison between how soccer and American football are played
19	Travel	1. Traveling to Beijing 2. Planning an Itinerary	1. Talk about your plans for summer vacation 2. Describe what kind of city Beijing is 3. Describe your travel itinerary 4. Ask for discounts, compare airfares and routes, and book an airplane ticket 5. Ask about seat assignments and request meal accommodations based on your dietary restrictions or preferences
20	At the Airport	1. Checking In at the Airport 2. Arriving in Beijing	1. Check in at the airport 2. Wish departing friends a safe journey and remind them to keep in touch 3. Greet guests at the airport 4. Compliment someone on his or her language ability 5. Ask about someone's health 6. Remind people to move on to the next event
That's How the Chinese Say It!			Review functional expressions from Lessons 16–20

Forms & Accuracy	Culture Highlights
1. Descriptive Complements (II) 2. Potential Complements 3. 就 (jiù) 4. Directional Complements (II)	Dating in China Valentine's Day in China Turning down a date the Chinese way Nightlife in China
1. Verb + 了 (le) + Numeral + Measure Word + Noun + 了 (le) 2. 连…都/也 (lián…dōu/yě) 3. Potential Complements with Verb + 不下 (bu xià) 4. 多 (duō) Indicating an Approximate Number 5. Question Pronouns with 都/也 (dōu/yě)	College dorms in China Renting an apartment in China Raising pets in China
1. Duration of Non-Action 2. 好/难 (hǎo/nán) + V 3. 下去 (xia qu) Indicating Continuation 4. Duration of Actions 5. The Particle 着 (zhe) 6. 被/叫/让 (bèi/jiào/ràng) in Passive-Voice Sentences	"Putting on weight" in China "Football" in China Morning exercises in China TV channels in China
1. 不得了 (bù déliǎo, extremely) 2. Question Pronouns as Indefinite References (Whoever, Whatever, etc.) 3. Numbers over One Thousand 4. Comparative Sentences with 比 (bǐ) (II)	Travel agencies in China Travel season in China
1. 的 (de), 得 (de), 地 (de) Compared 2. …的时候 (…de shíhou) and …以后 (…yǐhòu) Compared 3. 还 (hái) + Positive Adjective 4. Kinship Terms	Domestic flights in China Beijing Roast Duck in Chinese food culture
1. 一言为定 (yì yán wéi dìng, it's a deal; it's decided) 2. "Good," "Very good," "Excellent," "Extraordinary" 3. Greetings and Farewells	

Abbreviations of Grammatical Terms

adj	adjective
adv	adverb
conj	conjunction
interj	interjection
m	measure word
mv	modal verb
n	noun
nu	numeral
p	particle
pn	proper noun
pr	pronoun
prefix	prefix
prep	preposition
qp	question particle
qpr	question pronoun
t	time word
v	verb
vc	verb plus complement
vo	verb plus object

Cast of Characters

Back Row:

Mr. Fei:	**Gao Wenzhong:**	**Gao Xiaoyin:**	**Wang Peng:**	**Helen:**	**Li You:**
费先生	高文中	高小音	王朋	海伦	李友

Mr. Fei:
费先生
Owen Fields, Gao Xiaoyin's high school classmate.

Gao Wenzhong:
高文中
Winston Gore, an English student. His parents work in the United States. He says he enjoys singing and dancing. He is also a big fan of Chinese cooking. He has a secret crush on Bai Ying'ai.

Gao Xiaoyin:
高小音
Jenny Gore, Winston's older sister. She has already graduated from college, and is now a school librarian.

Wang Peng:
王朋
A Chinese freshman from Beijing. He has quickly adapted to American college life and likes to play and watch sports.

Helen:
海伦
Gao Wenzhong's cousin. She has a one-year-old son, Tom.

Li You:
李友
Amy Lee, an American student from New York State. She and Wang Peng meet each other on the first day of classes and soon become good friends.

Front Row:

Bai Ying'ai:
白英爱
Baek Yeung Ae, a friendly outgoing Korean student from Seoul. She finds Wang Peng very "cool" and very "cute".

Wang Hong:
王红
Wang Peng's younger sister. She is preparing to attend college in America.

Wang Peng's parents:
王朋的父母
From Beijing, in their late forties.

Chang laoshi:
常老师
(Chang Xiaoliang): Originally from China, in her forties. Chang Laoshi has been teaching Chinese in the United States for ten years.

LESSON 11

Talking about the Weather

第十一课 谈天气

Dì shíyī kè　Tán tiānqì

 LEARNING OBJECTIVES

In this lesson, you will learn to use Chinese to

- Employ basic terms for weather patterns and phenomena;
- Describe simple weather changes;
- Compare the weather of two places;
- Talk about what you may do in nice or bad weather;
- Present a simple weather forecast.

 RELATE AND GET READY

In your own culture/community—

1. What is the typical weather in spring, summer, autumn, and winter?

2. Where do people get information about weather?

3. What weather-related outdoor sports are popular, if any?

4. How do people feel about rain or snow?

Dialogue I: Tomorrow's Weather Will Be Even Better!

(Gao Xiaoyin is looking out the window.)

  今天天气比①昨天好，不下
雪了②。

 我约了朋友明天去公
园滑冰，不知道天气会③
怎么样？

 我刚才看了网上的天气预
报，明天天气比今天更好。
不但不会下雪，而且● 会暖
和一点儿④。

 是吗？太好了！

LANGUAGE NOTES

❶ In a sentence with the 不
但 (búdàn)···, 而且
(érqiě)··· (not only…,
but also…) structure, the
conjunction 而且 (érqiě)
in the second clause is
generally required, while the
conjunction 不但 (búdàn) in
the first clause is optional.

你约了谁去滑冰？

 白英爱。

 你约了白英爱？可是她今天早上坐飞机去纽约了。

 真的啊？那我明天怎么办？

 你还是在家看碟 吧!

❷ 碟 (dié) means a small plate or something that resembles a small plate. It is now often used to refer to DVDs. The phrase 看碟 (kàn dié) thus means to watch a movie or TV series on DVD.

 Jīntiān tiānqì bǐ① zuótiān hǎo, bú xià xuě le②.

 Wǒ yuē le péngyou míngtiān qù gōngyuán huá bīng, bù zhīdào tiānqì huì③ zěnmeyàng?

 Wǒ gāngcái kàn le wǎng shang de tiānqì yùbào, míngtiān tiānqì bǐ jīntiān gèng hǎo. Búdàn bú huì xià xuě, érqiě❶ huì nuǎnhuo yì diǎnr④.

 Shì ma? Tài hǎo le!

 Nǐ yuē le shéi qù huá bīng?

 Bái Yīng'ài.

 Nǐ yuē le Bái Yīng'ài? Kěshì tā jīntiān zǎoshang zuò fēijī qù Niǔyuē le.

 Zhēn de a? Nà wǒ míngtiān zěnmebàn?

 Nǐ háishi zài jiā kàn dié❷ ba!

VOCABULARY

1.	天气	tiānqì	n	weather
2.	比	bǐ	prep/v	(comparison marker); to compare [See Grammar 1.]
3.	下雪	xià xuě	vo	to snow
4.	约	yuē	v	to make an appointment
5.	公园	gōngyuán	n	park
6.	滑冰	huá bīng	vo	to ice skate
7.	会	huì	mv	will [See Grammar 3.]
8.	刚才	gāngcái	t	just now; a moment ago
9.	网上	wǎng shang		on the internet
10.	预报	yùbào	v	to forecast

天气预报
tiānqì yùbào

VOCABULARY

11.	更	gèng	adv	even more
12.	不但···，而且···	búdàn..., érqiě...	conj	not only..., but also...
13.	暖和	nuǎnhuo	adj	warm
14.	冷	lěng	adj	cold
15.	办	bàn	v	to handle; to do
16.	碟	dié	n	disc; small plate, dish, saucer

世界主要城市天气

城市	天气	气温(℃)	城市	天气	气温(℃)
华盛顿	☀	33/21	新德里		36/28
纽约	☀	31/21	德黑兰	☀	36/26
芝加哥	☁	30/20	莫斯科		23/15
洛杉矶	☁	25/18	圣彼得堡		23/15
旧金山	☁	21/13	伊斯坦布尔	☁	30/22
温哥华	☀	23/13	雅典	☁	35/22
蒙特利尔	☀	28/18	布拉格	☁	22/7
多伦多	☀	30/17	日内瓦	☁	26/14
阿卡波克	☁	23/12	法兰克福	☀	23/9
巴西利亚	☁	17/11	柏林	☁	21/10
里约热内卢	☁	21/16	慕尼黑	☁	23/8
布宜诺斯艾利斯	☁	13/5	巴黎	☀	23/12
圣地亚哥	☁	14/4	里昂	☀	29/20
东京	☁	29/11	都柏林	☀	22/12
曼谷		34/26	伦敦	☁	23/11
新加坡		30/25	斯德马尔摩	☁	22/13

纽约今天会不会下雪？
Niǔyuē jīntiān huì bú huì xià xuě?

Grammar

1. Comparative Sentences with 比 (bǐ) (I)

Specific comparison of two entities is usually expressed with the basic pattern

A + 比 (bǐ) + B + Adj

❶   李友比她大姐高。

Lǐ Yǒu bǐ tā dàjiě gāo.

(Li You is taller than her oldest sister.)

❷   今天比昨天冷。

Jīntiān bǐ zuótiān lěng.

(Today is colder than yesterday.)

❸   第十课的语法比第九课的语法容易。

Dì shí kè de yǔfǎ bǐ dì jiǔ kè de yǔfǎ róngyì.

(Lesson Ten's grammar is easier than Lesson Nine's grammar.)

There are two ways in which the basic comparative construction may be further modified: a) by adding a modifying expression after the adjective:

A + 比 (bǐ) + B + Adj + 一点儿/得多/多了 (yì diǎnr/de duō/duō le)

❹   今天比昨天冷一点。

Jīntiān bǐ zuótiān lěng yì diǎn.

(Today is a bit colder than yesterday.)

(4a)   *今天比昨天一点儿冷。

*Jīntiān bǐ zuótiān yì diǎnr lěng.

❺   明天会比今天冷得多。

Míngtiān huì bǐ jīntiān lěng de duō.

(Tomorrow will be much colder than today.)

❻ 纽约比这儿冷多了/冷得多。

Niǔyuē bǐ zhèr lěng duō le/lěng de duō.

(New York is much colder than here.)

Note that the modifying expression must be placed after the adjective, not before it.

(6a) *纽约比这儿很冷。

*Niǔyuē bǐ zhèr hěn lěng.

"Much colder" is 冷多了 (lěng duō le) or 冷得多 (lěng de duō), not 很冷 (hěn lěng, very cold).

b) by adding the adverb 更 (gèng) or the adverb 还 (hái) in front of the adjective:

A + 比 (bǐ) + B + 更/还 (gèng/hái) + Adj

❼ 昨天冷，今天比昨天更冷/今天比昨天还冷。

Zuótiān lěng, jīntiān bǐ zuótiān gèng lěng/jīntiān bǐ zuótiān hái lěng.

(Yesterday was cold. Today is even colder than yesterday.)

跟 (gēn) and 和 (hé) can be used in another type of comparative sentence:

A 跟/和 B（不）一样 + Adj (A gēn/hé B {bù} yíyàng + Adj)

However, unlike a comparative sentence with 比 (bǐ), a comparative sentence with 跟 (gēn) or 和 (hé) only indicates whether two things or persons exhibit the same degree of an attribute, without specifying which of the two exhibits it to a greater or lesser degree.

Compare (8a) with (8b) and (8c) with (8d).

❽ **a:** 这个教室和那个教室一样大。

Zhè ge jiàoshì hé nà ge jiàoshì yíyàng dà.

(This classroom and that classroom are the same size.)

b: 这个教室跟那个教室不一样大。

Zhè ge jiàoshì gēn nà ge jiàoshì bù yíyàng dà.

(This classroom and that classroom are not the same size.)

c: 这个教室比那个教室大。

Zhè ge jiàoshì bǐ nà ge jiàoshì dà.

(This classroom is larger than that classroom.)

d: 这个教室比那个教室大得多。

Zhè ge jiàoshì bǐ nà ge jiàoshì dà de duō.

(This classroom is much larger than that classroom.)

---

2. The Particle 了 (le) (III): 了 as a Sentence-Final Particle

[See also Grammar 5 in Lesson 5 and Grammar 5 in Lesson 8.]

When 了 (le) occurs at the end of a sentence, it usually indicates a change of status or the realization of a new situation.

❶   下雪了。

Xià xuě le.

(It's snowing now.)

❷   妹妹累了。

Mèimei lèi le.

(My sister has become tired.)

❸   我昨天没有空儿，今天有空儿了。

Wǒ zuótiān méiyǒu kòngr, jīntiān yǒu kòngr le.

(I didn't have time yesterday, but I do today.)

❹   你看，公共汽车来了。

Nǐ kàn, gōnggòng qìchē lái le.

(Look, the bus is here.)

When used in this sense, 了 (le) can still be used at the end of a sentence even if the sentence is in the negative.

❺   我没有钱了，不买了。

Wǒ méiyǒu qián le, bù mǎi le.

(I don't have any money [left]. I won't buy it anymore.)

Remember that to negate 有 (yǒu, to have), one uses 没 (méi), not 不 (bù).

3. The Modal Verb 会 (huì, will) (II) [See also Grammar 9 in Lesson 8.]

会 (huì) indicates an anticipated event or action.

❶ 白老师现在不在办公室，可是他明天会在。

Bái lǎoshī xiànzài bú zài bàngōngshì, kěshì tā míngtiān huì zài.

(Teacher Bai is not in the office now, but he will be tomorrow.)

❷ **A:** 你明年做什么？

Nǐ míngnián zuò shénme?

(What will you do next year?)

B: 我明年会去英国学英文。

Wǒ míngnián huì qù Yīngguó xué Yīngwén.

(I'll go to Britain to learn English next year.)

❸ 他说他晚上会给你发短信。

Tā shuō tā wǎnshang huì gěi nǐ fā duǎnxìn.

(He said he will send you a text message this evening.)

The negative form of 会 (huì) is 不会 (bú huì):

❹ 小王觉得不舒服，今天不会来滑冰了。

Xiǎo Wáng juéde bù shūfu, jīntiān bú huì lái huá bīng le.

(Little Wang is not feeling well. He won't come ice skating today after all.)

❺ 她这几天特别忙，晚上不会去听音乐会。

Tā zhè jǐ tiān tèbié máng, wǎnshang bú huì qù tīng yīnyuèhuì.

(She is very busy these days. She won't be going to the concert tonight.)

❻ 天气预报说这个周末不会下雪。

Tiānqì yùbào shuō zhè ge zhōumò bú huì xià xuě.

(The weather forecast says that it won't snow this weekend.)

4. Adj+（一）点儿 ({yì} diǎnr)

The expression （一）点儿 ({yì} diǎnr) can be placed after an adjective to indicate slight qualification. 一 (yī) is optional.

❶   前几天我很不高兴，昨天考试考得很好，我
高兴点儿了。

Qián jǐ tiān wǒ hěn bù gāoxìng, zuótiān kǎo shì kǎo de hěn hǎo, wǒ gāoxìng

diǎnr le.

(I was very unhappy a few days ago. I did very well on the exam yesterday.
I am a little bit happier now.)

❷   我妹妹比我姐姐高一点儿。

 Wǒ mèimei bǐ wǒ jiějie gāo yì diǎnr.

(My younger sister is a bit taller than my older sister.)

❸   你得快点儿，看电影要晚了。

Nǐ děi kuài diǎnr, kàn diànyǐng yào wǎn le.

(You'd better pick up the pace a bit, or you'll be late for the movie.)

❹   今天比昨天冷点儿。

Jīntiān bǐ zuótiān lěng diǎnr.

(Today is a bit colder than yesterday.)

❺   老师，请您说话说得慢一点儿。

Lǎoshī, qǐng nín shuō huà shuō de màn yì diǎnr.

(Teacher, would you please speak a little bit more slowly?)

（一）点儿 (yì diǎnr) does not precede the adjective. The following sentences are therefore incorrect:

(2a)   *我妹妹比我姐姐一点儿高。

　　　*Wǒ mèimei bǐ wǒ jiějie yì diǎnr gāo.

(4a)   *今天比昨天一点儿冷。

　　　*Jīntiān bǐ zuótiān yì diǎnr lěng.

(5a)   *老师，请您说话说得一点儿慢。

　　　*Lǎoshī, qǐng nín shuō huà shuō de yì diǎnr màn.

Language Practice

A. Let's Compare

a. Shopping for Shoes

You are helping a friend decide between two pairs of shoes. Please compare their colors, styles, and prices.

size: 8 $90

size: 8.5 $100

b. Blind Date

You are out on a blind date. Your date is telling you his/her preferences, and would like to know yours. Let's see how compatible you and your date are.

EXAMPLE: **Your date**

 >

好吃 (hǎochī, good to eat; delicious)

我觉得美国菜比中国菜好吃。你呢？

Wǒ juéde Měiguó cài bǐ Zhōngguó cài hǎochī. Nǐ ne?

1.   >   好喝   hǎohē (delicious to drink)

2.   >   难   nán

3.   >   慢   màn

B. Healthy Lifestyle Choices

Little Zhang decided to change his old habits in order to lead a healthier lifestyle. Let's see how he does things differently these days.

EXAMPLE:

past   present

他以前不吃早饭，
现在吃早饭了。

Tā yǐqián bù chī zǎofàn,

xiànzài chī zǎofàn le.

1.

2.

3.

C. Are You a Fan?

If you are a fan of Wang Peng, Li You, Bai Ying'ai, or Gao Wenzhong, and you know everything about them, what will you say when others ask questions about them? Let's practice using the structure 不但···而且··· (búdàn...érqiě...).

EXAMPLE:

Someone asks

A: 王朋帅吗？ 高   Wáng Péng shuài ma?   gāo

You, as a fan, will answer

B: 王朋不但很帅，   Wáng Péng búdàn hěn shuài,
而且很高。   érqiě hěn gāo.

Someone asks

A: 王朋喜欢看球吗？   Wáng Péng xǐhuan kàn qiú ma?

You, as a fan, will answer

B: 王朋不但喜欢看球，   Wáng Péng búdàn xǐhuan kàn qiú,
而且喜欢打球。   érqiě xǐhuan dǎ qiú.

1.

A: 高文中高吗？ 帅   Gāo Wénzhōng gāo ma?   shuài

B:

A: 高文中喜欢
唱歌吗？

Gāo Wénzhōng xǐhuan

chàng gē ma?

B:

2.

A: 白英爱写字写得快吗？
漂亮

Bái Yīng'ài xiě zì xiě de kuài ma?

piàoliang

B:

A: 白英爱会说英文吗？
中文

Bái Yīng'ài huì shuō Yīngwén ma?

Zhōngwén

B:

3.

A: 李友的衣服好看吗？
便宜

Lǐ Yǒu de yīfu hǎokàn ma?

piányi

B:

A: 李友常常复习生词
语法吗？
预习

Lǐ Yǒu chángcháng fùxí shēngcí

yǔfǎ ma?

yùxí

B:

D. Giving a Weather Report

Look at the illustrations and give simple descriptions of the weather possibilities for each city tomorrow.

北京   Běijīng

→ 天气预报说北京   Tiānqì yùbào shuō Běijīng
明天会下雪。   míngtiān huì xià xuě.

北京   Běijīng

→

纽约   Niǔyuē

→

纽约   Niǔyuē

→

E. Dating Dilemma

You can't make up your mind: "Who should I go out with, A or B?" A has numerous good qualities. Your friend points out that B at least equals A, if not in fact surpasses A. Or your friend reminds you that B trumps A in some other way.

EXAMPLE:

You:	我觉得A很帅/漂亮。	Wǒ juéde A hěn shuài/piàoliang.
Friend:	可是B跟A一样帅/漂亮。	Kěshì B gēn A yíyàng shuài/piàoliang.
	不，不，不，B比A帅/漂亮多了。	Bù, bù, bù, B bǐ A shuài/piàoliang duō le.

Possible attributes to consider:

1. 高
2. 钱　多
3. 学习　好
4. 打球打得好

1. gāo
2. qián duō
3. xuéxí　hǎo
4. dǎ qiú dǎ de hǎo

All considered:

_____比_____好。

_____ bǐ _____ hǎo.

F. Recap and Narrate

Working with a partner, recap the content of Dialogue I:

1. 昨天的天气好不好？
2. 昨天下雪了吗？

1. Zuótiān de tiānqì hǎo bù hǎo?
2. Zuótiān xià xuě le ma?

3. 今天的天气好吗？
明天呢？

4. 高文中约了谁去
公园滑冰？

5. 白英爱能跟高文中
去滑冰吗？为什么？

6. 高小音让高文中
明天做什么？

3. Jīntiān de tiānqì hǎo ma?

Míngtiān ne?

4. Gāo Wénzhōng yuē le shéi qù

gōngyuán huá bīng?

5. Bái Yīng'ài néng gēn Gāo

Wénzhōng qù huá bīng ma?

Wèishénme?

6. Gāo Xiǎoyīn ràng Gāo

Wénzhōng   míngtiān zuò

shénme?

Using the words and phrases in blue as prompts, connect your answers above to form a narrative like this example:

现在是冬天，昨天下雪了，今天的天气比昨天好，不下雪了。天气预报说明天的天气更好，不但不会下雪，而且会暖和一点儿。高文中很高兴，因为他约了白英爱去公园滑冰。可是高小音告诉他，白英爱今天早上坐飞机去纽约了。高文中不知道。他问高小音他明天怎么办？高小音让他在家看碟。

Xiànzài shì dōngtiān, zuótiān xià xuě le, jīntiān de tiānqì bǐ zuótiān hǎo, bú xià xuě le. Tiānqì yùbào shuō míngtiān de tiānqì gèng hǎo, búdàn bú huì xià xuě, érqiě huì nuǎnhuo yì diǎnr. Gāo Wénzhōng hěn gāoxìng, yīnwèi tā yuē le Bái Yīng'ài qù gōngyuán huá bīng. Kěshì Gāo Xiǎoyīn gàosù tā, Bái Yīng'ài jīntiān zǎoshang zuò fēijī qù Niǔyuē le. Gāo Wénzhōng bù zhīdào. Tā wèn Gāo Xiǎoyīn tā míngtiān zěnmebàn? Gāo Xiǎoyīn ràng tā zài jiā kàn dié.

Dialogue II: The Weather Here Is Awful!

（高文中在网上找白英爱聊天儿。）

  英爱，纽约那么好玩儿，你
怎么在网上，没出去？

 这儿的天气非常糟糕。

 怎么了？❶

 昨天下大雨，今天又⑤下雨了。

 这个周末这儿天气很好，你快一
点儿回来吧。

 这个周末纽约也会暖和一点儿。
我下个星期有一个面试，还不能
回去。

LANGUAGE NOTES

❶ 怎么了？(Zěnme le?)
is a question that may be
asked upon encountering an
unusual situation.

我在加州找了一个工作，你也去吧。加州冬天不冷，夏天不热，春天和秋天更舒服。

 加州好是好⑥，可是我更喜欢纽约。

(Gāo Wénzhōng zài wǎng shang zhǎo Bái Yīng'ài liáo tiānr.)

 Yīng'ài, Niǔyuē nàme hǎowánr, nǐ zěnme zài wǎng shang, méi chū qu?

 Zhèr de tiānqì fēicháng zāogāo.

 Zěnme le?❶

 Zuótiān xià dà yǔ, jīntiān yòu⑤ xià yǔ le.

 Zhè ge zhōumò zhèr tiānqì hěn hǎo, nǐ kuài yì diǎnr huí lai ba.

 Zhè ge zhōumò Niǔyuē yě huì nuǎnhuo yì diǎnr. Wǒ xià ge xīngqī yǒu yí ge miànshì, hái bù néng huí qu.

 Wǒ zài Jiāzhōu zhǎo le yí ge gōngzuò, nǐ yě qù ba. Jiāzhōu dōngtiān bù lěng, xiàtiān bú rè, chūntiān hé qiūtiān gèng shūfu.

 Jiāzhōu hǎo shì hǎo⑥, kěshì wǒ gèng xǐhuan Niǔyuē.

 VOCABULARY

1.	那么	nàme	pr	(indicating degree) so, such
2.	好玩儿	hǎowánr	adj	fun, amusing, interesting
3.	出去	chū qu	vc	to go out
4.	非常	fēicháng	adv	very, extremely, exceedingly
5.	糟糕	zāogāo	adj	in a terrible mess; how terrible
6.	下雨	xià yǔ	vo	to rain
7.	又	yòu	adv	again [See Grammar 5.]

VOCABULARY

8.	面试	miànshì	v/n	to interview; interview
9.	回去	huí qu	vc	to go back; to return
10.	冬天	dōngtiān	n	winter
11.	夏天	xiàtiān	n	summer
12.	热	rè	adj	hot
13.	春天	chūntiān	n	spring
14.	秋天	qiūtiān	n	autumn; fall
15.	舒服	shūfu	adj	comfortable

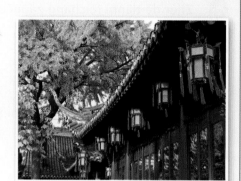

Proper Nouns

16.	加州	Jiāzhōu		California

这是哪个城市的天气预报？
Zhè shì nǎ ge chéngshì de tiānqì yùbào?

Grammar

5. The Adverb 又 (yòu, again)

又 (yòu, again) indicates recurrence of an action.

1 昨天早上下雪，今天早上又下雪了。

Zuótiān zǎoshang xià xuě, jīntiān zǎoshang yòu xià xuě le.

(It snowed yesterday morning. It snowed again this morning.)

2 妈妈上个星期给我打电话，这个星期又给我打电话了。

Māma shàng ge xīngqī gěi wǒ dǎ diànhuà, zhè ge xīngqī yòu gěi wǒ dǎ

diànhuà le.

(My mom called me last weekend. She called me again this weekend.)

3 他昨天复习了第八课的语法，今天又复习了。

Tā zuótiān fùxí le dì bā kè de yǔfǎ, jīntiān yòu fùxí le.

(He reviewed the grammar in Lesson Eight yesterday, and he reviewed it again today.)

Both 又 (yòu, again) and 再 (zài, again) indicate repetition of an action, but in a sentence with 又 (yòu, again), usually both the original action and the repetition occurred in the past, whereas 再 (zài, again) indicates an anticipated repetition of an action in general.

4 我上个周末去跳舞了，昨天我又去跳舞了。

Wǒ shàng ge zhōumò qù tiào wǔ le, zuótiān wǒ yòu qù tiào wǔ le.

(I went dancing last weekend. Yesterday I went dancing again.)

5 我昨天去跳舞了，我想明天晚上再去跳舞。

Wǒ zuótiān qù tiào wǔ le, wǒ xiǎng míngtiān wǎnshang zài qù tiào wǔ.

(I went dancing yesterday. I'm thinking of going dancing again tomorrow night.)

6. Adj / V + 是 (shì) + Adj / V, + 可是／但是 … (kěshì／dànshì…)

Sentences in this pattern usually imply that the speaker accepts the validity of a certain point of view but wishes to offer an alternative perspective or emphasize a different aspect of the matter.

❶ A: 滑冰难不难？

Huá bīng nán bu nán?

(Is ice skating difficult?)

B: 滑冰难是难，可是很有意思。

Huá bīng nán shì nán, kěshì hěn yǒu yìsi.

(It *is* difficult, but it is very interesting.)

❷ A: 在高速公路上开车，你紧张吗？

Zài gāosù gōnglù shang kāi chē, nǐ jǐnzhāng ma?

(Do you get nervous driving on the highway?)

B: 紧张是紧张，可是也很好玩儿。

Jǐnzhāng shì jǐnzhāng, kěshì yě hěn hǎowánr.

(I do get nervous, but I find it a lot of fun, too.)

❸ A: 明天学校开会，你去不去？

Míngtiān xuéxiào kāi huì, nǐ qù bu qù?

(There is a meeting at school tomorrow. Will you go?)

B: 我去是去，可是会晚一点儿。

Wǒ qù shì qù, kěshì huì wǎn yì diǎnr.

(I'll go, but I will be a little bit late.)

④ A: 你喜欢这张照片吗？

Nǐ xǐhuan zhè zhāng zhàopiàn ma?

(Do you like this picture?)

B: 喜欢是喜欢，可是这张照片太小了。

Xǐhuan shì xǐhuan, kěshì zhè zhāng zhàopiàn tài xiǎo le.)

(I like it, but this picture is too small.)

This pattern can be used only when the adjective or verb in it has already been mentioned, e.g., 难 (nán) in (1), 紧张 (jǐnzhāng) in (2), 去 (qù) in (3), and 喜欢 (xǐhuan) in (4). In this regard, it is different from the pattern 虽然… 可是/但是… (suīrán...kěshì/dànshì...).

Language Practice

G. Plan B

When you plan something and the weather does not cooperate, then what do you do? Ask and answer the following questions with your partner, and see if you can settle on an alternative.

EXAMPLE:

A: 我想出去玩儿， 可是下雨了。

Wǒ xiǎng chū qu wánr, kěshì xià yǔ le.

B: 别出去了！还是 在家看电视吧。

Bié chū qu le! Háishi zài jiā kàn diànshì ba.

1. A: 我想去买点儿东西， 可是雪下得很大。

Wǒ xiǎng qù mǎi diǎnr dōngxi, kěshì xuě xià de hěn dà.

B: ___别去买东西了！还_____

2. A: 我想出去看朋友， 可是天气很糟糕。

Wǒ xiǎng chū qu kàn péngyou, kěshì tiānqì hěn zāogāo.

B: _____

3. **A:** 我想去公园打球，
     但是太热。

   Wǒ xiǎng qù gōngyuán dǎ qiú,

   dànshì tài rè.

B: _____

H. Little Zhang's Routine

The following chart shows what Little Zhang did last week. Let's recap by using
又 (yòu).

Monday	Tuesday	Wednesday	Thursday	Friday	Saturday

EXAMPLE:

→   小张星期一看碟，
     星期五又看碟。

Xiǎo Zhāng xīngqīyī kàn dié,

xīngqīwǔ **yòu** kàn dié.

1.

  →

2.

  →

I. Two Sides to Every Coin

Things are rarely simple. Take turns reminding each other to consider another factor.

EXAMPLE:

加州　　漂亮

Jiāzhōu　　piàoliang

A: 加州很漂亮。

A: Jiāzhōu hěn piàoliang.

B: 加州漂亮是漂亮，
可是东西太贵了。

B: Jiāzhōu piàoliang shì piàoliang,
kěshì dōngxi tài guì le.

How about the following

1. 纽约	有意思	Niǔyuē	yǒu yìsi
2. 坐地铁	便宜	zuò dìtiě	piányi
3. 坐公共汽车	慢	zuò gōnggòng qìchē	màn
4. 北京的冬天	下雪	Běijīng de dōngtiān	xià xuě

(handwritten above 坐地铁: tě)
(handwritten above 便宜: pián yì)

J. Beijing Weather

The following is a three-day weather forecast for Beijing. Give a report on which days the weather will be colder/warmer and how the weather will change, and compare it with the weather in your town.

next Monday

next Tuesday

next Wednesday

28°F   37°F   40°F

K. **Recap and Narrate**

Work with a partner, recap the content of Dialogue II:

1. 高文中说纽约
   好玩儿吗？

2. 白英爱在纽约为什么
   在房间里上网，
   没出去？

3. 高文中为什么让
   白英爱周末快
   一点儿回学校？

4. 白英爱这个周末
   能回学校吗？

5. 高文中在哪儿找了
   一个工作？

6. 高文中说那儿的天气
   怎么样？

7. 白英爱觉得那儿
   怎么样？

1. Gāo Wénzhōng shuō Niǔyuē
   hǎowánr ma?

2. Bái Yīng'ài zài Niǔyuē wèishénme
   zài fángjiān li shàng wǎng,
   méi chū qu?

3. Gāo Wénzhōng wèishénme ràng
   Bái Yīng'ài zhōumò kuài
   yì diǎnr huí xuéxiào?

4. Bái Yīng'ài zhè ge zhōumò
   néng huí xuéxiào ma?

5. Gāo Wénzhōng zài nǎr zhǎo le
   yí ge gōngzuò?

6. Gāo Wénzhōng shuō nàr de tiānqì
   zěnmeyàng?

7. Bái Yīng'ài juéde nàr
   zěnmeyàng?

Using the words and phrases in blue as prompts, connect your answers above to form a narrative like this example:

纽约很好玩儿，可是那儿现在的天气非常糟糕，昨天下大雨，今天又下大雨了。高文中说学校这儿周末的天气很好，让白英爱快一点儿回来。可是白英爱说纽约周末的天气也会好一点儿，而且她下个星期有一个面试，还不能回去。高文中在加州找了一个工作，他告诉英爱加州的天气很好，冬天不冷，夏天不热，春天和秋天更舒服，希望白英爱也去加州。英爱说，加州好是好，可是她更喜欢纽约。

Niǔyuē hěn hǎowánr, kěshì nàr xiànzài de tiānqì fēicháng zāogāo, zuótiān xià dà yǔ, jīntiān yòu xià dà yǔ le. Gāo Wénzhōng shuō xuéxiào zhèr zhōumò de tiānqì hěn hǎo, ràng Bái Yīng'ài kuài yì diǎnr huí lai. Kěshì Bái Yīng'ài shuō Niǔyuē zhōumò de tiānqì yě huì hǎo yì diǎnr, érqiě tā xià gè xīngqī yǒu yí ge miànshì, hái bù néng huí qu. Gāo Wénzhōng zài Jiāzhōu zhǎo le yí ge gōngzuò, tā gàosù Yīng'ài Jiāzhōu de tiānqì hěn hǎo, dōngtiān bù lěng, xiàtiān bú rè, chūntiān hé qiūtiān gèng shūfu, xīwàng Bái Yīng'ài yě qù Jiāzhōu. Yīng'ài shuō, Jiāzhōu hǎo shì hǎo, kěshì tā gèng xǐhuan Niǔyuē.

HOW ABOUT YOU?

How's the weather where you are?

1.	潮湿	cháoshī	adj	wet; humid
2.	闷热	mēnrè	adj	hot and stifling
3.	凉快	liángkuai	adj	pleasantly cool
4.	晴天	qíngtiān	n	sunny day
5.	阴天	yīntiān	n	overcast day
6.	风	fēng	n	wind

If there are other terms that you wish to use to describe the weather, please ask your teacher and make a note here:

_____

Culture Highlights

❶ For measuring temperature, China uses the Celsius rather than the Fahrenheit system. For measuring length and weight, China uses the metric system, even though some people still use the old system. The basic unit of length in the old Chinese system is 里 (lǐ), which equals half a kilometer, or 0.311 mile. The basic unit of weight in the old Chinese system is 斤 (jīn), which equals half a kilogram, or 1.102 pounds.

❷ In China, the climatic conditions differ drastically from one part of the country to another. Generally speaking, just as in America, the north is cold and snowy in winter; the south, hot and wet in summer. Three cities, 重庆 (Chóngqìng), 武汉 (Wǔhàn), and 南京 (Nánjīng), are nicknamed "furnaces" for their notoriously hot temperatures in summer. Some other cities, such as 昆明 (Kūnmíng), are known for their year-round balmy weather. In the lower 长江 (Chángjiāng, the longest river in China, also known as the Yangtze) valley, there is a 黄梅 (huángméi, literally, yellow plum) season in May and June characterized by copious rain and high humidity. But the major rainy season for most of southern China is in July and August, when almost all the rivers swell to flood levels. In winter, the island of 海南 (Hǎinán) provides warmth and appealing resorts for tourists from the north, while many southerners brave the cold and pour into the northern city of 哈尔滨 (Hā'ěrbīn) for its annual exhibition of ice sculptures.

❸ Some Chinese names for Western places were invented by early Chinese immigrants, e.g., 旧金山 (Jiùjīnshān, literally, Old Gold Mountain) for San Francisco. But the vast majority of names for Western places are transliterations. Massachusetts, for instance, is transliterated as 麻萨诸塞 (Másàzhūsài), which is in turn abbreviated to 麻州 (Mázhōu), with the character 州 (zhōu) meaning "state." Similarly, California is transliterated as 加利福尼亚 (Jiālìfúníyà), which is often shortened to 加州 (Jiāzhōu).

❹ China now boasts more internet users than any other country. Many Chinese urbanites have residential internet access, but many youngsters prefer to use the internet at a type of commercial facility called 网吧 (wǎngbā, internet bar). As 网吧 (wǎngbā) provide not only internet access but also snacks and beverages, they are favorite social venues for these young internet users. One can easily locate a 网吧 (wǎngbā) in a commercial area in any Chinese city. In Taiwan, 网吧 (wǎngbā) is commonly known as 网咖 (wǎngkā).

English Text

Dialogue I

Gao Xiaoyin: Today's weather is better than yesterday's. It's not snowing anymore.

Gao Wenzhong: I asked a friend to go ice skating in the park tomorrow. I wonder what the weather is going to be like.

Gao Xiaoyin: I looked up the forecast on the internet. Tomorrow's weather will be even better than today. Not only will it not snow, it'll be a bit warmer, too.

Gao Wenzhong: Really? Fantastic!

Gao Xiaoyin: Whom did you ask to go ice skating?

Gao Wenzhong: Bai Ying'ai.

Gao Xiaoyin: You asked Bai Ying'ai? But she flew to New York this morning.

Gao Wenzhong: Really? Then what do I do tomorrow?

Gao Xiaoyin: Why don't you watch a DVD at home?

Dialogue II

(Gao Wenzhong is chatting with Bai Ying'ai online.)

Gao Wenzhong: Ying'ai, New York is so much fun. How come you're online and not out and about?

Bai Ying'ai: The weather here is awful.

Gao Wenzhong: How come?

Bai Ying'ai: Yesterday it poured. It rained again today.

Gao Wenzhong: The weather here is great this weekend. You'd better come back as soon as you can.

Bai Ying'ai: It's going to be warmer in New York this weekend. Next week I have an interview. I can't come back just yet.

Gao Wenzhong: I found a job in California. Go with me. It's not cold in the winter in California, or hot in the summer. Spring and fall are even more comfortable.

Bai Ying'ai: California is great, but I like New York more.

PROGRESS CHECKLIST

Before proceeding to Lesson 12, be sure you can complete the following tasks in Chinese:

I am able to—

- ☑ Provide a simple description of the weather;
- ☐ Describe the climate in the place where I live;
- ☐ Describe basic weather changes;
- ☐ Compare the weather in two places;
- ☐ Talk about what I may do if the weather is not nice and I cannot go out.

LESSON 12

Dining

第十二课 吃饭

Dì shí'èr kè   Chī fàn

 LEARNING OBJECTIVES

In this lesson, you will learn to use Chinese to

- Ask if there are seats available in a restaurant;
- Order Chinese dishes;
- Tell the waiter your dietary preferences and restrictions;
- Ask the restaurant to recommend dishes;
- Rush your order;
- Pay for your meal;
- Get the correct change after your payment.

 RELATE AND GET READY

In your own culture/community—

1. Do people order and eat their own dishes when dining out, or do they share their dishes with others?
2. Do people order hot or cold beverages to go with their meals?
3. Do people have their soup before or after their main dish?
4. How is being a vegetarian different from being a vegan?
5. How do most people pay for their meal: in cash, with a credit card, or by check?
6. Do people typically get a receipt after paying for a meal?

Dialogue I: Dining Out

（在饭馆儿）

 请进，请进。

人怎么这么多？好像一个位子都^① 没有了。

服务员，请问，还有没有位子？

有，有，有。那张桌子没有人。

*　*　*

两位想吃点儿什么？

王朋，你点菜吧。

LANGUAGE NOTES

❶ In Beijing, 这么 (zhème) is commonly pronounced as zème.

❷ In a restaurant, one may address a staff member, either male or female, as 服务员 (fúwùyuán, waiter). In Beijing, however, some customers would address a young waiter as 小伙子 (xiǎohuǒzi, young man) and a young waitress as 小妹 (xiǎomèi, lit., little sister), while some older or middle-aged people would call a young waitress 姑娘 (gūniang, girl; miss). In Taiwan, it is proper to address a waiter as 先生 (xiānsheng) and a waitress as 小姐 (xiǎojiě).

好。先给我们两盘饺子，要素的。

除了饺子以外，还要什么？

李友，你说呢？

还要一盘家常豆腐，不要放肉，我吃素。

我们的家常豆腐没有肉。

还要两碗酸辣汤③，请别放味精，少② 放点儿盐。有小白菜吗？

对不起，小白菜刚③卖完④。

那就不要青菜了。

那喝点儿④ 什么呢？

我要一杯冰茶。李友，你喝什么？

我很渴，请给我一杯可乐，多放点儿冰。

好，两盘饺子，一盘家常豆腐，两碗酸辣汤，一杯冰茶，一杯可乐，多放冰。还要别的吗？

不要别的了，这些够⑤了。
服务员，我们都饿了，请上菜快一点儿。

没问题，菜很快就能做好⑤。

③ Nouns for containers or vessels such as 碗 (wǎn, bowl), 杯 (bēi, cup/glass), and 盘 (pán, plate/dish) can serve as measure words, e.g., 一碗饭 (yì wǎn fàn, a bowl of rice), 一杯水 (yì bēi shuǐ, a glass of water), and 一盘饺子 (yì pán jiǎozi, a plate of dumplings).

④ 点儿 (diǎnr) here is the abbreviated form of 一点儿 (yì diǎn). When used to modify nouns, (一) 点儿 ({yì} diǎnr) can soften the tone and therefore make the sentence more polite.

⑤ As an adjective, 够 (gòu) functions only as a predicate, and never as an attributive before nouns. Thus one says 我的钱不够 (wǒ de qián bú gòu, my money is not enough), but never *我没有够钱 (*wǒ méi yǒu gòu qián).

(Zài fànguǎnr)

 Qǐng jìn, qǐng jìn.

 Rén zěnme zhème❶ duō? Hǎoxiàng yí ge wèizi dōu① méiyǒu le.

 Fúwùyuán❷, qǐng wèn, hái yǒu méiyǒu wèizi?

 Yǒu, yǒu, yǒu. Nà zhāng zhuōzi méiyǒu rén.

*   *   *

 Liǎng wèi xiǎng chī diǎnr shénme?

 Wáng Péng, nǐ diǎn cài ba.

 Hǎo. Xiān gěi wǒmen liǎng pán jiǎozi, yào sù de.

 Chúle jiǎozi yǐwài, hái yào shénme?

 Lǐ Yǒu, nǐ shuō ne?

 Hái yào yì pán jiācháng dòufu, bú yào fàng ròu, wǒ chī sù.

 Wǒmen de jiācháng dòufu méiyǒu ròu.

 Hái yào liǎng wǎn suānlàtāng❸, qǐng bié fàng wèijīng, shǎo② fàng diǎnr yán. Yǒu xiǎo báicài ma?

 Duìbuqǐ, xiǎo báicài gāng③ mài wán④.

 Nà jiù bú yào qīngcài le.

 Nà hē diǎnr❹ shénme ne?

 Wǒ yào yì bēi bīngchá. Lǐ Yǒu, nǐ hē shénme?

 Wǒ hěn kě, qǐng gěi wǒ yì bēi kělè, duō fàng diǎnr bīng.

 Hǎo, liǎng pán jiǎozi, yì pán jiācháng dòufu, liǎng wǎn suānlàtāng, yì bēi bīngchá, yì bēi kělè, duō fàng bīng. Hái yào bié de ma?

 Bú yào bié de le, zhè xiē gòu❺ le. Fúwùyuán, wǒmen dōu è le, qǐng shàng cài kuài yì diǎnr.

 Méi wèntí, cài hěn kuài jiù néng zuò hǎo⑤.

VOCABULARY

1.	饭馆（儿）	fànguǎn(r)	n	restaurant
2.	好像	hǎoxiàng	v	to seem; to be like
3.	位子	wèizi	n	seat
4.	服务员	fúwùyuán	n	waiter; attendant
	服务	fúwù	v	to serve; to provide service
5.	桌子	zhuōzi	n	table
6.	点菜	diǎn cài	vo	to order food
7.	盘	pán	n	plate; dish
8.	饺子	jiǎozi	n	dumplings (with vegetable and/or meat filling)
9.	素	sù	adj	vegetarian; made from vegetables
10.	家常	jiācháng	n	home-style
11.	豆腐	dòufu	n	tofu; bean curd
12.	放	fàng	v	to put; to place
13.	肉	ròu	n	meat
14.	碗	wǎn	n	bowl
15.	酸辣汤	suānlàtāng	n	hot and sour soup
	酸	suān	adj	sour
	辣	là	adj	spicy; hot
	汤	tāng	n	soup
16.	味精	wèijīng	n	monosodium glutamate (MSG)
17.	盐	yán	n	salt
18.	白菜	báicài	n	bok choy

VOCABULARY

19.	刚	gāng	adv	just [See Grammar 3.]
20.	卖完	mài wán	vc	to be sold out [See Grammar 4.]
	完	wán	c	finished
21.	青菜	qīngcài	n	green/leafy vegetable
22.	冰茶	bīngchá	n	iced tea
	冰	bīng	n	ice
23.	渴	kě	adj	thirsty
24.	些	xiē	m	(measure word for an indefinite amount); some
25.	够	gòu	adj	enough
26.	饿	è	adj	hungry
27.	上菜	shàng cài	vo	to serve food

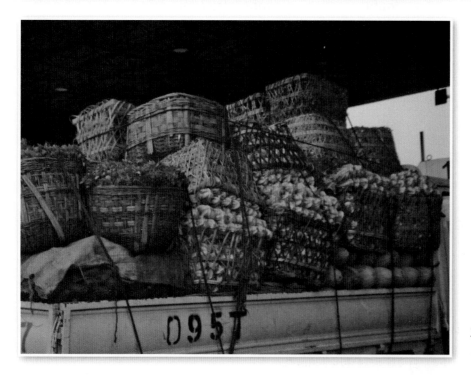

这么多青菜！
Zhème duō qīngcài!

青菜
qīngcài

牛肉
niúròu
(beef, see
Dialogue II)

饺子
jiǎozi

豆腐
dòufu

Grammar

1. 一…也/都…不/没… (yì…yě/dōu…bù/méi)

These structures are used to form an emphatic negation meaning "not at all" or "not even one."

A. Subject + 一 (yī) + **Measure Word** + **Object** + 也/都 (yě/dōu) + 不/没 (bù/méi) + **Verb**

❶ 小李一个朋友也没有。

Xiǎo Lǐ yí ge péngyou yě méiyǒu.

(Little Li does not have a single friend.)

❷ 爸爸今天一杯茶都没喝。

Bàba jīntiān yì bēi chá dōu méi hē.

(My father didn't have a single cup of tea today.)

B. Topic (+ Subject) + 一 **(yī) + Measure Word +** 也/都 **(yě/dōu) +** 不/没 **(bù/méi) + Verb**

❸   这些衬衫我一件也不喜欢。

Zhè xiē chènshān wǒ yí jiàn yě bù xǐhuan.

(I don't like any of these shirts.)

❹   哥哥的鞋，弟弟一双都不能穿。

Gēge de xié, dìdi yì shuāng dōu bù néng chuān.

(The younger brother cannot wear any of his older brother's shoes.)

C. Subject + 一点儿 **(yì diǎnr) + Object +** 也/都 **(yě/dōu) +** 不/没 **(bù/méi) + Verb**

❺   他去了商店，可是一点儿东西也没买。

Tā qù le shāngdiàn, kěshì yì diǎnr dōngxi yě méi mǎi.

(He went to the store, but he didn't buy anything at all.)

❻   妈妈做菜一点儿味精都不放。

Māma zuò cài yì diǎnr wèijīng dōu bú fang.

(Mom doesn't use any MSG in her cooking.)

If the noun after 一 (yī) is countable, a proper measure word should be used between 一 (yī) and the noun, as in (1), (2), (3), and (4). If the noun is uncountable, the phrase 一点儿 (yì diǎnr) is usually used instead, as in (5) and (6).

The following sentences are incorrect:

(1a) *小李没有一个朋友。

*Xiǎo Lǐ méiyǒu yí ge péngyou.

(3a) *这些衬衫我不喜欢一件。

*Zhè xiē chènshān wǒ bù xǐhuan yí jiàn.

(5a) *他东西没买一点儿。

*Tā dōngxī méi mǎi yì diǎnr.

The construction 一点儿 (yìdiǎnr) + 也/都 (yě/dōu) + 不 (bù/méi) can also be used before an adjective to express emphatic negation.

❼ 这儿的冬天一点儿也不冷。

Zhèr de dōngtiān yì diǎnr yě bù lěng.

(Winter here is not cold at all.)

❽ 那个学校一点儿也不漂亮。

Nà ge xuéxiào yì diǎnr yě bú piàoliang.

(That school is not pretty at all.)

❾ 这杯冰茶一点儿都不好喝。

Zhè bēi bīngchá yì diǎnr dōu bù hǎohē.

(This glass of iced tea doesn't taste good at all.)

2. Adverb 多/少 (duō/shǎo) + V

多 (duō) and 少 (shǎo) are two adjectives whose usage is rather unusual. To express the idea of doing something "more" or "less," one places 多 (duō) or 少 (shǎo) before the verb.

❶ 爸爸告诉妈妈做菜的时候少放盐，多放点儿糖。

Bàba gàosu māma zuò cài de shíhou shǎo fàng yán, duō fàng diǎnr táng.

(Dad asked Mom to add less salt and more sugar when she cooks.)

❷ 上中文课得多说中文，少说英文。

Shàng Zhōngwén kè děi duō shuō Zhōngwén, shǎo shuō Yīngwén.

(In Chinese class, one should speak more Chinese and less English.)

This "多/少 (duō/shǎo) + verb" construction can sometimes denote a deviation from the correct amount or number.

❸ 你多找了我一块钱。

Nǐ duō zhǎo le wǒ yí kuài qián.

(You gave me one dollar too many.)

❹ 老师说要写五十个字，我写了四十五个，少
写了五个。

Lǎoshī shuō yào xiě wǔshí ge zì, wǒ xiě le sìshíwǔ ge, shǎo xiě le wǔ ge.

(The teacher told us to write fifty characters. I wrote forty-five. I was five short.)

---

3. 刚 (gāng) vs. 刚才 (gāngcái)

As an adverb, 刚 (gāng) denotes that the action or change in situation took place in the most recent past.

❶ 我哥哥刚从中国来，一个朋友都没有。

Wǒ gēge gāng cóng Zhōngguó lái, yí ge péngyou dōu méiyǒu.

(My older brother just came from China. He doesn't have a single friend here.)

❷ 我刚洗完澡，舒服极了。

Wǒ gāng xǐ wán zǎo, shūfu jí le.

(I just showered, and feel so great.)

刚才 (gāngcái) is a noun that refers to the time shortly before the act of speaking.

❸ A: 你知道王朋在哪儿吗？

Nǐ zhīdào Wáng Péng zài nǎr ma?

(Do you know where Wang Peng is?)

B: 他刚才在这儿，我不知道他去哪儿了。

Tā gāngcái zài zhèr, wǒ bù zhīdao tā qù nǎr le.

(He was here a moment ago. I don't know where he went.)

❹ 弟弟刚才吃了十五个饺子，喝了两碗
酸辣汤。

Dìdi gāngcái chī le shíwǔ ge jiǎozi, hē le liǎng wǎn suānlàtāng.

(My younger brother finished fifteen dumplings and two bowls of hot and sour soup a moment ago.)

Although 刚 (gāng) and 刚才 (gāngcái) are similar in meaning, they are classified as different parts of speech and are therefore used differently.

a. 刚 (gāng) can be followed by an expression that indicates the duration of time.

❺ 他刚走了两天。

Tā gāng zǒu le liǎng tiān.

(He left only two days ago.)

*他刚才走了两天。

*Tā gāng cái zǒu le liǎng tiān.

Unlike 刚才 (gāngcái), 刚 (gāng) cannot be followed by the negation words 不 (bù) or 没 (méi).

❻ A: 你刚才为什么没说？

Nǐ gāngcái wèishénme méi shuō?

(Why didn't you say it a moment ago?)

*你刚为什么没说？

*Nǐ gāng wèishénme méi shuō?

B: 我刚才不想说。

Wǒ gāngcái bù xiǎng shuō.

(I didn't want to say it a moment ago.)

*我刚不想说。

*Wǒ gāng bù xiǎng shuō.

b. A sentence that includes 刚才 (gāngcái) often ends with 了 (le), but a sentence including 刚 (gāng) cannot have 了 (le) at the end.

❼ A: 你刚才去哪儿了？老师要你去办公室找他。

Nǐ gāngcái qù nǎr le? Lǎoshī yào nǐ qù bàngōngshì zhǎo tā.

(Where were you a moment ago? The teacher wanted you to go to his office.)

B: 我刚才去图书馆了。

Wǒ gāngcái qù túshūguǎn le.

(I went to the library.)

❽ A: 明天的考试你开始准备了吗？

Míngtiān de kǎo shì nǐ kāishǐ zhǔnbèi le ma?

(Have you started preparing for tomorrow's test?)

B: 刚开始准备。

Gāng kāishǐ zhǔnbèi.

(I just got started.)

*刚开始准备了。

*Gāng kāishǐ zhǔnbèi le.

4. Resultative Complements (I)

Following a verb, an adjective or another verb can be used to denote the result of the action, hence the term resultative complement.

❶ 小白菜卖完了。

Xiǎo báicài mài wán le.

(Baby bok choy is sold out.)

❷ 你找错钱了。

Nǐ zhǎo cuò qián le.

(You gave me the incorrect change.)

❸ 那个人是谁你看清楚了吗？

Nà ge rén shì shéi nǐ kàn qīngchu le ma?

(Did you see clearly who that person was?)

[清楚 qīngchu, clear: see Dialogue II]

④ 太好了，这个字你写对了。

Tài hǎo le, zhè ge zì nǐ xiě duì le.

(Great! You wrote this character correctly.)

Generally, the negative form of a resultative complement is formed by placing 没 (méi, no, not) or 没有 (méiyǒu, have not) before the verb.

⑤ 小白菜还没卖完。

Xiǎo báicài hái méi mài wán.

(Baby bok choy is not sold out yet.)

⑥ 那个人我没看清楚。

Nà ge rén wǒ méi kàn qīngchu.

(I didn't see clearly who that person was.)

⑦ 糟糕，这个字你没有写对。

Zāogāo, zhè ge zì nǐ méiyǒu xiě duì.

(Shoot! You didn't write this character correctly.)

Following certain verbs, the use of an adjective as the resultative complement is not random. In those cases, it is advisable to take the combination of the verb and the complement as a whole unit.

5. 好 (hǎo) as a Resultative Complement

好 (hǎo) can serve as a complement following a verb, indicating the completion of an action. It often indicates readiness to start the next action or event.

① 饭做好了，快来吃吧。

Fàn zuò hǎo le, kuài lái chī ba.

(The food is ready. Come and eat.)

② 功课做好了，我要睡觉了。

Gōngkè zuò hǎo le, wǒ yào shuì jiào le.

(My homework is done. I want to go to bed.)

❸   衣服我已经帮你买好了，明天晚会你就可以
穿了。

Yīfu wǒ yǐjīng bāng nǐ mǎi hǎo le, míngtiān wǎnhuì nǐ jiù kěyǐ chuān le.

(I've already bought the dress for you. You can wear it for the party tomorrow night.)

Language Practice

A. Picky Shopper

Your boyfriend/girlfriend is hard to please. You take him/her shopping. As it turns out, he/she doesn't like any of the items in the shopping center. Tell your friends what happened.

EXAMPLE:

→ 那儿的衬衫他/她一件都
不喜欢，一件都没买。

Nàr de chènshān tā yí jiàn dōu bù xǐhuan, yí jiàn dōu méi mǎi.

1.

2.

3.

4.

5.

B. How Was Your Day?

Today is not Wang Peng's lucky day. He rode the wrong bus, wore the wrong clothes, and did the wrong homework. But Li You had a great day today. She understood what the teacher said, finished her homework, and saw her good friend Bai Ying'ai.

Let's recap what happened to Wang Peng and Li You.

EXAMPLE: (rode the wrong bus)

王朋今天坐错车了。   Wáng Péng jīntiān zuò cuò chē le.

1. 王朋今天穿了错衣服了。

2. 王朋今天做错

1. _____

2. _____

3. _____

C. Ready, Set, Go!

Suppose you have a Chinese test tomorrow. Express your readiness by saying that you have completed all of the following actions.

EXAMPLE: 练习汉字   liànxí Hànzì

→ 我练习汉字练习好了。   Wǒ liànxí Hànzì liànxí hǎo le.

or   or

汉字我练习好了。   Hànzì wǒ liànxí hǎo le.

1. 做功课   zuò gōngkè

2. 复习生词语法   fùxí shēngcí yǔfǎ

3. 准备考试   zhǔnbèi kǎo shì

If you are not ready, what will you say?
Ask the classmate next to you if he/she is ready.

D. Course Evaluation

The following is a wish list of a Chinese language teacher who hopes his students can change some of their habits. As a Chinese language student, powwow with your partner and come up with your own list of what you would like your teacher to do differently.

老师希望学生：   Lǎoshī xīwàng xuésheng:

多来上课   duō lái shàng kè

多预习课文   duō yùxí kèwén

多听录音   duō tīng lùyīn

多复习生词语法   duō fùxí shēngcí yǔfǎ

多练习写汉字   duō liànxí xiě Hànzì

少说英文   shǎo shuō Yīngwén

少玩儿   shǎo wánr

学生希望老师：

Xuésheng xīwàng lǎoshī:

_____

_____

_____

_____

E. Recap and Narrate

Working with a partner, recap the content of Dialogue I:

1. 王朋和李友到
饭馆儿的时候，
那儿的人多吗？

1. Wáng Péng hé Lǐ Yǒu dào
fànguǎnr de shíhou,
nàr de rén duō ma?

2. 李友让王朋点菜，
他点了些什么？

2. Lǐ Yǒu ràng Wáng Péng diǎn cài,
tā diǎn le xiē shénme?

3. 李友点了些什么？

3. Lǐ Yǒu diǎn le xiē shénme?

4. 服务员说他们的
家常豆腐有肉吗？

4. Fúwùyuán shuō tāmen de
jiācháng dòufu yǒu ròu ma?

5. 李友点酸辣汤的时候，
跟服务员说了什么？

5. Lǐ Yǒu diǎn suānlàtāng de shíhou,
gēn fúwùyuán shuō le shénme?

6. 王朋和李友点
青菜了吗？

6. Wáng Péng hé Lǐ Yǒu diǎn
qīngcài le ma?

7. 王朋和李友要喝什么？

7. Wáng Péng hé Lǐ Yǒu yào hē
shénme?

8. 李友为什么要服务员
上菜快一点儿？

8. Lǐ Yǒu wèishénme yào fúwùyuán
shàng cài kuài yì diǎnr?

Using the words and phrases in blue as prompts, connect your answers above to form a narrative like this example:

王朋和李友去一家中国饭馆儿吃饭，饭馆儿的人很多。王朋先点了两盘素饺子，李友点了一盘家常豆腐，她告诉服务员家常豆腐不要放肉，因为她吃素。除了饺子和家常豆腐以外，他们还点了两碗酸辣汤。服务员问他们喝点儿什么，王朋要了一杯冰茶，李友要了一杯可乐，还告诉服务员多放一点儿冰。因为他们都饿了，所以让服务员上菜快一点儿。服务员说没问题，菜很快就能做好。

Wáng Péng hé Lǐ Yǒu qù yì jiā Zhōngguó fànguǎnr chī fàn, fànguǎnr de rén hěn duō. Wáng Péng xiān diǎn le liǎng pán sù jiǎozi, Lǐ Yǒu diǎn le yì pán jiācháng dòufu, tā gàosù fúwùyuán jiācháng dòufu bú yào fàng ròu, yīnwèi tā chī sù. Chúle jiǎozi hé jiācháng dòufu yǐwài, tāmen hái diǎn le liǎng wǎn suānlàtāng. Fúwùyuán wèn tāmen hē diǎnr shénme, Wáng Péng yào le yì bēi bīngchá, Lǐ Yǒu yào le yì bēi kělè, hái gàosù fúwùyuán duō fàng yì diǎnr bīng. Yīnwèi tāmen dōu è le, suǒyǐ ràng fúwùyuán shàng cài kuài yì diǎnr. Fúwùyuán shuō méi wèntí, cài hěn kuài jiù néng zuò hǎo.

一盘饺子
yì pán jiǎozi

Dialogue II: Eating in a Cafeteria

（今天是星期四，学生餐厅有中国菜，师傅是上海人。）

Liu Xin

师傅❶，请问今天晚饭有什么好吃的？

我们今天有糖醋鱼，甜甜的⑥、酸酸的，好吃极了❷，你买一个吧。

好。今天有没有红烧牛肉？

没有。你已经要鱼了，别吃肉了。来⑦个凉拌黄瓜吧？

好。再来一碗米饭。一共多少钱？

糖醋鱼，四块五，凉拌黄瓜，一块七；一碗米饭，五毛钱。一共六块七。

LANGUAGE NOTES

❶ 师傅 (shīfu, master worker) is a common term to address a stranger, especially a blue-collar worker such as a taxi driver or a chef.

❷ When used after an adjective or a verb, 极了 (jí le) usually indicates the superlative degree: 今天热极了。(Jīntiān rè jí le, it is extremely hot today.) 他高兴极了。(Tā gāoxìng jí le, he is overjoyed.)

师傅，糟糕，我忘了带饭卡了。
这是十块钱。

 找你三块三。

 师傅，钱你找错了，多找了我一
块钱。

 对不起，我没有看清楚。

 没关系❸。

 下个星期四再来。

 好，再见。

❸ 没关系 (méi guānxi, it doesn't matter): When someone apologizes by saying 对不起 (duìbuqǐ), it is common to respond by saying 没关系 (méi guānxi, it doesn't matter.)

(Jīntiān shì xīngqīsì, xuéshēng cāntīng yǒu Zhōngguó cài, shīfu shì Shànghǎi rén.)

 Shīfu❶, qǐng wèn jīntiān wǎnfàn yǒu shénme hàochī de?

 Wǒmen jīntiān yǒu tángcùyú, tián tián de⑥, suān suān de, hǎochī jí le❷, nǐ mǎi yí ge ba.

 Hǎo. Jīntiān yǒu méiyǒu hóngshāo niúròu?

 Méiyǒu. Nǐ yǐjīng yào yú le, bié chī ròu le. Lái⑦ ge liángbàn huánggua ba?

 Hǎo. Zài lái yì wǎn mǐfàn. Yígòng duōshao qián?

 Tángcùyú, sì kuài wǔ, liángbàn huánggua, yí kuài qī; Yì wǎn mǐfàn, wǔ máo qián. Yígòng liù kuài qī.

 Shīfu, zāogāo, wǒ wàng le dài fànkǎ le. Zhè shì shí kuài qián.

 Zhǎo nǐ sān kuài sān.

 Shīfu, qián nǐ zhǎo cuò le, duō zhǎo le wǒ yí kuài qián.

 Duìbuqǐ, wǒ méiyǒu kàn qīngchu.

 Méi guānxi. ❸

 Xià ge xīngqīsì zài lái.

 Hǎo, zàijiàn.

学生在学生餐厅点菜。
Xuésheng zài xuéshēng cāntīng diǎn cài.

 VOCABULARY

1.	师傅	shīfu	n	master worker
2.	好吃	hǎochī	adj	delicious
3.	糖醋鱼	tángcùyú	n	fish in sweet and sour sauce
	糖	táng	n	sugar
	醋	cù	n	vinegar
4.	甜	tián	adj	sweet
5.	酸	suān	adj	sour
6.	极	jí	adv	extremely
7.	红烧	hóngshāo	v	to braise in soy sauce

VOCABULARY

8.	牛肉	niúròu	n	beef
	牛	niú	n	cow; ox
9.	鱼	yú	n	fish
10.	凉拌	liángbàn	v	(of food) cold "blended"; cold tossed
11.	黄瓜	huánggua	n	cucumber
12.	米饭	mǐfàn	n	cooked rice
13.	忘	wàng	v	to forget
14.	带	dài	v	to bring; to take; to carry; to come with
15.	饭卡	fànkǎ	n	meal card
16.	错	cuò	adj	wrong
17.	清楚	qīngchu	adj	clear
18.	没关系	méi guānxi		it doesn't matter

Proper Nouns

19.	上海	Shànghǎi	Shanghai

上海 Shànghǎi

学生食堂就是学生餐厅。
Xuéshēng shítáng jiù shì xuéshēng cāntīng.

Grammar

6. Reduplication of Adjectives

Some Chinese adjectives can be reduplicated. When monosyllabic adjectives are reduplicated, the accent usually falls on the second occurrence. When the reduplicated monosyllabic adjective takes a "r" suffix, like 慢慢儿 (màn mānr, slow), its second occurrence is usually pronounced in the first tone, regardless what the adjective's original tone is. Reduplication of adjectives often suggests an approving and appreciative attitude on the speaker's part.

❶   王朋高高的，很帅。

　　Wáng Péng gāo gāo de, hěn shuài.

　　(Wang Peng is tall and handsome.)

❷   可乐凉凉的，很好喝。

　　Kělè liáng liáng de, hěn hǎo hē.

　　(The cola is nicely chilled and tastes good.)

❸   酸辣汤酸酸的、辣辣的，非常好喝。

　　Suānlà tāng suān suān de, là là de, fēicháng hǎo hē.

　　(The hot and sour soup is a bit sour and a bit hot; it tastes great.)

Reduplication of adjectives usually does not appear in the negative form.

7. The Verb 来 (lái)

In colloquial expressions, the verb 来 (lái) can serve as a substitute for certain verbs, mostly in imperative sentences:

❶ 先生，你们想吃点儿什么？

Xiānsheng, nǐmen xiǎng chī diǎnr shénme?

(Sir, what would you like?)

来一盘糖醋鱼，一碗酸辣汤，和一碗米饭。

Lái yì pán tángcùyú, yì wǎn suānlàtāng, hé yì wǎn mǐfàn.

(Give me a plate of sweet and sour fish, a bowl of hot and sour soup, and a bowl of rice, please.)

❷ (At a party, when someone has sung a song)

再来一个！

Zài lái yí ge!

(Encore!)

The use of 来 (lái) in this sense is rather limited. It is usually used in restaurants and stores, especially when buying small things or coaxing someone to sing a song.

Language Practice

F. Special of the Day

Pretend that you are a waiter in a restaurant; you need to recommend and promote your dishes/drinks to the customers. Let's see how enthusiastic you can be.

EXAMPLE:

→ 我们的青菜好吃极了。Wǒmen de qīngcài hǎochī jí le.

1.

2.

3.

4.

5.

G. Placing Your Order

Imagine that you are in a restaurant in China, and the waiter is asking you what you want to have. The easiest way to place your order in a Chinese restaurant is by using 来 (lái). Let's practice.

EXAMPLE: X 2

→ 服务员，来两杯冰茶。 Fúwùyuán, lái liǎng bēi bīngchá.

1.   x3

2.   x1

3.   x1

4.   x2

5.   x2

H. Special Requests

Tell the waitperson that you have special dietary requirements and ask that the chef not use certain ingredients. Make sure to use 一···也/都不···(yī...yě/dōu bù...) in your request.

EXAMPLE: salt

→ 我不吃盐，请师傅   Wǒ bù chī yán, qǐng shīfu
一点儿盐都不要/别放。 yì diǎnr yán dōu bú yào/bié fàng.

1. MSG

2. meat

3. vinegar

4. sugar

I. Recap and Narrate

Working with a partner, recap the content of Dialogue II:

1. 星期几学生餐厅有
中国菜？师傅是
哪儿人？

1. Xīngqījǐ xuéshēng cāntīng yǒu
Zhōngguó cài? Shīfù shì
nǎr rén?

2. 师傅告诉王朋今天
有什么好吃的？

2. Shīfu gàosù Wáng Péng jīntiān
yǒu shénme hàochī de?

3. 今天有没有红烧牛肉？

3. Jīntiān yǒu méiyǒu hóngshāo
niúròu?

4. 师傅让王朋再来
个什么菜？

4. Shīfu ràng Wáng Péng zài lái
ge shénme cài?

5. 王朋要米饭了吗？

6. 王朋一共花了
   多少钱？

7. 王朋忘了带饭卡，
   给了师傅多少钱？

8. 师傅找了他多少钱？

9. 师傅找钱找对了吗？

10. 师傅说为什么
    他找钱找错了？

5. Wáng Péng yào mǐfàn le ma?

6. Wáng Péng yígòng huā le
   duōshao qián?

7. Wáng Péng wàng le dài fànkǎ,
   gěi le shīfu duōshao qián?

8. Shīfu zhǎo le tā duōshao qián?

9. Shīfu zhǎo qián zhǎo duì le ma?

10. Shīfu shuō wèishénme
    tā zhǎo qián zhǎo cuò le?

Using the words and phrases in blue as prompts, connect your answers above to form a narrative like this example:

每个星期四学生餐厅都有中国菜，今天是星期四，所以王朋去学生餐厅吃饭。餐厅的师傅是上海人，他告诉王朋今天有糖醋鱼，甜甜的、酸酸的，好吃极了。王朋还想吃红烧牛肉，师傅说今天没有红烧牛肉，来个凉拌黄瓜吧。王朋还要了一碗米饭，一共花了六块七。因为他忘了带饭卡，就给了师傅十块钱，师傅多找了他一块钱。王朋告诉师傅钱找错了。师傅说对不起，他没有看清楚。王朋说没关系。

Měige xīngqīsì xuéshēng cāntīng dōu yǒu Zhōngguó cài, jīntiān shì xīngqīsì, suǒyǐ Wáng Péng qù xuéshēng cāntīng chī fàn. Cāntīng de shīfu shì Shànghǎi rén, tā gàosù Wáng Péng jīntiān yǒu tángcùyú, tiántián de, suānsuān de, hǎochī jí le. Wáng Péng hái xiǎng chī hóngshāo niúròu, shīfu shuō jīntiān méiyǒu hóngshāo niúròu, lái ge liángbàn huánggua ba. Wáng Péng hái yào le yì wǎn mǐfàn, yígòng huā le liù kuài qī. Yīnwèi tā wàng le dài fànkǎ, jiù gěi le shīfu shí kuài qián, shīfu duō zhǎo le tā yí kuài qián. Wáng Péng gàosù shīfu qián zhǎo cuò le. Shīfù shuō duìbuqǐ, tā méiyǒu kàn qīngchu. Wáng Péng shuō méi guānxi.

HOW ABOUT YOU?

What's on your grocery list?

1.	鸡	jī	n	chicken
2.	猪肉	zhūròu	n	pork
3.	羊肉	yángròu	n	lamb; mutton
4.	虾	xiā	n	shrimp
5.	蛋	dàn	n	egg
6.	胡萝卜	húluóbo	n	carrot
7.	洋葱	yángcōng	n	onion

What other grocery items would you like to know? Please ask your teacher and make a note here:

_____

What's your favorite Chinese dish?

1.	宫保鸡丁	gōngbǎo jīdīng	n	Kung Pao chicken
2.	麻婆豆腐	mápó dòufu	n	Mapo tofu
3.	蛋花汤	dànhuātāng	n	egg drop soup
4.	炒面	chǎomiàn	n	stir-fried noodles

What other Chinese dishes do you like? If you don't know their names in Chinese, please ask your teacher and make a note here:

_____

Culture Highlights

❶ The word 中国菜 (Zhōngguó cài) covers all varieties of Chinese food in different styles. There are different ways of delineating Chinese cooking styles. Among the principal regional cuisines in China are the Shandong school, which originated in the northern province of Shandong; the Shanghainese school, favored by people in the lower Yangtze valley; and the Cantonese and Sichuanese schools, based respectively in the southern provinces of Guangdong and Sichuan. A Chinese restaurant usually specializes in only one cooking style, but some are more eclectic.

❷ In a Chinese meal, rice is the 主食 (zhǔshí, staple, or principal food), particularly in the traditional rice-growing region of the country, the south. In the north, 主食 (zhǔshí) often consists of 面 (miàn, noodles), 饺子 (jiǎozi, dumplings), and 馒头 (mántou, Chinese bread) instead.

❸ In Chinese food culture, knives (刀 dāo) belong in the kitchen, not at the dining table. The cook preempts the diner's need for a knife by

主食 Rice and Noodle

泰国香米饭 Thai Flavor Rice	3元/碗
高级知识份子面 Gao's Noodles with Tomato Sauce	36元
过桥米线 Cross Bridge Rice Noodle	38元
小锅米线 Spicy and Sour Rice Noodle in Small Pot	16元
腾冲大救驾 Stir Fried Rice Pie	26元
贵州炒粉 Guizhou Fried Rice Noodle	26元

cutting up the food, especially the meat, into small pieces before cooking. As everyone knows, most Chinese people eat not with a fork but with a pair of chopsticks (筷子 kuàizi).

4 Since the 1990s, American fast food restaurants such as KFC (肯德基, Kěndéjī), McDonald's (麦当劳, Màidāngláo), and Pizza Hut (必胜客, Bìshèngkè) have been popping up in Chinese cities like mushrooms. Many of them have enjoyed flourishing business. The dubious reputation of American fast food as a "fattener" does not scare most Chinese customers away, and it is popular, especially among young people and children, to hang out with friends in an American fast food restaurant. The success of these American restaurants in China has been, at least in part, due to efforts they have made to adapt to local tastes. KFC, for instance, now offers 豆浆 (dòujiāng, soybean milk) and 油条 (yóutiáo, deep-fried dough sticks) for breakfast. McDonald's now sells 鸡卷 (jījuǎn, chicken rolls).

油条
yóutiáo

English Text

Dialogue I

(In a restaurant)

Waiter: Come in! Please come in!

Li You: How come there are so many people? It doesn't look like there's a table left.

Wang Peng: Waiter, are there any tables left?

Waiter: Yes, yes. That table is not taken.

* * *

Waiter: What would you like to order?

Li You: Wang Peng, why don't you order?

Wang Peng: All right. Give us two plates of dumplings, to start things off. Vegetarian dumplings.

Waiter: What else would you like besides dumplings?

Wang Peng: Li You, what do you say?

Li You: Family-style tofu with no meat in it. I'm a vegetarian.

Waiter: Our family-style tofu has no meat in it.

Li You: Also two bowls of hot and sour soup with no MSG. Not too salty. Do you have baby bok choy?

Waiter: I'm sorry. We've just sold out baby bok choy.

Wang Peng: Then we'll do without green vegetables.

Waiter: What would you like to drink?

Wang Peng: I'd like a glass of iced tea. Li You, what would you like to drink?

Li You: I'm really thirsty. Please give me a cola, with lots of ice.

Waiter: OK. Two plates of dumplings, family-style tofu, two hot and sour soups, a glass of iced tea, a cola with lots of ice. Anything else?

Li You: That'll be all. That's more than enough. Waiter, we're both really hungry. Could you please bring the food as soon as possible?

Waiter: No problem. The dishes will be done in no time.

辣的凉拌黄瓜
là de liángbàn huánggua

不辣的凉拌黄瓜
bú là de liángbàn huánggua

Dialogue II

(It's Thursday. The student cafeteria is serving Chinese food. The chef is from Shanghai.)

Wang Peng: Chef, what's good for dinner today?

Chef: We've got sweet and sour fish. It's a little sweet and a little sour. It's delicious. Why don't you get that?

Wang Peng: Great. Do you have beef braised in soy sauce today?

Chef: No, we don't. You've already got fish, so there's no need to have meat. How about a cucumber salad?

Wang Peng: All right. Give me a bowl of rice. How much all together?

Chef: Sweet and sour fish is $4.50, cucumber salad $1.70; one bowl of rice, 50 cents. All together $6.70.

Wang Peng: Shoot, Chef. I forgot my meal card. Here's $10.

Chef: $3.30 is your change.

Wang Peng: Chef, you've given the wrong change. You gave me one dollar extra.

Chef: I'm sorry. I didn't see it clearly.

Wang Peng: That's all right.

Chef: Come again next Thursday.

Wang Peng: OK. Bye.

PROGRESS CHECKLIST

Before proceeding to Lesson 13, be sure you can complete the following tasks in Chinese:

I am able to—

- ☑ Ask the restaurant host if there are seats available;
- ☐ Name some Chinese dishes and place an order;
- ☐ Tell the waiter my meal preferences and dietary restrictions;
- ☐ Ask the waiter to recommend dishes and to rush the order if I'm in a hurry;
- ☐ Pay the bill after my meal;
- ☐ Get the correct change after my payment.

LESSON 13

Asking Directions

第十三课　问路

Dì shísān kè　Wèn lù

 LEARNING OBJECTIVES

In this lesson, you will learn to use Chinese to

- Ask for and give directions;
- Identify locations by using landmarks as references;
- Describe whether two places are close to or far away from one another;
- State where you are heading and the purpose of going there.

 RELATE AND GET READY

In your own culture/community—

1. Besides the basics such as "hello," "how are you," "what's up," and so on, what are some other common greetings?

2. What phrases do people often use when giving directions?

3. What do people usually say to indicate that they don't have a good sense of direction?

Dialogue I: Where Are You Off To?

 小白，下课了？上哪儿
去①？

您好，常老师。我想去学校
的电脑中心，不知道怎么
走，听说就在运动场旁边①。

电脑中心没有② 运动场
那么③ 远。你知道学校图
书馆在哪里② 吗？

知道，离王朋的宿舍不远。

电脑中心离图书馆很近，就
在图书馆和学生活动中心中
间。

LANGUAGE NOTES

① 上哪儿去 (shàng nǎr qu) is a more casual way of asking 去哪儿 (qù nǎr).

② Here 哪里 (nǎli) is a question word meaning "where." It is interchangeable with 哪儿 (nǎr). People in northern China, especially in Beijing, speak with an "儿 (ér) ending" quite often. For example, some people say 明儿 (míngr) for "tomorrow" instead of 明天 (míngtiān), and 这儿 (zhèr) for "here" instead of 这里 (zhèli).

常老师，您去哪儿呢？

 我想到学校书店去买书④。

 书店在什么地方？

 就在学生活动中心里边。
我们一起走吧。

 好。

③什么地方 (shénme dìfang, lit., what place) is generally interchangeable with 哪儿 (nǎr) or 哪里 (nǎli).

 Xiǎo Bái, xià kè le? Shàng nǎr qu?

 Nín hǎo, Cháng lǎoshī. Wǒ xiǎng qù xuéxiào de diànnǎo zhōngxīn, bù zhīdào zěnme zǒu, tīngshuō jiù zài yùndòngchǎng pángbiān.

 Diànnǎo zhōngxīn méiyǒu yùndòngchǎng nàme yuǎn. Nǐ zhīdào xuéxiào túshūguǎn zài nǎli ma?

 Zhīdào, lí Wáng Péng de sùshè bù yuǎn.

 Diànnǎo zhōngxīn lí túshūguǎn hěn jìn, jiù zài túshūguǎn hé xuéshēng huódòng zhōngxīn zhōngjiān.

 Cháng lǎoshī, nín qù nǎr ne?

 Wǒ xiǎng dào xuéxiào shūdiàn qù mǎi shū④.

 Shūdiàn zài shénme dìfang?

Jiù zài xuéshēng huódòng zhōngxīn lǐbian. Wǒmen yìqǐ zǒu ba.

Hǎo.

VOCABULARY

1.	上	shàng	v	to go [colloq.]
2.	中心	zhōngxīn	n	center
3.	听说	tīngshuō	v	to be told; to hear of
4.	运动	yùndòng	n	sports
5.	场	chǎng	n	field
6.	旁边	pángbiān	n	side [See Grammar 1.]
7.	远	yuǎn	adj	far
8.	离	lí	prep	away from
9.	近	jìn	adj	near
10.	活动	huódòng	n	activity
11.	中间	zhōngjiān	n	middle
12.	书店	shūdiàn	n	bookstore
13.	地方	dìfang	n	place
14.	里边	lǐbian	n	inside [See Grammar 1.]

Grammar

1. Direction and Location Words

Direction words 上/下/前/后/左/右/东/南/西/北/里/外/旁 (shàng/xià/qián/hòu/zuǒ/yòu/dōng/nán/xī/běi/lǐ/wài/páng) often combine with suffixes such as 边 (biān), 面 (miàn), and 头 (tóu). As shown below, such compounds become location words. The suffixes 边 (biān), 面 (miàn), and 头 (tóu) are all pronounced in the neutral tone, with the exception of the 边 (biān) in 旁边 (pángbiān), which remains in the full first tone.

上边/面/头
shàngbian/mian/tou
(top)

前边/面/头
(qiánbian/mian/tou)
(front)

后边/面/头
hòubian/mian/tou
(back)

下边/面/头
xiàbian/mian/tou
(bottom)

里边/面/头
lǐbian/mian/tou
(inside)

外边/面/头
wàibian/mian/tou
(outside)

中间

zhōngjiān

(middle)

左边/面

zuǒbian/mian

(left side)

右边/面

yòubian/mian

(right side)

旁边

pángbiān

(side)

北边/面

běibian/mian

(north side)

西边/面

xībian/mian

(west side)

东边/面

dōngbian/mian

(east side)

南边/面

nánbian/mian

(south side)

The direction word 上 (shàng, on) or 里 (lǐ, in) combines with a noun to form a location expression, e.g., 桌子上 (zhuōzi shang, on the table), 衣服上 (yīfu shang, on the clothes), 书上 (shū shang, in/on the book), 学校里 (xuéxiào li, in the school), 办公室里 (bàngōngshì li, in the office), 教室里 (jiàoshì li, in the classroom), 电视里 (diànshì li, on TV). The word 里 (lǐ) cannot be used after some proper nouns such as the name of a country or a city.

Compare:

学校里有很多学生。

Xuéxiào li yǒu hěn duō xuésheng.

(There are many students at school.)

北京有很多学生。

Běijīng yǒu hěn duō xuésheng.

(There are many students in Beijing.)

It is incorrect to say:

*北京里有很多学生。

*Běijīng li yǒu hěn duō xuésheng.

The combination of a direction word plus 边 (biān) /面 (miàn) /头 (tóu) can follow a noun to indicate a location, e.g., 图书馆(的)旁边 (túshūguǎn {de} pángbiān, near the library); 学校(的)里面 (xuéxiào {de} lǐmian, inside the school); 桌子(的)上头 (zhuōzi {de} shàngtou, on the table); 教室(的)外面 (jiàoshì {de} wàimian, outside the classroom); 城市(的)北边 (chéngshì {de} běibian, north of the city). In these expressions the particle 的 (de) following the noun is optional.

2. Comparative Sentences with 没（有）(méi{yǒu})

Besides using 比 (bǐ), another way to make a comparison is to use 没（有）(méi{yǒu}). In a comparative sentence with 没有 (méiyǒu), the pronoun 那么 (nàme) is sometimes added to the sentence. [See more on 那么 (nàme) below.]

❶   我弟弟没有我高。

Wǒ dìdi méiyǒu wǒ gāo.

(My younger brother is not as tall as I am.)

[I am taller than my brother.]

❷　北京没有上海热。

Běijīng méiyǒu Shānghǎi rè.

(It is not as hot in Beijing as in Shanghai.)

❸　他姐姐没有他妹妹那么喜欢买东西。

Tā jiějie méiyǒu tā mèimei nàme xǐhuan mǎi dōngxi.

(His older sister does not like shopping as much as his younger sister does.)

[His older sister might like shopping too, but not as much as his younger sister.]

❹　我没有她那么喜欢刷卡。

Wǒ méiyǒu tā nàme xǐhuan shuā kǎ.

(I don't like to use credit cards as much as she does.)

[I do use credit cards, but she likes to use them more than I do.]

A 没有 (méiyǒu) B... vs. A 不比 (bù bǐ) B...

While 没有 (méiyǒu) ... is used to say that one thing is of a lesser degree than another, 不比 (bù bǐ) ... means "no more than..." The two things being compared may be equal, but what is specifically stated is that A is *no more* than B. Compare the following sentences:

❺　**A:** 今天比昨天热吗？

Jīntiān bǐ zuótiān rè ma?

(Is today hotter than yesterday?)

　　B: 今天不比昨天热。

Jīntiān bù bǐ zuótiān rè.

(Today is not any hotter than yesterday.)

[It could be the same temperature or cooler than yesterday.]

　　C: 今天没有昨天热。

Jīntiān méiyǒu zuótiān rè.

(Today is not as hot as yesterday.)

[Today is cooler.]

❻ **A:** 这篇课文比那篇课文短吗？

Zhè piān kèwén bǐ nà piān kèwén duǎn ma?

(Is this text shorter than that one?)

B: 这篇课文不比那篇课文短，两篇一样长。

Zhè piān kèwén bù bǐ nà piān kèwén duǎn, liǎng piān yíyàng cháng.)

(This text is not any shorter than that one. They are the same length.)

C: 是吗？我觉得这篇课文没有那篇长。

Shì ma? Wǒ juéde zhè piān kèwén méiyǒu nà piān cháng.

(Really? I think this text is not as long as that one.)

[This text is shorter than that one.]

A Quick Summary of Comparative Sentences

A 比 (bǐ)   B 大 (dà)   A>B
A 不比 (bù bǐ)   B 大 (dà)   A≤B
A 没有 (méiyǒu)   B 大 (dà)   A<B

---

3. 那么 (nàme) Indicating Degree

那么 (nàme) is often placed before adjectives or verbs such as 想 (xiǎng), 喜欢 (xǐhuan), 会 (huì), 能 (néng), and 希望 (xīwàng), to denote a high degree.

❶ 你那么不喜欢写日记，就别写了吧。

Nǐ nàme bù xǐhuan xiě rìjì, jiù bié xiě le ba.

(Since you dislike writing journals so much, why don't you quit doing it?)

没有···那么··· (méiyǒu... nàme...) means "not reaching the point of."

❷ 弟弟没有哥哥那么帅，那么酷。

Dìdi méiyǒu gēge nàme shuài, nàme kù.

(The younger brother is not as handsome and cool as the older brother.)

❸   坐地铁没有坐公共汽车那么麻烦。

Zuò dìtiě méiyǒu zuò gōnggòng qìchē nàme máfan.

(Riding the subway is not as much of a hassle as riding the bus.)

❹   这个样子没有你说的那么合适。

Zhè ge yàngzi méiyǒu nǐ shuō de nàme héshì.

(This style is not as suitable as you said.)

❺   这张地图没有那张地图那么新。

Zhè zhāng dìtú méiyǒu nà zhāng dìtú nàme xīn.

This map is not as new as that one.)

By using 那么(nàme), the speaker affirms the certain attribute of something or somebody in question. By stating that the younger brother does not reach the same standard of handsomeness and coolness as the older brother, (2), for instance, acknowledges that the older brother is handsome and cool.

---

4. 到 (dào) + Place + 去 (qù) + Action

In this structure, the combination of "到 (dào) + Place + 去 (qù) + Action" denotes the purpose of going somewhere.

❶   我要到电脑中心去上网。

Wǒ yào dào diànnǎo zhōngxīn qù shàng wǎng.

(I want to go to the computer center to use the internet.)

❷   他到朋友的宿舍去聊天儿了。

Tā dào péngyou de sùshè qù liáo tiānr le.

(He went to his friend's dorm to chat.)

❸   我们到飞机场去送李小姐。

Wǒmen dào fēijīchǎng qù sòng Lǐ xiǎojiě.

(We went to the airport to see Miss Li off.)

Language Practice

A. Xiao Peng's Room

The following is Xiao Peng's room. Xiao Peng claims he cannot find his stuff and keeps asking "Where are my things?" Xiao Peng's mother has to tell him where things are. Pair up with a partner and role-play Xiao Peng and his mother.

EXAMPLE:

Xiao Peng: 我的电脑呢？   Wǒ de diànnǎo ne?

Mother: 你的电脑在   Nǐ de diànnǎo zài
　　　　桌子上。   zhuōzi shang.

1.

2.

3.

4.

B. Compare and Contrast

Based on the clues given, make comparisons using 没有···（那么）···(méiyǒu…
{nàme}…, not as…)

EXAMPLE: today   yesterday
                40º F   55º F

 今天没有昨天
（那么）暖和。

Jīntiān méiyǒu zuótiān

(nàme) nuǎnhuo.

1.

2.

¥ 45.00   ¥ 60.00

2008

3.

2009

4.

size 30

size 32

5.

C. Geography Bee

Locate each city on the map and work with your partner to ask and answer whether each city is close to or far away from the place where you are.

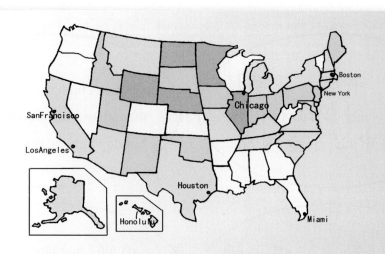

EXAMPLE: 纽约   Niǔyuē

→ A: 纽约离我们
这儿远吗？

Niǔyuē lí wǒmen
zhèr yuǎn ma?

B: 纽约离我们这儿
很远/不远/很近。

Niǔyuē lí wǒmen zhèr
hěn yuǎn/bù yuǎn/hěn jìn.

1. Boston
2. Chicago
3. Houston
4. Los Angeles
5. Miami
6. San Francisco
7. Honolulu

D. Plans for the Weekend

Your friend is coming to visit you at school this weekend, and you want to show him/her around. Your choices of places and activities are shown below. Work with a partner to come up with suggestions.

公园　书店　运动场
商店　图书馆　宿舍
活动中心　老师家

gōngyuán　shūdiàn　yùndòngchǎng
shāngdiàn　túshūguǎn　sùshè
huódòng zhōngxīn　lǎoshī jiā

打球　滑冰　喝咖啡
看碟　上网　吃饺子
聊天　听音乐

dǎ qiú　huá bīng　hē kāfēi
kàn dié　shàng wǎng　chī jiǎozi
liáo tiān　tīng yīnyuè

EXAMPLE: if you choose 公园 (gōngyuán) from the first group and 滑冰 (huá bīng) from the second group, then you will suggest

我们到公园去
滑冰，好吗？

Wǒmen dào gōngyuán qù
huá bīng, hǎo ma?

or

我们去公园
滑冰，好吗？

Wǒmen qù gōngyuán
huá bīng, hǎo ma?

1.

2.

3.

4.

5.

E. The Inside Scoop

Your partner always knows where to find the most stylish clothing, delicious food, and fun activities. Ask where he/she goes to buy clothes, to go out to eat, etc.

1. 你喜欢到哪儿
去跳舞？

   Nǐ xǐhuan dào nǎr

   qù tiào wǔ?

2. 你周末晚上常常
到哪儿去吃饭？

   Nǐ zhōumò wǎnshang chángcháng

   dào nǎr qù chī fàn?

3. 你喜欢到哪儿
去看电影？

   Nǐ xǐhuan dào nǎr

   qù kàn diànyǐng?

4. 你常常到哪儿
去买衣服？

   Nǐ chángcháng dào nǎr

   qù mǎi yīfu?

F. Recap and Narrate

Working with a partner, recap the content of Dialogue I:

1. 白英爱要去
什么地方？

   1. Bái Yīng'ài yào qù

      shénme dìfāng?

2. 白英爱知道学校的
电脑中心怎么走
吗？

   2. Bái Yīng'ài zhīdào xué xiào de

      diànnǎo zhōngxīn zěnme zǒu

      ma?

3. 电脑中心有
运动场远吗？

   3. Diànnǎo zhōngxīn yǒu

      yùndòngchǎng yuǎn ma?

4. 电脑中心在哪儿？

   4. Diànnǎo zhōngxīn zài nǎr?

5. 常老师去哪儿？

   5. Cháng lǎoshī qù nǎr?

6. 常老师为什么让
白英爱跟她一起走？

   6. Cháng lǎoshī wèishénme ràng

      Bái Yīng'ài gēn tā yìqǐ zǒu?

Using the words and phrases in blue as prompts, connect your answers above to form a narrative like this example:

白英爱要去学校的电脑中心，她不知道怎么走，但是听说电脑中心就在运动场旁边。她看见了常老师。常老师告诉她电脑中心没有运动场那么远，离图书馆很近，就在图书馆和学生活动中心中间。白英爱知道图书馆离王朋的宿舍不远，所以现在知道去电脑中心怎么走了。常老师要到学校的书店去买书，书店就在学生活动中心里边，所以她让白英爱跟她一起走。

Bái Yīng'ài yào qù xuéxiào de diànnǎo zhōngxīn, tā bù zhīdào zěnme zǒu, dànshì tīngshuō diànnǎo zhōngxīn jiù zài yùndòngchǎng pángbiān. Tā kàn jiàn le Cháng lǎoshī. Cháng lǎoshī gàosù tā diànnǎo zhōngxīn méiyǒu yùndòngchǎng nàme yuǎn, lí túshūguǎn hěn jìn, jiù zài túshūguǎn hé xuéshēng huódòng zhōngxīn zhōngjiān. Bái Yīng'ài zhīdao túshūguǎn lí Wáng Péng de sùshè bù yuǎn, suǒyǐ xiànzài zhīdao qù diànnǎo zhōngxīn zěnme zǒu le. Cháng lǎoshī yào dào xuéxiào de shūdiàn qù mǎi shū, shūdiàn jiù zài xuéshēng huódòng zhōngxīn lǐbian, suǒyǐ tā ràng Bái Yīng'ài gēn tā yìqǐ zǒu.

Dialogue II: Going to Chinatown

我们去中国城吃中国饭吧！

我没去过⑤中国城，不知道
中国城在哪儿。

没问题❶，你开车，我告诉你
怎么走。

你有地图吗？给我看看⑥。

地图在宿舍里，我忘了拿来了。

没有地图，走错了怎么办？

没有地图没关系，中国城我去过
很多次，不用地图也能找到⑦。

LANGUAGE NOTES

❶ 没问题 (méi wèntí, no problem) vs. 没关系 (méi guānxi, it doesn't matter): One uses 没问题 (méi wèntí) to assure someone that their request will be met or a problem will be solved, e.g. "开车送你去机场？没问题！" (Kāi chē sòng nǐ qù jīchǎng? Méi wèntí. Drive you to the airport? No problem!) 没关系 (méi guānxi), on the other hand, downplays the severity or impact of an issue, and is often used in response to someone's apology for a minor mistake.

你从这儿一直往南开，过三个路口，往西一拐就^⑧到了。

 哎，我不知道东南西北^❸。

 那你一直往前开，过三个红绿灯，往右一拐就到了。

（过了三个路口）

 不对，不对。你看，这个路口只能往左拐，不能往右拐。

 那就是下一个路口。往右拐，再往前开。到了，到了，你看见了吗？前面有很多中国字。

 那不是中文，那是日文，我们到了小东京了。

 是吗？那我们不吃中国饭了，吃日本饭吧！

❷ 拐 (guǎi), in the sense of "to turn," is used mainly in northern China. In the south, 转 (zhuǎn) is more commonly used instead, which is also the more formal substitute for 拐 (guǎi) in the north.

❸ Chinese speakers customarily mention the four directions in a set sequence, 东南西北 (dōng nán xī běi) or 东西南北 (dōng xī nán běi). For southeast and northeast, one says 东南 (dōng nán) and 东北 (dōng běi), never *南东 (nán dōng) or *北东 (běi dōng). Similarly, for southwest and northwest, one says 西南 (xī nán) and 西北 (xī běi), never *南西 (nán xī) or *北西 (běi xī).

 Wǒmen qù Zhōngguóchéng chī Zhōngguó fàn ba!

 Wǒ méi qù guo^⑤ Zhōngguóchéng, bù zhīdào Zhōngguóchéng zài nǎr.

 Méi wèntí^❶, nǐ kāi chē, wǒ gàosù nǐ zěnme zǒu.

 Nǐ yǒu dìtú ma? Gěi wǒ kàn kan^⑥.

 Dìtú zài sùshè li, wǒ wàng le ná lai le.

 Méiyǒu dìtú, zǒu cuò le zěnmebàn?

 Méiyǒu dìtú méi guānxi, Zhōngguóchéng wǒ qù guo hěn duō cì, bú yòng dìtú yě néng zhǎo dào^⑦. Nǐ cóng zhèr yìzhí wǎng nán kāi, guò sān ge lùkǒu, wǎng xī yì guǎi^❷ jiù^⑧ dào le.

 Āi, wǒ bù zhīdào dōng nán xī běi^❸.

Nà nǐ yìzhí wǎng qián kāi, guò sān ge hónglǜdēng, wǎng yòu yì guǎi jiù dào le.

(Guò le sān ge lùkǒu)

 Bú duì, bú duì. Nǐ kàn, zhè ge lùkǒu zhǐ néng wǎng zuǒ guǎi, bù néng wǎng yòu guǎi.

 Nà jiù shì xià yí ge lùkǒu. Wǎng yòu guǎi, zài wǎng qián kāi. Dào le, dào le, nǐ kàn jiàn le ma? Qiánmian yǒu hěn duō Zhōngguó zì.

 Nà bú shì Zhōngwén, nà shì Rìwén, wǒmen dào le Xiǎo Dōngjīng le.

 Shì ma? Nà wǒmen bù chī Zhōngguó fàn le, chī Rìběn fàn ba.

 ## VOCABULARY

1.	过	guo	p	(particle used after a verb to indicate a past experience) [See Grammar 5.]
2.	中国城	Zhōngguóchéng	n	Chinatown
	城	chéng	n	town; city
3.	地图	dìtú	n	map
4.	拿	ná	v	to take; to get
5.	次	cì	m	(measure word for frequency)
6.	从	cóng	prep	from
7.	一直	yìzhí	adv	straight; continuously
8.	往	wǎng	prep	towards
9.	南	nán	n	south
10.	过	guò	v	to pass
11.	路口	lùkǒu	n	intersection

VOCABULARY

12.	西	xī	n	west
13.	拐	guǎi	v	to turn
14.	哎	āi	excl	(exclamatory particle to express surprise or dissatisfaction)
15.	东	dōng	n	east
16.	北	běi	n	north
17.	前	qián	n	forward; ahead
18.	红绿灯	hónglǜdēng	n	traffic light
	灯	dēng	n	light
19.	右	yòu	n	right
20.	左	zuǒ	n	left
21.	前面	qiánmian	n	ahead; in front of

Proper Nouns

22.	日文	Rìwén		Japanese (language)
23.	东京	Dōngjīng		Tokyo
24.	日本	Rìběn		Japan

北海公园在故宫的哪一边？
Běihǎi Gōngyuán zài Gùgōng de nǎ yì biān?

Grammar

5. The Dynamic Particle 过 (guo)

The dynamic particle 过 (guo) is used to denote a past experience or occurrence that did not continue to the present but, typically, had an impact on the present.

❶   我在中国城工作过一年，所以我知道怎么走。

Wǒ zài Zhōngguóchéng gōngzuò guo yì nián, suǒyǐ wǒ zhīdào zěnme zǒu.

(I worked in Chinatown for a year, so I know how to get there.)

[The fact that the speaker worked in Chinatown for a year is the reason why he/she knows how to get there.]

❷   我见过李友，(所以知道)她很高。

Wǒ jiàn guo Lǐ Yǒu, (suǒyǐ zhīdào) tā hěn gāo.

(I've met Li You before, (so I know) she is tall.)

❸ **A:** 运动场远不远，你知道吗？

Yùndòngchǎng yuǎn bù yuǎn, nǐ zhīdào ma?

(Do you know if the sports field is far from here?)

A: 运动场我去过，(所以我知道)不远，很近。

Yùndòngchǎng wǒ qù guo, (suǒyǐ wǒ zhīdào) bù yuǎn, hěn jìn.

(I've been to the sports field, (so I know) it is not far away. It's very close.)

In this kind of sentence, expressions of time are often either unspecified or completely absent. If there is no time expression, the implied time for the action or event is 以前 (yǐqián, before; previously). Sometimes 以前 (yǐqián) can appear in the sentence as well.

❹   我以前去过中国城，知道怎么走。

Wǒ yǐqián qù guo Zhōngguóchéng, zhīdào zěnme zǒu.

(I've been to Chinatown before. I know how to get there.)

❺   以前我们见过面，可是没说过话。

Yǐqián wǒmen jiàn guo miàn, kěshì méi shuō guo huà.

(We've met before, but we've never spoken to each other.)

An expression indicating a specific time can also occasionally appear in a sentence with 过 (guo).

❻ **A:** 你见过李小姐吗？

Nǐ jiàn guo Lǐ xiǎojiě ma?

(Have you ever met Miss Li?)

B: 见过，上个月还见过她。

Jiàn guo, shàng ge yuè hái jiàn guo tā.

(Yes. I saw her as recently as last month.)

6. Reduplication of Verbs

Like adjectives [see Grammar 3 in Lesson 12], verbs can also be reduplicated. Reduplication of a verb in this lesson refers to an anticipated or requested action, and it makes the tone of the sentence milder.

❶ 老师，您再说说什么时候用"了"，好吗？

Lǎoshī, nín zài shuō shuo shénme shíhou yòng "le", hǎo ma?

(Teacher, would you say a bit more about when to use "le", please?)

❷ 妈，您看看，我这样写对不对？

Mā, nín kàn kan, wǒ zhèyàng xiě duì bu duì?

(Mom, take a look—did I write this correctly or not?)

❸ 我用用你的电脑可以吗？

Wǒ yòng yong nǐ de diànnǎo kěyǐ ma?

(May I use your computer for a minute?)

❹ 你帮我找找我的笔，好吗？

Nǐ bāng wǒ zhǎo zhao wǒ de bǐ, hǎo ma?

(Could you help me look for my pen for a second?)

❺ 你考完试，我们一起去公园走走，聊聊天儿。

Nǐ kǎo wán shì, wǒmen yìqǐ qù gōngyuán zǒu zou, liáo liao tiānr.

(Let's take a walk in the park and have a chat after your exam.)

If a sentence includes both a modal verb and an action verb, only the action verb can be reduplicated.

❻ 她想看看我的新手机。

Tā xiǎng kàn kan wǒ de xīn shǒujī.

(She wants to take a look at my new cell phone.)

7. Resultative Complements (II)

Let's review all the resultative complements that we have introduced so far, and learn some new ones that can be formed from the verbs and complements you already know.

a. 完 (wán):

看完	(kàn wán)	(finish reading)
吃完	(chī wán)	(finish eating)
喝完	(hē wán)	(finish drinking)
考完	(kǎo wán)	(finish taking a test)
买完	(mǎi wán)	(finish buying)
卖完	(mài wán)	(sell out)

b. 到 (dào):

找到	(zhǎo dào)	(find [something or someone] successfully)
看到	(kàn dào)	(see [something or someone])
听到	(tīng dào)	(hear [something or someone])
买到	(mǎi dào)	(buy [something] successfully)

c. 见 (jiàn):

看见	(kàn jiàn)	(see [something or someone]) — same as 看到 (kàn dào)
听见	(tīng jiàn)	(hear [something or someone]) — same as 听到 (tīng dào)

d. 好 (hǎo):

做好	(zuò hǎo)	(complete doing something, which is now ready)
买好	(mǎi hǎo)	(complete buying something, which is now ready)
准备好	(zhǔnbèi hǎo)	(prepare something, which is ready)

e. 错 (cuò):

买错	(mǎi cuò)	(buy the wrong thing)
找错	(zhǎo cuò)	(give the wrong change; find the wrong person or thing)
写错	(xiě cuò)	(write [something] incorrectly)
说错	(shuō cuò)	(say [something] incorrectly)
走错	(zǒu cuò)	(go the wrong way)

f. 懂 (dǒng):

听懂	(tīng dǒng)	(comprehend what one hears)
看懂	(kàn dǒng)	(comprehend what one reads or sees)

g. 清楚 (qīngchu):

看清楚	(kàn qīngchu)	(see [something] clearly)
听清楚	(tīng qīngchu)	(hear [something] clearly)

h. 会 (huì):

学会	(xué huì)	(acquire the skills [for doing something that one was previously unable to do])

The collocation of a verb with its resultative complement is not random; one has to memorize the whole expression of verb plus resultative complement. Some resultative complements are semantically related to the verb. For instance, in the sentence 我昨天看见她了 (Wǒ zuótiān kàn jiàn tā le, I saw her yesterday), the complement is semantically related to 看 (kàn), the verb of the sentence. Some resultative complements are semantically related to the object. In the sentence 我写错了两个字 (Wǒ xiě cuò le liǎng ge zì, I wrote two characters incorrectly), for instance, it is the object "characters" 字 (zì) that are "wrong" 错 (cuò). Some resultative complements are related to the subject, e.g., in the sentence 我学会了 (Wǒ xué huì le, I have learned it), the complement 会 (huì) is semantically related to 我 (wǒ), the subject of the sentence.

8. 一···就··· (yī...jiù..., as soon as...then...)

This structure connects two actions. It can be used to combine actions in two different types of situations: habitual situations or one-time situations. In a habitual situation, whenever the first action occurs, the second action immediately follows:

❶   他一上课就想睡觉。

Tā yí shàng kè jiù xiǎng shuì jiào.

(He feels sleepy every time the class starts.)

❷   小张平常只吃青菜，一吃肉就不舒服。

Xiǎo Zhāng píngcháng zhǐ chī qīngcài, yì chī ròu jiù bù shūfu.

(Little Zhang normally eats only vegetables. He feels sick whenever he eats meat.)

❸   李律师一累就喝咖啡。

Lǐ lùshī yí lèi jiù hē kāfēi.

(Attorney Li drinks coffee whenever he feels tired.)

In a one-time situation, the second action takes place as soon as the first is completed:

❹   我们一进饭馆儿，服务员就告诉我们没位子了。

Wǒmen yí jìn fànguǎnr, fúwùyuán jiù gàosù wǒmen méi wèizi le.

(As soon as we got into the restaurant, the waiter told us there were no seats available.)

❺   这课的语法很容易，我一看就懂。

Zhè kè de yǔfǎ hěn róngyì, wǒ yí kàn jiù dǒng.

(The grammar in this lesson was very easy. I understood it the moment I read it.)

6 活动中心离这儿不远，到第二个路口，往右一拐就到了。

Huódòng zhōngxīn lí zhèr bù yuǎn, dào dì èr ge lùkǒu, wǎng yòu yì guǎi jiù dào le.

(The activity center is not far from here. Turn right at the second intersection, and you'll be there.)

Language Practice

F. Experience Inventory

Ask your partner if he/she has ever tried the activities or tasted the foods shown below. Ask a follow-up question if the answer is affirmative. Ask if he/she wishes to try them if the answer is negative.

EXAMPLE 1:

→ A: 你打过球吗？   A: Nǐ dǎ guo qiú ma?

B: 我打过（球）。   B: Wǒ dǎ guo (qiú).

A: 你觉得打球   A: Nǐ juéde dǎ qiú
   有意思吗？   yǒu yìsi ma?

B: 我觉得打球很   B: Wǒ juéde dǎ qiú hěn
   有意思/没有意思。   yǒu yìsi/méi yǒu yìsi.

1.

2.

3.

4.

5.

EXAMPLE 2:

A: 你吃过家常豆腐吗？

B: 我吃过（家常豆腐）。

A: 你觉得家常豆腐
好吃吗？

B: 我觉得家常豆腐
很好吃/不好吃。

A: Nǐ chī guo jiācháng dòufu ma?

B: Wǒ chī guo (jiācháng dòufu).

A: Nǐ juéde jiācháng dòufu
hàochī ma?

B: Wǒ juéde jiācháng dòufu
hěn hàochī/bù hàochī.

20/
20

1.

A:你吃过糖醋鱼吗？   A你觉得糖醋鱼好吃吗？
B：我吃过。   B 我觉得糖醋鱼好吃。

饺子

2.

A:你吃过饺子吗？   A:你觉得饺子好吃吗？
B:我吃过饺子。   B:我觉得饺子好吃。

A:你吃过小白菜吗？   A:你觉得小白菜好吃吗？
B:我吃过。   B:我觉得小白菜好吃。

3.

G. One Thing After Another

Work with your partner and take turns asking each other:

1. **A:** 你平常一吃完早饭
就做什么？

   Nǐ píngcháng yì chī wán zǎofàn
jiù zuò shénme?

   B: 我平常一吃完早饭就要去上学 。

2. **A:** 你平常一下中文
课就做什么？

   Nǐ píngcháng yí xià Zhōngwén
kè jiù zuò shénme?

   B: 我平常一下中文课就回家吃中饭 。

3. **A:** 你平常一高兴就
做什么？

   Nǐ píngcháng yì gāoxìng jiù
zuò shénme?

   B: 我平常一高兴就唱歌 。

4. **A:** 你昨天早上一
起床就做什么？

   Nǐ zuótiān zǎoshang yì
qǐ chuáng jiù zuò shénme?

   B: 我昨天一起床后就吃早饭 。

5. **A:** 你昨天一回家就
做什么？

   Nǐ zuótiān yì huí jiā jiù
zuò shénme?

   B: 我昨天一回家就上网了 。

H. Location, Location, Location

Locate some of the buildings using different landmarks.

EXAMPLE: 图书馆   túshūguǎn

A: 请问图书馆在哪儿？   Qǐng wèn, túshūguǎn zài nǎr?

B: 图书馆在运动场   Túshūguǎn zài yùndòngchǎng
的北边。   de běibian.

or

图书馆在教室和   Túshūguǎn zài jiàoshì hé
咖啡馆的中间。   kāfēiguǎn de zhōngjiān.

1. 公园   gōngyuán

2. 餐厅   cāntīng

3. 运动场   yùndòngchǎng

4. 公共汽车站   gōnggòng qìchē zhàn

I. How Do I Get There?

Using the map from the previous exercise, practice with your partner how to ask for and give directions.

EXAMPLE: 公园 ➜ 老师办公室   gōngyuán ➜ lǎoshī bàngōngshì

A: 从公园到老师办公室怎么走？

B: 你从公园出来，上五行路，往北走，到了第一个路口，往东拐，过两个路口，到了第三个路口往左一拐，就到了/老师办公室就在你的右边儿。

A: Cóng gōngyuán dào lǎoshī bàngōngshì zěnme zǒu?

B: Nǐ cóng gōngyuán chū lai, shàng Wǔxínglù, wǎng běi zǒu, dào le dì yī ge lùkǒu, wǎng dōng guǎi, guò liǎng ge lùkǒu, dào le dì sān ge lùkǒu wǎng zuǒ yì guǎi, jiù dào le/lǎoshī bàngōngshì jiù zài nǐ de yòubianr.

1. 电脑中心 ➜ 运动场

2. 学生宿舍 ➜ 公共汽车站

3. 书店 ➜ 花店 (florist's shop)

1. diànnǎo zhōngxīn ➜ yùndòngchǎng

2. xuéshēng sùshè ➜ gōnggòng qìchē zhàn

3. shūdiàn ➜ huādiàn

J. Recap and Narrate

Working with a partner, recap the content of Dialogue II:

1. 王朋和高文中
   一起去什么地方？

   1. Wáng Péng hé Gāo Wénzhōng
      yìqǐ qù shénme dìfang?

2. 谁开车？

   2. Shéi kāi chē?

3. 王朋知道去
   中国城
   怎么走吗？

   3. Wáng Péng zhīdào qù
      Zhōngguóchéng
      zěnme zǒu ma?

4. 高文中说他带
   地图了吗？

   4. Gāo Wénzhōng shuō tā dài
      dìtú le ma?

5. 高文中说他知道
   去中国城怎么
   走吗？

   5. Gāo Wénzhōng shuō tā zhīdào
      qù Zhōngguóchéng zěnme
      zǒu ma?

6. 高文中说去
   中国城怎么走？

   6. Gāo Wénzhōng shuō qù
      Zhōngguóchéng zěnme zǒu?

7. 王朋知道东南
   西北吗？

   7. Wáng Péng zhīdào dōng nán
      xī běi ma?

8. 高文中告诉
   王朋的路对吗？

   8. Gāo Wénzhōng gàosù
      Wáng Péng de lù duì ma?

Using the words and phrases in blue as prompts, connect your answers above to form a narrative like this example:

王朋和高文中一起开车去中国城吃中国饭，王朋不知道怎么走，问高文中带地图了没有。高文中忘了带地图，他说他不用地图也能找到中国城。他说一直往南开，过三个路口，往西一拐就到了。可是王朋说他不知道东南西北。高文中又说一直往前开，过三个红绿灯，往右一拐就到了。可是，他们最后开到了小东京。

Wáng Péng hé Gāo Wénzhōng yìqǐ kāi chē qù Zhōngguóchéng chī Zhōngguó fàn, Wáng Péng bù zhīdào zěnme zǒu, wèn Gāo Wénzhōng dài dìtú le méiyǒu. Gāo Wénzhōng wàng le dài dìtú, tā shuō tā bú yòng dìtú yě néng zhǎo dào Zhōngguóchéng. Tā shuō yìzhí wǎng nán kāi, guò sān ge lùkǒu, wǎng xī yì guǎi jiù dào le. Kěshì Wáng Péng shuō tā bù zhīdào dōng nán xī běi. Gāo Wénzhōng yòu shuō yìzhí wǎng qián kāi, guò sān ge hónglǜdēng, wǎng yòu yì guǎi jiù dào le. Kěshì, tāmen zuìhòu kāi dào le xiǎo Dōngjīng.

HOW ABOUT YOU?

Where do you walk?

1.	单行道	dānxíngdào	n	one-way street
2.	斑马线	bānmǎxiàn	n	zebra crossing; pedestrian crosswalk
3.	天桥	tiānqiáo	n	pedestrian overpass
4.	地下（通）道	dìxià (tōng)dào	n	pedestrian underpass

What other traffic-related terms would you like to know how to say? Please ask your teacher and make a note here: _____

Culture Highlights

❶ In Chinese culture, a common and cordial way to greet someone is by asking a casual question about the routine activity that the other person is engaged in at the moment. Thus, upon seeing a friend on her way to a grocery store, one could ask 买菜呀? (Mǎi cài ya? Going grocery shopping, eh?) Running into a fellow student who is leaving a classroom, one could ask 下课了? (Xià kè le? Just had your class?) As the situation is usually very obvious, the speaker does not expect, and is not interested in, an elaborate answer. Nor are these questions considered intrusive or personal.

❷ In many cities in China, the array of traffic lights includes an electronic display of the number of seconds before the light turns from green to red, which enables drivers and pedestrians to better manage their time in getting through the intersection.

❸ Both 中国话 (Zhōngguó huà) and 中文 (Zhōngwén) refer to the Chinese language. However, while 中文 (Zhōngwén) covers both spoken and written Chinese, 中国话 (Zhōngguó huà) stresses spoken Chinese. 中国字 (Zhōngguó zì) is synonymous with 汉字 (Hànzì). Similarly, both 日语 (Rìyǔ) and 日文 (Rìwén) mean the Japanese language. While 日文 (Rìwén) covers both spoken and written Japanese, 日语 (Rìyǔ) stresses spoken Japanese. 日本话 (Rìběn huà) is synonymous with 日语 (Rìyǔ), but it is more informal.

English Text

Dialogue I

Teacher Chang: Are classes over, Little Bai? Where are you off to?

Bai Ying'ai: Hi, Teacher Chang. I want to go to the school computer center, but I don't know how to get there. I heard it's next to the sports field.

Teacher Chang: The computer center is not as far as the sports field. You know where the school library is?

Bai Ying'ai: Yes, I do. It's not far from Wang Peng's dorm.

Teacher Chang: The computer center is near the library. It's between the library and the student activity center.

Bai Ying'ai: Teacher Chang, where are you headed?

Teacher Chang: I'd like to get some books at the school bookstore.

Bai Ying'ai: Where's the bookstore?

Teacher Chang: It's in the student activity center. We can walk together.

Bai Ying'ai: Wonderful.

Dialogue II

Gao Wenzhong: Let's go to Chinatown to have some Chinese food.

Wang Peng: I've never been to Chinatown. I don't know where Chinatown is.

Gao Wenzhong: No problem. You drive, and I'll tell you how to get there.

Wang Peng: Do you have a map? Let me take a look.

Gao Wenzhong: The map is in the dorm. I forgot to bring it.

Wang Peng: Without the map, what will we do if we go the wrong way?

Gao Wenzhong: It doesn't matter if we don't have the map. I've been to Chinatown many times. I can find it without a map. Go south from here. After three blocks, turn west, and we'll be there.

Wang Peng: Oh, I don't have any sense of direction.

Gao Wenzhong: Then drive straight ahead. After three traffic lights, turn right, and you'll be there.

(After three blocks)

Wang Peng: This isn't right. See, you can only turn left here. You can't turn right.

Gao Wenzhong: Then it'll be the next block. Turn right. Keep going further. We're there, we're there. See, there are lots of Chinese characters in front of us.

Wang Peng: That's not Chinese, that's Japanese. We're in Little Tokyo.

Gao Wenzhong: Really? Then let's not have Chinese food, let's have Japanese food instead.

PROGRESS CHECKLIST

Before proceeding to Lesson 14, be sure you can complete the following tasks in Chinese:

I am able to—

- ☑ Ask for directions;
- ☐ Give directions;
- ☐ Locate places using landmark references;
- ☐ Tell someone whether a place is far away from or close to another place;
- ☐ Provide information about where I am going and why.

LESSON 14

Birthday Party

第十四课 生日晚会

Dì shísì kè Shēngrì wǎnhuì

 LEARNING OBJECTIVES

In this lesson, you will learn to use Chinese to

- Ask a friend to go to a party with you;
- Suggest things to take to a get-together;
- Offer someone a ride and arrange a time and place to meet;
- Thank people for their gifts;
- Describe a duration of time;
- Talk about the year of your birth and your Chinese zodiac sign;
- Give a simple description of someone's facial features.

 RELATE AND GET READY

In your own culture/community—

1. How are birthdays usually celebrated?
2. What do people bring to a birthday party?
3. Are there any taboos about gift giving?
4. Are people supposed to open gifts in front of the gift giver?
5. What kinds of facial features are considered attractive?

Dialogue I: Let's Go to a Party!

（李友给王朋打电话。）

  王朋，你做什么呢①？

我看书呢。

 今天高小音过生日❶，晚上我们在她家开舞会，你能去吗？

 能去。几点？

 七点。我们先吃饭，吃完饭再唱歌跳舞。

 有哪些人？

LANGUAGE NOTES

❶ Apart from 过生日 (guò shēngrì, to celebrate one's birthday), the verb 过 (guò, to live [a life]; to observe [a holiday]; to celebrate [a festival]) appears in many other expressions such as 过年 (guò nián, to celebrate the New Year), 过节 (guò jié, to celebrate a festival), and 过日子 (guò rìzi, to live one's life; to live from day to day).

小音和她的男朋友，小音的
表姐❷，白英爱，你妹妹王红，
听说还有小音的中学同学。

你要送给小音什么生日礼物？

我买了一本书送给她。

那我带什么东西？

饮料或者水果都可以。

那我带一些饮料，再买一把花儿。

小音爱吃水果，我再买一些苹果、
梨和西瓜吧。

你住的地方② 离小音家很远，水果
很重，我开车来接你，我们一起去
吧。

好，我六点半在楼下等你。

❷ The kinship term 表姐 (biǎojiě) is more narrowly defined than its translation "older female cousin" would suggest. One's "older female cousin" will be a 表姐 (biǎojiě) if she is a daughter of one's father's sister or one's mother's sister or brother. But if she is one's paternal uncle's daughter, she will then be a 堂姐 (tángjiě) instead of a 表姐 (biǎojiě). For more Chinese kinship terms, see Grammar 4 in Lesson 20.

(Lǐ Yǒu gěi Wáng Péng dǎ diànhuà.)

Wáng Péng, nǐ zuò shénme ne①?

Wǒ kàn shū ne.

Jīntiān Gāo Xiǎoyīn guò shēngrì❶, wǎnshang wǒmen zài tā jiā kāi wǔhuì, nǐ néng qù ma?

Néng qù. Jǐ diǎn?

Qī diǎn. Wǒmen xiān chī fàn, chī wán fàn zài chàng gē tiào wǔ.

Yǒu nǎ xiē rén?

Xiǎoyīn hé tā de nánpéngyou, Xiǎoyīn de biǎojiě❷, Bái Yīng'ài, nǐ mèimei Wáng Hóng, tīngshuō hái yǒu Xiǎoyīn de zhōngxué tóngxué.

Nǐ yào sòng gěi Xiǎoyīn shénme shēngrì lǐwù?

Wǒ mǎi le yì běn shū sòng gěi tā.

Nà wǒ dài shénme dōngxi?

Yǐnliào huòzhě shuǐguǒ dōu kěyǐ.

Nà wǒ dài yì xiē yǐnliào, zài mǎi yì bǎ huār.

Xiǎoyīn ài chī shuǐguǒ, wǒ zài mǎi yì xiē píngguǒ, lí hé xīgua ba.

Nǐ zhù de dìfang② lí Xiǎoyīn jiā hěn yuǎn, shuǐguǒ hěn zhòng, wǒ kāi chē lái jiē nǐ, wǒmen yìqǐ qù ba.

Hǎo, wǒ liù diǎn bàn zài lóu xià děng nǐ.

VOCABULARY

1.	舞会	wǔhuì	n	dance party; ball
2.	表姐	biǎojiě	n	older female cousin
3.	中学	zhōngxué	n	middle school; secondary school
4.	送	sòng	v	to give as a gift
5.	礼物	lǐwù	n	gift; present
6.	本	běn	m	(measure word for books)
7.	饮料	yǐnliào	n	beverage
8.	水果	shuǐguǒ	n	fruit
9.	把	bǎ	m	(measure word for bunches of things, and chairs)
10.	花	huā	n	flower
11.	爱	ài	v	to love; to like; to be fond of
12.	苹果	píngguǒ	n	apple

VOCABULARY

13.	梨	lí	n	pear
14.	西瓜	xīgua	n	watermelon
15.	住	zhù	v	to live (in a certain place)
16.	重	zhòng	adj	heavy; serious
17.	接	jiē	v	to catch; to meet; to welcome
18.	楼	lóu	n	multi-storied building; floor (of a multi-level building)

Proper Nouns

19.	王红	Wáng Hóng	(a personal name)

附餐飲料	冰	熱
咖啡		
紅茶		
果汁		

你想喝什么饮料？热的还是凉的？
Nǐ xiǎng hē shénme yǐnliào? Rè de háishi liáng de?

Grammar

1. 呢 (ne) Indicating an Action in Progress

呢 (ne), at the end of a sentence, indicates that the action is in progress. It is like 在 (zài), which is never used at the end of a sentence, but rather before a verb.

❶   你写什么呢？

Nǐ xiě shénme ne?

(What are you writing?)

❷   你找什么呢？

Nǐ zhǎo shénme ne?

(What are you looking for?)

呢 (ne) can be used in conjunction with 在 (zài):

❸   你在写什么呢？

Nǐ zài xiě shénme ne?

(What are you writing?)

❹   你在找什么呢？

Nǐ zài zhǎo shénme ne?

(What are you looking for?)

在 (zài) can be preceded by 正 (zhèng). The phrase 正在 (zhèngzài) places extra emphasis on the progressive nature of an action.

❺   我昨天给他打电话的时候，他正在做功课呢。

Wǒ zuótiān gěi tā dǎ diànhuà de shíhou, tā zhèngzài zuò gōngkè ne.

(When I called him yesterday, he was right in the middle of doing his homework.)

6   别去找他，他正在睡觉呢。

Bié qù zhǎo tā, tā zhèngzài shuì jiào ne.

(Don't go look for him. He is sleeping.)

在 (zài) alone indicates that an action is in progress; therefore, the 呢 (ne) in (3) and (4) above can be omitted.

2. Verbal Phrases and Subject-Predicate Phrases Used as Attributives

In Chinese, attributives, often followed by the particle 的 (de), always appear before the elements that they modify. Verbs, verbal phrases, and subject-object phrases can all serve as attributives.

1   吃的东西

chī de dōngxi

(things to eat)

2   穿的衣服

chuān de yīfu

(clothes to wear, or clothes being worn)

3   新买的饭卡

xīn mǎi de fànkǎ

(newly-bought meal cards)

4   昨天来的同学

zuótiān lái de tóngxué

(the classmate{s} who came yesterday)

5   以前认识的朋友

yǐqián rènshi de péngyou

(the friend{s} one got acquainted with in the past)

6   我妈妈做的豆腐

wǒ māma zuò de dòufu

(the tofu dish that my mother makes/made)

❼ 老师给我们的功课

lǎoshī gěi wǒmen de gōngkè

(the homework the teacher assigned us)

❽ 朋友送的苹果

péngyou sòng de píngguǒ

(the apples given by a friend)

❾ 请你跳舞的那个人

qǐng nǐ tiào wǔ de nà gè rén

(that person who asked you to dance)

❿ 我妹妹爱的那个很帅的男人

wǒ mèimei ài de nà ge hěn shuài de nánren

(that very handsome man that my sister loves)

Language Practice

A. What Are They Doing?

With a partner, use the pictures to ask and answer what these people are doing.

EXAMPLE:

→ **A:** 他（在）做什么呢？　Tā (zài) zuò shénme ne?

B: 他（在）喝汤呢。　Tā (zài) hē tāng ne.

1.

2.

3.

4.

5.

B. Oh, That One!

Combine the two short sentences into one, using the highlighted verb or verb phrase as an attributive:

EXAMPLE:

他买了一件衣服   Tā **mǎi** le yí jiàn yīfu

那件衣服很贵   nà jiàn yīfu **hěn guì**

→ 他买的那件衣服很贵。   Tā **mǎi** de nà jiàn yīfu **hěn guì**.

1. 他写了一个字
   那个字很漂亮

2. 她买了一件衬衫
   那件衬衫是红的

3. 我哥哥给了我一枝笔
   那枝笔是黑的

4. 妹妹带了一些水果
   那些水果很贵

5. 表姐卖了一些花
   那些花很漂亮

1. Tā xiě le yí ge zì

   nà ge zì hěn piàoliang

2. Tā mǎi le yí jiàn chènshān

   nà jiàn chènshān shì hóng de

3. Wǒ gēge gěi le wǒ yì zhī bǐ

   nà zhī bǐ shì hēi de

4. Mèimei dài le yì xiē shuǐguǒ

   nà xiē shuǐguǒ hěn guì

5. Biǎojiě mài le yì xiē huā

   nà xiē huā hěn piàoliang

C. Who's Who?

Help your new teacher match the names on the class roster with your classmates.

EXAMPLE 1:

A: Jamal 是谁？
B: Jamal 是那个穿黑色
衬衫的学生。

Jamal shì shéi?
Jamal shì nà ge chuān hēisè
chènshān de xuésheng.

EXAMPLE 2:

A: Katy 是谁？
B: Katy 是那个正在看书
的女孩。

Katy shì shéi?
Katy shì nà ge zhèngzài kàn shū
de nǚ hái.

1. Classmate 1

2. Classmate 2

3. Classmate 3

4. Classmate 4

5. Classmate 5

D. **Recap and Narrate**

Working with a partner, recap the content of Dialogue I:

1. 高小音哪天过生日？

2. 李友他们晚上要做什么？

3. 他们吃晚饭以后还要做什么？

4. 哪些人去高小音家？

5. 李友买了什么送给小音？

6. 王朋要带什么东西？

7. 李友要带什么？

8. 王朋为什么要开车接李友？

1. Gāo Xiǎoyīn nǎ tiān guò shēngrì?

2. Lǐ Yǒu tāmen wǎnshang yào zuò shénme?

3. Tāmen chī wǎnfàn yǐhòu hái yào zuò shénme?

4. Nǎ xiē rén qù Gāo Xiǎoyīn jiā?

5. Lǐ Yǒu mǎi le shénme sòng gěi Xiǎoyīn?

6. Wáng Péng yào dài shénme dōngxi?

7. Lǐ Yǒu yào dài shénme?

8. Wáng Péng wèishénme yào kāi chē jiē Lǐ Yǒu?

Using the words and phrases in blue as prompts, connect your answers above to form a narrative like this example:

李友告诉王朋今天是高小音的生日，晚上在小音家开生日舞会。除了小音的男朋友、表姐以外，小音的中学同学和白英爱也会去。她问王朋能不能去，王朋说他能去。他要带饮料和花，李友买了一本书送给小音，还要带一些苹果、梨和西瓜。因为李友住的地方离高小音家很远，水果很重，所以王朋要开车接李友一起去。李友说她六点半在楼下等王朋。

Lǐ Yǒu gàosù Wáng Péng jīntiān shì Gāo Xiǎoyīn de shēngrì, wǎnshang zài Xiǎoyīn jiā kāi shēngrì wǔhuì. Chúle Xiǎoyīn de nánpéngyou, biǎojiě yǐwài, Xiǎoyīn de zhōngxué tóngxué hé Bái Yīng'ài yě huì qù. Tā wèn Wáng Péng néng bù néng qù, Wáng Péng shuō tā néng qù. Tā yào dài yǐnliào hé huā, Lǐ Yǒu mǎi le yì běn shū sòng gěi Xiǎoyīn, hái yào dài yì xiē píngguǒ, lí hé xīgua. Yīnwèi Lǐ Yǒu zhù de dìfang lí Gāo Xiǎoyīn jiā hěn yuǎn, shuǐguǒ hěn zhòng, suǒyǐ Wáng Péng yào kāi chē jiē Lǐ Yǒu yìqǐ qù. Lǐ Yǒu shuō tā liù diǎn bàn zài lóu xià děng Wáng Péng.

This is a store's name. What do you think the store wants people to buy?

Dialogue II: Attending a Birthday Party

（在高小音家）

  王朋，李友，快进来。

 小音，祝你生日快乐！
这是送给你的生日礼物。

 谢谢！(She opens the gift.) 太好了！
我一直想买这本书。带这么
多东西，你们太客气了。

 哥哥，李友，你们来了❶。

 啊。小红，你怎么样？

 我很好。每天都在学英文。

LANGUAGE NOTES

❶ 你们来了 (Nǐmen lái le, You're here) not only acknowledges the visitors' arrival, but also serves as a casual greeting.

小红，你每天练习英文练习多长时间③？

三个半钟头②。还看两个钟头的英文电视。

哎，你们两个是什么时候到的④？

刚到。

白英爱没跟你们一起来吗？

她还⑤没来？我以为③她已经来了。

王朋，李友，来，我给你们介绍一下，这是我表姐海伦，这是她的儿子汤姆。

你好，海伦。

你好，王朋。文中和小音都说你又聪明④又用功⑥。

哪里，哪里。你的中文说得真好，是在哪儿学的？

在暑期班⑤学的。

❷ 钟头 (zhōngtóu) is the colloquial equivalent of 小时 (xiǎoshí).

❸ 以为 (yǐwéi) is often used to signify an understanding or judgment which has proved to be erroneous. If someone has realized that she was mistaken in assuming someone else to be vegetarian, she could say to that person: 我以为你吃素 (Wǒ yǐwéi nǐ chī sù. I thought you were a vegetarian).

❹ About the formation of the adjective 聪明 (cōngming; clever): 聪 (cōng) literally means "able to hear well," and 明 (míng) means "able to see clearly," among other things. Therefore, 聪明 describes someone who is perceptive or bright.

❺ The Chinese words 班 (bān) and 课 (kè) denote two different concepts that are represented by the same word, "class," in English. While 课 (kè) refers to a course or a meeting time for the course, 班 (bān) is the term for the group of students who take a course together. Thus one says "我今天有电脑课" (Wǒ jīntiān yǒu diànnǎo kè, I have a computer class today), but "我的电脑班有二十个人" (Wǒ de diànnǎo bān yǒu èrshí ge rén, There are twenty people in my computer class).

哎，汤姆长⑥得真可爱！你们看，他笑了。他几岁了？

刚一岁，是去年生的，属狗。

你们看，他的脸圆圆的，眼睛大大的，鼻子高高的，嘴不大也不小，长得很像海伦。

妈妈这么漂亮，儿子长大一定也很帅。

来，来，来，我们吃蛋糕吧。

等等白英爱吧。她最爱吃蛋糕。

⑥ The character 长 (zhǎng / cháng) has two different meanings and pronunciations. As a verb, it is pronounced "zhǎng," meaning "to grow." When used as an adjective, it is pronounced "cháng," and means "long."

(Zài Gāo Xiǎoyīn jiā)

Wáng Péng, Lǐ Yǒu, kuài jìn lai.

Xiǎoyīn, zhù nǐ shēngrì kuàilè! Zhè shì sòng gěi nǐ de shēngrì lǐwù.

Xièxiè! (She opens the gift.) Tài hǎo le! Wǒ yìzhí xiǎng mǎi zhè běn shū. Dài zhème duō dōngxi, nǐmen tài kèqi le.

Gēge, Lǐ Yǒu, nǐmen lái le❶.

À. Xiǎo Hóng, nǐ zěnmeyàng?

Wǒ hěn hǎo. Měitiān dōu zài xué Yīngwén.

Xiǎo Hóng, nǐ měitiān liànxí Yīngwén liànxí duō cháng shíjiān③?

Sān ge bàn zhōngtóu❷. Hái kàn liǎng ge zhōngtóu de Yīngwén diànshì.

Āi, nǐmen liǎng ge shì shénme shíhou dào de④?

Gāng dào.

Bái Yīng'ài méi gēn nǐmen yìqǐ lái ma?

Tā hái⑤ méi lái? Wǒ yǐwéi❸ tā yǐjīng lái le.

Wáng Péng, Lǐ Yǒu, lái, wǒ gěi nǐmen jièshào yí xià, zhè shì wǒ biǎojiě Hǎilún, zhè shì tā de érzi Tāngmǔ.

Nǐ hǎo, Hǎilún.

Nǐ hǎo, Wáng Péng. Wénzhōng hé Xiǎoyīn dōu shuō nǐ yòu cōngming④ yòu yònggōng⑥.

Nǎli, nǎli. Nǐ de Zhōngwén shuō de zhēn hǎo, shì zài nǎr xué de?

Zài shǔqī bān⑤ xué de.

Āi, Tāngmǔ zhǎng⑥ de zhēn kě'ài! Nǐmen kàn, tā xiào le. Tā jǐ suì le?

Gāng yí suì, shì qùnián shēng de, shǔ gǒu.

Nǐmen kàn, tā de liǎn yuán yuán de, yǎnjing dà dà de, bízi gāo gāo de, zuǐ bú dà yě bù xiǎo, zhǎng de hěn xiàng Hǎilún.

Māma zhème piàoliang, érzi zhǎng dà yídìng yě hěn shuài.

Lái, lái, lái, wǒmen chī dàngāo ba.

Děng děng Bái Yīng'ài ba. Tā zuì ài chī dàngāo.

 ## VOCABULARY

1.	钟头	zhōngtóu	n	hour
2.	以为	yǐwéi	v	to assume erroneously
3.	聪明	cōngming	adj	smart; bright; clever
4.	用功	yònggōng	adj	hard-working; diligent; studious
5.	暑期	shǔqī	n	summer term
6.	班	bān	n	class
7.	长	zhǎng	v	to grow; to appear
8.	可爱	kě'ài	adj	cute; lovable
9.	去年	qùnián	t	last year
10.	属	shǔ	v	to belong to

VOCABULARY

11.	狗	gǒu	n	dog
12.	脸	liǎn	n	face
13.	圆	yuán	adj	round
14.	眼睛	yǎnjing	n	eye
15.	鼻子	bízi	n	nose
16.	嘴	zuǐ	n	mouth
17.	像	xiàng	v	to be like; to look like; to take after
18.	长大	zhǎng dà	vc	to grow up
19.	一定	yídìng	adj/adv	certain(ly); definite(ly)
20.	蛋糕	dàngāo	n	cake
21.	最	zuì	adv	most, (of superlative degree) -est

Proper Nouns

22.	海伦	Hǎilún		Helen
23.	汤姆	Tāngmǔ		Tom

眼睛 (yǎnjing, eye)

鼻子 (bízi, nose)

嘴 (zuǐ, mouth)

头发 (tóufa, hair)

耳朵 (ěrduo, ears)

眉毛 (méimao, eyebrows)

牙齿 (yáchǐ, teeth)

Grammar

3. Time Duration

To indicate the duration of an action, the following structure is used:

Subject + Verb + (Object + Verb) + （了） + Duration of time

❶   老高想在上海住一年。

Lǎo Gāo xiǎng zài Shànghǎi zhù yì nián.)

(Old Gao wishes to live in Shanghai for a year.)

❷   我每天在书店工作三个钟头。

Wǒ měitiān zài shūdiàn gōngzuò sān ge zhōngtóu.

(I work in a bookstore for three hours every day.)

❸   昨天下雪下了二十分钟。

Zuótian xià xuě xià le èrshí fēnzhōng.

(It snowed for twenty minutes yesterday.)

❹   你上暑期班上了多长时间？

Nǐ shàng shǔqī bān shàng le duō cháng shíjiān?

(How long were you in summer school?)

Sentences in this pattern must be in the affirmative. If the verb takes an object, the verb has to be repeated, as in (3) and (4). If the verb has an object, the following alternative pattern can be used to express the same idea.

Subject + Verb + （了） + Duration of time + （的） + Object

❺   昨天下了二十分钟（的）雪。

Zuótian xià le èrshí fēnzhōng (de) xuě.

(It snowed for twenty minutes yesterday.)

❻ 我上了四个星期（的）暑期班。

Wǒ shàng le sì ge xīngqī (de) shǔqī bān.

(I was in summer school for four weeks.)

The phrase for the length of time must not be put before the verb:

(6a) *我四个星期上了暑期班。

*Wǒ sì ge xīngqī shàng le shǔqī bān.

---

4. Sentences with 是…的 (shì…de)

To describe or inquire about the time, the place, the manner, or the initiator of an action that we know already happened, we need to use the 是…的 (shì…de) structure. The use of 是 (shì), however, is optional.

❶ **A:** 你去过北京吗？

Nǐ qù guo Běijīng ma?

(Have you been to Beijing?)

B: 我去过北京。

Wǒ qù guo Běijīng.

(Yes, I've been to Beijing.)

Person A now becomes aware of Person B's action of 去北京 (qù Běijīng, went to Beijing), and wants to find out when, how, and with whom that action was performed:

A: 你是跟谁一起去的？

Nǐ shì gēn shéi yìqǐ qù de?

(With whom did you go?)

B: 我是跟我表姐一起去的。

Wǒ shì gēn wǒ biǎojiě yìqǐ qù de.

(I went with my cousin.)

A: 你们是什么时候去的？

Nǐmen shì shénme shíhou qù de?

(When did you go?)

B: 我们是寒假去的 。

Wǒmen shì hánjià qù de.

(We went during the winter break.)

A: 你们是怎么去的？

Nǐmen shì zěnme qù de?

(How did you go?)

B: 我们是坐飞机去的。

Wǒmen shì zuò fēijī qù de.

(We went there by airplane.)

❷ A: 你看过这张碟吗？

Nǐ kàn guo zhè zhāng dié ma?

(Have you watched this DVD?)

B: 看过。

Kàn guo.

(Yes, I have.)

A: 是什么时候看的？

Shì shénme shíhou kàn de?

(When did you watch it?)

[A already knows that the action 看 (kàn) was completed.]

B: 上个周末看的。

Shàng ge zhōumò kàn de.

(I watched it last weekend.)

[It was last weekend that I watched it.]

❸ A: 你这条裤子真好看。是在哪儿买的？

Nǐ zhè tiáo kùzi zhēn hǎokàn. Shì zài nǎr mǎi de?

(These pants of yours look great. Where did you get them?)

[It's assumed that one generally buys pants (as opposed to making them at home, etc.), so the action 买 (mǎi) is already known.]

❹ A: 你吃饭了吗？

Nǐ chī fàn le ma?

(Have you eaten yet?)

B: 吃了。

Chī le.

(Yes, I have.)

[The action 吃 (chī) is now known.]

A: 在哪儿吃的？

Zài nǎr chī de?

(Where did you eat?)

B: 在学生餐厅吃的。

Zài xuéshēng cāntīng chī de.

(In the student cafeteria.)

❺ A: 你学过电脑吗？

Nǐ xué guo diànnǎo ma?

(Have you ever studied computers?)

B: 学过。

Xué guo.

(Yes, I have.)

A: 是跟谁学的？

Shì gēn shéi xué de?

(With whom did you study?)

B: 是跟王老师学的。

Shì gēn Wáng lǎoshī xué de.

(With Teacher Wang.)

5. 还 (hái, **still**)

还 (hái), as an adverb, can mean "still."

❶ 上午十一点了，他还在睡觉。

Shàngwǔ shíyī diǎn le, tā hái zài shuì jiào.

(It's 11 a.m., and he is still sleeping.)

❷ 今天的功课，我还没写完。

Jīntiān de gōngkè, wǒ hái méi xiě wán.

(I'm still not done with today's homework.)

❸ 这个语法老师教了，可是我还不懂。

Zhè ge yǔfǎ lǎoshī jiāo le, kěshì wǒ hái bù dǒng.

(The teacher has gone over this grammar point, but I still don't understand it.)

6. 又···又··· (yòu...yòu...., **both...and...**)

The two adjectives used in this structure are either both positive or both negative in meaning, e.g., 又聪明又用功 (yòu cōngming yòu yònggōng, smart and hardworking) [both adjectives are positive in meaning], 又多又难 (yòu duō yòu nán, too much and difficult) [both adjectives are negative in meaning].

Language Practice

E. Where Did You Get That?

You love your friend's print of an Ansel Adams photograph. You want to find out where and when he or she bought it, how much he or she spent on it, and whether he or she bought it himself or herself. You will start by saying:

这张照片真好看…   Zhè zhāng zhàopiàn zhēn hǎokàn…

and then you will ask

（是）在哪儿买的？   (Shì) zài nǎr mǎi de?

（是）什么时候买的？   (Shì) shénme shíhou mǎi de?

（是）谁买的？   (Shì) shéi mǎi de?

（是）多少钱买的？   (Shì) duōshao qián mǎi de?

Now you are checking out other classmates' shoes, shirts, jeans, pens, cars, etc., and you want to know as much as possible about each of those things.

F. Older or Younger

Go around the class and interview your classmates. Find out everyone's birthplace, birth year, and Chinese zodiac sign. Then report to the class how many classmates are older than you, how many are younger than you, how many were born in the same state/province/city as you were, and which zodiac sign is most common in the class.

1. 你是在哪儿生的？   1. Nǐ shì zài nǎr shēng de?

2. 你是哪一年生的？   2. Nǐ shì nǎ yì nián shēng de?

3. 你属什么？   3. Nǐ shǔ shénme?

G. Travel Interview

Work with a partner to discuss where you have traveled. Take turns asking each other:

1. 你去过(a city or country)吗？   **1.** Nǐ qù guo (a city or country) ma?

2. 你（是）什么时候去的？   **2.** Nǐ (shì) shénme shíhou qù de?

3. 你（是）跟谁一起去的？   **3.** Nǐ (shì) gēn shéi yìqǐ qù de?

4. 你（是）怎么去的？   **4.** Nǐ (shì) zěnme qù de?

H. Fantasy Trip or Boot Camp?

Imagine that you've signed up to go on a whirlwind tour of China during summer break. You just got your itinerary, and the travel schedule looks very intense. The trip leaders have scheduled each day down to the minute. Answer your classmates' questions on how much time you'll have for each activity.

EXAMPLE: 7:30am–7:45am

→ **A:** 你每天洗澡能洗多长时间？   Nǐ měitiān xǐ zǎo néng xǐ duō cháng shíjiān?

B: 我每天洗澡只能洗十五分钟。   Wǒ měitiān xǐ zǎo zhǐ néng xǐ shíwǔ fēnzhōng.

1.   1:30pm–2:45pm

2.   5:30pm–6:00pm

3.   11:00pm–5:00am

I. Last Night

Move around the class and ask your classmates how they spent their time last night.

EXAMPLE: **Emily**

A: Emily, 你昨天晚上做什么了？

B: 我昨天晚上看电视了。

A: 你昨天晚上看电视看了多长时间？

B: 我昨天晚上看电视看了半个钟头。

A: Emily, nǐ zuótiān wǎnshang zuò shénme le?

B: Wǒ zuótiān wǎnshang kàn diànshì le.

A: Nǐ zuótiān wǎnshang kàn diànshì kàn le duō cháng shíjiān?

B: Wǒ zuótiān wǎnshang kàn diànshì kàn le bàn ge zhōngtóu.

Then record your findings.

Emily 昨天晚上看电视看了半个钟头。

Emily zuótiān wǎnshang kàn diànshì kàn le bàn ge zhōngtóu.

1. Classmate 1
2. Classmate 2
3. Classmate 3
4. Classmate 4

J. Is the Baby Cute or What?

Work with your partner to describe the baby's features, and comment on whether the baby is cute.

K. Let's Plan a Party!

Find out among your classmates whose birthday is coming up by asking 谁的生日快到了? (Shéi de shēngrì kuài dào le?) Everyone should take a turn to ask that person what he or she likes to eat, drink, and do. Then work as a class to plan a birthday party together, and decide who will bring what to the party.

L. Recap and Narrate

Working with a partner, recap the content of Dialogue II:

1. 王朋和李友给高小音生日礼物的时候，高小音说什么了？

1. Wáng Péng hé Lǐ Yǒu gěi Gāo Xiǎoyīn shēngrì lǐwù de shíhou, Gāo Xiǎoyīn shuō shénme le?

2. 王红每天练习英文练习多长时间？

2. Wáng Hóng měitiān liànxí Yīngwén liànxí duō cháng shíjiān?

3. 白英爱来了吗？

3. Bái Yīng'ài lái le ma?

4. 高小音的表姐叫什么名字？表姐的儿子叫什么名字？

4. Gāo Xiǎoyīn de biǎojiě jiào shénme míngzi? Biǎojiě de érzi jiào shénme míngzi?

5. 表姐是在哪儿学的中文？

5. Biǎojiě shì zài nǎr xué de Zhōngwén?

6. 表姐的儿子几岁了？

6. Biǎojiě de érzi jǐ suì le?

7. 表姐的儿子长得什么样？

7. Biǎojiě de érzi zhǎng de shénme yàng?

8. 高文中为什么要等白英爱吃蛋糕？

8. Gāo Wénzhōng wèishénme yào děng Bái Yīng'ài chī dàngāo?

Using the words and phrases in blue as prompts, connect your answers above to form a narrative like this example:

今天晚上高小音家开生日舞会。王朋和李友是一起去的，他们送给了小音生日礼物，高小音很高兴，说王朋和李友太客气了。王朋的妹妹王红在高小音家住，每天练习三个半小时的英文，还看两个小时电视。高小音的表姐叫海伦，她的儿子叫汤姆。海伦在暑期班学过中文，她的中文说得很好。汤姆是去年生的，刚一岁，属狗。他长得很可爱，脸圆圆的，眼睛大大的，鼻子高高的，嘴不大也不小，很像海伦。高小音让大家吃蛋糕，可是高文中说要等白英爱，因为白英爱最爱吃蛋糕。真是这样吗？还是因为他喜欢白英爱了？

Jīntiān wǎnshang Gāo Xiǎoyīn jiā kāi shēngrì wǔhuì. Wáng Péng hé Lǐ Yǒu shì yìqǐ qù de, tāmen sòng gěi le Xiǎoyīn shēngrì lǐwù, Gāo Xiǎoyīn hěn gāoxìng, shuō Wáng Péng hé Lǐ Yǒu tài kèqi le. Wáng Péng de mèimei Wáng Hóng zài Gāo Xiǎoyīn jiā zhù, měitiān liànxí sān ge bàn xiǎoshí de Yīngwén, hái kàn liǎng ge xiǎoshí diànshì. Gāo Xiǎoyīn de biǎojiě jiào Hǎilún, tā de érzi jiào Tāngmǔ. Hǎilún zài shǔqī bān xué guo Zhōngwén, tā de Zhōngwén shuō de hěn hǎo. Tāngmǔ shì qùnián shēng de, gāng yí suì, shǔ gǒu. Tā zhǎng de hěn kě'ài, liǎn yuán yuán de, yǎnjing dà dà de, bízi gāo gāo de, zuǐ bú dà yě bù xiǎo, hěn xiàng Hǎilún. Gāo Xiǎoyīn ràng dàjiā chī dàngāo, kěshì Gāo Wénzhōng shuō yào děng Bái Yīng'ài, yīnwèi Bái Yīng'ài zuì ài chī dàngāo. Zhēn shì zhèyàng ma? Háishi yīnwèi tā xǐhuan Bái Yīng'ài le?

HOW ABOUT YOU?

What's your favorite fruit?

1.	香蕉	xiāngjiāo	n
2.	草莓	cǎoméi	n
3.	橘子	júzi	n
4.	桃儿	táor	n
5.	葡萄	pútao	n

If your favorite fruit is not listed above, please ask your teacher and make a note here:

_____

What would you bring to a birthday party?

1.	气球	qìqiú	n	balloons
2.	卡片	kǎpiàn	n	card
3.	汽水（儿）	qìshuǐ(r)	n	soft drink; soda pop
4.	零食	língshí	n	snacks
5.	饼干	bǐnggān	n	cookies; crackers
6.	糖（果）	táng (guǒ)	n	candy

What other things could one bring to a party? Please ask your teacher and make a note here:

_____

Culture Highlights

❶ Potluck dinner parties are not as popular in China as they are in the United States. The Chinese host or hostess will usually prepare everything for the dinner and not count on the guests for any contributions. But a visitor can still bring something as a token of his or her appreciation, like a fruit basket, a bottle of wine, or a bouquet of flowers.

❷ Nowadays, when Chinese people sing for fun, they usually sing karaoke (卡拉 OK, kǎlā'ōukēi) style. Many people in mainland China and Taiwan regularly go to karaoke bars to have a good time or celebrate someone's birthday. They can order food and beverages and reserve private rooms for their parties. Some people even have karaoke equipment at home.

❸ The Chinese usually express their appreciation of a gift profusely, typically by saying "你太客气了！" (Nǐ tài kèqi le, You're really too kind!). However, most Chinese people would refrain from opening the present immediately in front of the gift giver lest they appear too greedy. Flowers make good gifts, but for happy occasions one should avoid bouquets of white flowers, which are typically for funerals. Another taboo is giving a clock to an elderly person as a present, because the phrase 送钟 (sòng zhōng, to give a clock as a present) is ominously homophonous with 送终 (sòng zhōng), which means to attend someone's burial.

❹ There are twelve animal signs in the Chinese zodiac, each representing one year in a twelve-year cycle. According to a popular but unscientific theory, one's personality and temperament have much to do with the animal that represents the year of one's birth. It might be surprising that the twelve-year cycle should start with the year of the rat, the smallest and perhaps the least likable of the twelve animals. At the beginning, as the story goes, there was a bitter quarrel among the animals as to who should represent the first year of the cycle. Finally, they decided to settle the dispute with a race. The robust ox was in the lead all the way, but he did not notice that the tiny rat was taking a ride on his back. As the ox was approaching the end, the rat jumped down and hit the finish line first, while the disappointed ox had to settle for second place. The indolent pig finished last in the race, and accordingly was assigned to the final year of the cycle. The following is a list of the twelve animal signs and the years in recent decades that each of them represents:

1.	鼠	shǔ	rat	1948, 1960, 1972, 1984, 1996, 2008
2.	牛	niú	ox; cow	1949, 1961, 1973, 1985, 1997, 2009
3.	虎	hǔ	tiger	1950, 1962, 1974, 1986, 1998, 2010
4.	兔	tù	rabbit; hare	1951, 1963, 1975, 1987, 1999, 2011
5.	龙	lóng	dragon	1952, 1964, 1976, 1988, 2000, 2012
6.	蛇	shé	snake; serpent	1953, 1965, 1977, 1989, 2001, 2013
7.	马	mǎ	horse	1954, 1966, 1978, 1990, 2002, 2014
8.	羊	yáng	sheep; goat; ram	1955, 1967, 1979, 1991, 2003, 2015
9.	猴	hóu	monkey	1956, 1968, 1980, 1992, 2004, 2016
10.	鸡	jī	rooster; chicken	1957, 1969, 1981, 1993, 2005, 2017
11.	狗	gǒu	dog	1958, 1970, 1982, 1994, 2006, 2018
12.	猪	zhū	pig; boar	1959, 1971, 1983, 1995, 2007, 2019

English Text

Dialogue I

(Li You is on the phone with Wang Peng.)

Li You: Wang Peng, what are you doing?

Wang Peng: I'm reading.

Li You: Today is Gao Xiaoyin's birthday. Tonight we're having a dance party at her place. Can you go?

Wang Peng: Yes. What time?

Li You: Seven o'clock. We'll eat first. After dinner we'll sing and dance.

Wang Peng: Who will be there?

Li You: Xiaoyin and her boyfriend, Xiaoyin's cousin, Bai Ying'ai, your sister Wang Hong, and Xiaoyin's middle school classmates, I hear.

Wang Peng: What birthday gift are you giving Xiaoyin?

Li You: I bought a book to give to her.

Wang Peng: What should I bring?

Li You: Either beverages or fruit would do.

Wang Peng: Then I'll bring some beverages. I'll also get some flowers.

Li You: Xiaoyin loves fruit. I'll get some apples, pears and a watermelon.

Wang Peng: Your place is very far from Xiaoyin's house, and the fruit will be heavy. I'll come to pick you up. Let's go together.

Li You: OK, I'll wait for you downstairs at six-thirty.

Dialogue II

(At Gao Xiaoyin's house)

Gao Xiaoyin: Wang Peng, Li You, come in.

Li You: Happy birthday, Xiaoyin. This is a birthday gift for you.

Gao Xiaoyin: Thank you. (She opens the gift.) I always wanted to buy this book. You brought so many things with you. You're really too kind.

Wang Hong: Hey brother, Li You, you're here.

Li You: Xiao Hong, how are you?

Wang Hong: I'm fine. I'm studying English every day.

Wang Peng: Xiao Hong, how much time do you spend practicing English every day?

Wang Hong: Three and half hours, plus I watch two hours of English-language TV.

Gao Wenzhong: When did you two get here?

Li You: Just now.

Gao Wenzhong: Didn't Bai Ying'ai come with you?

Li You: She's still not here? I thought she'd already gotten here.

Gao Xiaoyin: Wang Peng, Li You, let me introduce you. This is my cousin Helen. This is her son Tom.

Wang Peng: Hello, Helen.

Helen: Hello, Wang Peng. Wenzhong and Xiaoyin say that you're very smart and very hardworking.

Wang Peng: You flatter me. Your Chinese is great. Where did you learn it?

Helen: At summer school.

Wang Peng: Hey, Tom is really cute. Look, he's smiling now. How old is he?

Helen: He just turned one. He was born last year, the year of the dog.

Li You: Look, he's got a round face, big eyes, and a straight nose. His mouth is not too big, and not too small. He looks just like Helen.

Wang Hong: With such a gorgeous mom, the son will definitely be very handsome.

Gao Xiaoyin: Come, let's eat the cake.

Gao Wenzhong: Why don't we wait for Bai Ying'ai? She loves cake.

PROGRESS CHECKLIST

Before proceeding to Lesson 15, be sure you can complete the following tasks in Chinese:

I am able to—

- ☑ Ask a friend to attend a party;
- ☐ Offer a ride and set up a place and time for picking up someone;
- ☐ Talk about the duration of an action;
- ☐ Thank someone for his or her gift;
- ☐ Ask someone about his or her birth year and Chinese zodiac sign, and talk about my own;
- ☐ Give a basic description of someone's facial features.

牛年
Niú nián (the Year of the Ox)

LESSON 15

Seeing a Doctor

第十五课 看病
Dì shíwù kè   Kàn bìng

 LEARNING OBJECTIVES

In this lesson, you will learn to use Chinese to

- Talk about basic symptoms of a cold;
- Describe common symptoms of allergies;
- Understand and repeat instructions on when and how often to take medications;
- Talk about why you do or don't want to see the doctor;
- Urge others to see a doctor when they are not feeling well.

 RELATE AND GET READY

In your own culture/community—

1. Can you see a doctor without an appointment?

2. Do you have to pay an office visit fee before seeing a doctor?

3. Is it common to see the doctor and pay for medication at the same place?

4. Apart from medication, what other kinds of treatment might a doctor recommend?

5. Is everyone covered by health insurance?

Dialogue I: My Stomachache Is Killing Me!

（病人去医院看病）

医生，我肚子疼死①了。

你昨天吃什么东西了？

我姐姐上个星期过生日，蛋糕没吃完。昨天晚上我
吃了几口②，夜里肚子就疼起来了③，今天早上上了
好几次②厕所。

你把④蛋糕放在哪儿了？

放在冰箱里了。

放了几天了？

五、六❶天了。

 发烧吗？

 不发烧。

 你躺下。先检查一下。

* * *

 你吃蛋糕把肚子吃坏了。

 要不要打针？

 不用打针，吃这种药❷
就可以。一天三次，一次
两片。

 医生，一天吃几次？请您
再说一遍。

 一天三次，一次两片。

 好！饭前❸吃还是饭后
吃？

 饭前饭后都可以。不过，
你最好二十四小时不吃
饭。

 那我要饿死了。不行，这
个办法不好！

LANGUAGE NOTES

❶ A combination of two adjacent numbers can be used to denote an approximate number, e.g., 五十六、七岁 (wǔshí liù, qī suì, fifty-six or fifty-seven years old), 十八、九块钱 (shí bā, jiǔ kuài qián, eighteen or nineteen dollars), 三、四天 (sān, sì tiān, three or four days), 两、三枝笔 (liǎng, sān zhī bǐ, two or three pens). However, the numbers nine and ten cannot be used this way since it could lead to ambiguity: it would be difficult to distinguish 九、十天 (jiǔ, shí tiān) from 九十天 (jiǔshí tiān, ninety days) in speech.

❷ "To take medicine" is 吃药 (chī yào), literally "to eat medicine." A more formal expression is 服药 (fú yào), which is commonly written on prescriptions and prescription instructions.

❸ 前 (qián, before) in 饭前 (fàn qián, before meals) and 后 (hòu, after) in 饭后 (fàn hòu; after meals) are the shortened forms of 以前 (yǐqián, before) and 以后 (yǐhòu, after) respectively.

(Bìngrén qù yīyuàn kàn bìng)

 Yīshēng, wǒ dùzi téng sǐ① le.

 Nǐ zuótiān chī shénme dōngxi le?

 Wǒ jiějie shàng ge xīngqī guò shēngrì, dàngāo méi chī wán. Zuótiān wǎnshang wǒ chī le jǐ kǒu②, yè li dùzi jiù téng qi lai le③, jīntiān zǎoshang shàng le hǎo jǐ cì② cèsuǒ.

 Nǐ bǎ④ dàngāo fàng zài nǎr le?

 Fàng zài bīngxiāng lǐ le.

 Fàng le jǐ tiān le?

 Wǔ, liù❶ tiān le.

 Fā shāo ma?

 Bù fā shāo.

 Nǐ tǎng xia. Xiān jiǎnchá yí xià.

* * *

 Nǐ chī dàngāo bǎ dùzi chī huài le.

 Yào bú yào dǎ zhēn?

 Búyòng dǎ zhēn, chī zhè zhǒng yào② jiù kěyǐ. Yì tiān sān cì, yí cì liǎng piàn.

 Yīshēng, yì tiān chī jǐ cì? Qǐng nín zài shuō yí biàn.

 Yì tiān sān cì, yí cì liǎng piàn.

 Hǎo! Fàn qián❸ chī háishi fàn hòu chī?

 Fàn qián fàn hòu dōu kěyǐ. Búguò, nǐ zuìhǎo èrshí sì xiǎoshí bù chī fàn.

 Nà wǒ yào è sǐ le. Bù xíng, zhè ge bànfǎ bù hǎo!

VOCABULARY

1.	病人	bìngrén	n	patient
	病	bìng	n/v	illness; to become ill
2.	医院	yīyuàn	n	hospital
3.	看病	kàn bìng	vo	to see a doctor; (of a doctor) to see a patient
4.	肚子	dùzi	n	belly; abdomen
5.	疼死	téng sǐ	adj + c	really painful [See Grammar 1.]
	疼	téng	adj	aching
	死	sǐ	v/c	to die; (a complement indicating an extreme degree)
6.	夜里	yèli	n	at night
7.	好几	hǎo jǐ		quite a few
8.	厕所	cèsuǒ	n	restroom, toilet
9.	把	bǎ	prep	(indicating a thing is disposed of) [See Grammar 4.]
10.	冰箱	bīngxiāng	n	refrigerator
11.	发烧	fā shāo	vo	to have a fever
12.	躺下	tǎng xia	vc	to lie down
	躺	tǎng	v	to lie
13.	检查	jiǎnchá	v	to examine
14.	吃坏	chī huài	vc	to get sick because of bad food
	坏	huài	adj	bad
15.	打针	dǎ zhēn	vo	to get an injection
	针	zhēn	n	needle
16.	药	yào	n	medicine

VOCABULARY

17.	片	piàn	m	(measure word for tablet; slice)
18.	遍	biàn	m	(measure word for complete courses of an action or instances of an action)
19.	最好	zuìhǎo	adv	had better
20.	小时	xiǎoshí	n	hour
21.	办法	bànfǎ	n	method; way (of doing something)

内服藥用法

請按「✓」項指示方法服用

□ 每日4次，三餐飯前後及睡前各＿次，每次＿＿粒包

✓ 每日3次，三餐飯前後各｜次，每次｜粒包

□ 每日2次，早、晚飯前後各次，每次＿＿粒包

□ 每日1次，飯前後服＿＿粒包

□ 每＿＿小時服＿＿粒包

□ 每晚睡前服＿＿粒包

请问，药每天吃几次？饭前吃还是饭后吃？

Qǐng wèn, yào měitiān chī jǐ cì? Fàn qián chī háishi fàn hòu chī?

Grammar

1. 死 (sǐ) Indicating an Extreme Degree

Placed after an adjective, 死 (sǐ) can serve as a complement to indicate an extreme degree of the condition named by the adjective.

❶ 打针疼死了。

Dǎ zhēn téng sǐ le.

(It's extremely painful to get a shot.)

❷ 我饿死了。

Wǒ è sǐ le.

(I'm starving.)

❸ 今天热死了。

Jīntiān rè sǐ le.

(It's awfully hot today.)

死 (sǐ) often follows an adjective with a pejorative meaning and therefore the combination carries a negative connotation, as shown in the examples above. Occasionally, however, it may also be used in a positive context.

❹ 知道了这件事，他高兴死了。

Zhīdào le zhè jiàn shì, tā gāoxìng sǐ le.

(He was tickled pink when he learned about this.)

Most complimentary adjectives cannot be followed by 死 (sǐ). People therefore seldom say:

❺ *那件衣服漂亮死了。

*Nà jiàn yīfu piàoliang sǐ le.

❻ *他跟他女朋友好死了。

*Tā gēn tā de nǚ péngyou hǎo sǐ le.

2. Times of Actions

次 (cì) is the measure word most frequently used to indicate that an action is performed a certain number of times. The "number + 次 (cì)" combination follows the verb.

❶ 上午我打了两次电话。

Shàngwǔ wǒ dǎ le liǎng cì diànhuà.

(I made two phone calls in the morning.)

❷ 昨天我吃了三次药。

Zuótiān wǒ chī le sān cì yào.

(I took the medicine three times yesterday.)

If the object is not a person or a place, 次 (cì) should be placed between the verb and the object. If the object represents a person or a place, 次 (cì) can go either between the verb and the object or after the object.

❸ A: 去年我去了一次中国。你呢？

Qùnián wǒ qù le yí cì Zhōngguó. Nǐ ne?

(Last year I went to China once. How about you?)

B: 去年我去了中国两次。

Qùnián wǒ qù le Zhōngguó liǎng cì.

(Last year I went to China twice.)

❹ A: 昨天我找了三次王医生。

Zuótiān wǒ zhǎo le sān cì Wáng yīshēng.

(I went looking for Dr. Wang three times yesterday.)

B: 是吗？昨天我也找了王医生三次。

Shì ma? Zuótiān wǒ yě zhǎo le Wáng yīshēng sān cì.

(Is that right? I also went looking for Dr. Wang three times yesterday.)

If the object is a personal pronoun, however, 次 (cì) must follow the object.

❺   我昨天找了他两次，他都不在。

Wǒ zuótiān zhǎo le tā liǎng cì, tā dōu bú zài.

(Yesterday I went looking for him twice, but he was not in either time.)

遍 (biàn) is another measure word for occurrences of actions, but it pertains to the entire course of the action from the beginning to the end.

❻   请你念一遍课文。

Qǐng nǐ niàn yí biàn kèwén.

(Please read the text [from the beginning to the end] once).

Nouns denoting body parts involved in the actions can also sometimes serve as measure words for occurrences of actions. One example is from Dialogue I of the current lesson:

昨天晚上我吃了几口…

Zuótiān wǎnshang wǒ chī le jǐ kǒu…

(I ate a few mouthfuls last night…)

3. 起来 (qi lai) Indicating the Beginning of an Action

起来 (qi lai) indicates the moment when something static becomes dynamic, that is, it signifies the beginning of an action or state.

❶   我们一见面就聊了起来。

Wǒmen yí jiàn miàn jiù liáo le qi lai

(We began chatting as soon as we met.)

❷   他一回家就写起信来。

Tā yì huí jiā jiù xiě qi xìn lai.

(He began to write a letter as soon as he got home.)

❸ 下了课以后，学生们打起球来。

Xià le kè yǐhòu, xuésheng men dǎ qi qiú lai.

(The students started to play ball after the class was over.)

Note that the object is placed between 起 (qi) and 来 (lai), rather than after 起来 (qi lai).

---

4. 把 (bǎ) Construction (I)

Sentences with 把 (bǎ) are common in Chinese. The basic construction is as follows:

Subject + 把 (bǎ) + Object + Verb + Other Element (Complement/ 了 {le}, etc.)

In the 把 (bǎ) construction, what follows the position 把 (bǎ) and precedes the verb serves as both the object of 把 (bǎ) and the object of the verb. In general, a sentence in the 把 (bǎ) construction highlights the subject's disposal of or impact upon the object, with the result of the disposal or impact indicated by the element following the verb.

❶ 我把你要的书找到了。

Wǒ bǎ nǐ yào de shū zhǎo dào le.

(I have found the books that you wanted.)

[The resultative complement 到 (dào) serves as the "other element."]

In (1), the subject 我 (wǒ) exerts an impact on the book through the action of 找 (zhǎo), of which 到 (dào) is the result.

❷ 你把这个字写错了。

Nǐ bǎ zhè ge zì xiě cuò le.

(You wrote this character incorrectly.)

[The resultative complement 错 (cuò) serves as the "other element."]

In (2), the subject 你 (nǐ) exerts an impact on the character through the action of 写 (xiě), of which 错 (cuò) is the result.

❸ 请把那条裤子给我。

Qǐng bǎ nà tiáo kùzi gěi wǒ.

(Please pass me that pair of pants.)

[The indirect object 我 (wǒ) serves as the "other element."]

❹ 你把这篇课文看看。

Nǐ bǎ zhè piān kèwén kàn kan.

(Would you take a look at this text?)

[The reduplicated verb 看 (kàn) serves as the "other element."]

❺ 把这杯咖啡喝了！

Bǎ zhè bēi kāfēi hē le!

(Finish up this cup of coffee!)

❻ 你怎么把女朋友的生日忘了？

Nǐ zěnme bǎ nǚpéngyou de shēngrì wàng le?

(How did you manage to forget your girlfriend's birthday?)

[In (5) and (6), the particle 了 (le) serves as the "other element."]

(3), (4), and (5) suggest what the listener is requested to do to the objects (the pants, the text, and the coffee). The other element could be a complement as in (1) and (2), an indirect object as in (3), a reduplicated verb as in (4), or the particle 了 (le) as in (5) and (6).

In the 把 (bǎ) construction, the object is often something already known to both the speaker and the listener. For example, 你要的书 (nǐ yào de shū) in (1), 这个字 (zhè ge zì) in (2), 那条裤子 (nà tiáo kùzi) in (3), and 女朋友的生日 (nǚpéngyou de shēngrì) in (6) are all things that are already known. Compare the following two sentences:

❼ 老王给了小张一些钱。

Lǎo Wáng gěi le Xiǎo Zhāng yì xiē qián.

(Old Wang gave Little Zhang some money.)

8 老王把钱给小张了。

Lǎo Wáng bǎ qián gěi Xiǎo Zhāng le.

(Old Wang gave the money to Little Zhang.)

The object in (7), "some money," is unspecified. However, in (8), the speaker expects the listener to know what money is being referred to.

If the subject of a sentence is given, the object is something known to both the speaker and listener, and the verb is followed by a complement in the form of a prepositional phrase with 在 (zài) or 到 (dào), that sentence *must* appear in the 把 (bǎ) construction. For example:

你把笔放在桌子上。

Nǐ bǎ bǐ fàng zài zhuōzi shang.

(Put the pen on the desk.)

请你把这封信送到律师的办公室。

Qǐng nǐ bǎ zhè fēng xìn sòng dào lǜshī de bàngōngshì.

(Please deliver this letter to the attorney's office.)

The following sentences are therefore incorrect:

*你放笔在桌子上。

*Nǐ fàng bǐ zài zhuōzi shang.

*请你送这封信到律师的办公室。

*Qǐng nǐ sòng zhè fēng xìn dào lǜshī de bàngōngshì.

Language Practice

A. Extreme Cases

EXAMPLE:

→ 他渴死了。 Tā kě sǐ le.

1. →

2. $250 →

3. →

B. Study Habits

Work with your partner and find out each other's daily routine for studying Chinese. Then find out what happened yesterday.

EXAMPLE: 听录音   tīng lùyīn

→ A: 你每天听几遍/次   Nǐ měitiān tīng jǐ biàn/cì
       录音？   lùyīn?

   B: 我每天听_____录音。   Wǒ měitiān tīng _____ lùyīn.

   A: 昨天呢？   Zuótiān ne?

   B: 我昨天听了_____   Wǒ zuótiān tīng le _____
       录音。   lùyīn.

1. 念课文   niàn kèwén

2. 复习生词语法   fùxí shēngcí yǔfǎ

3. 写汉字   xiě Hànzì

C. Moving Day

Your friend has offered to help you move into your new apartment, and wants to know where everything should go.

EXAMPLE:

→ A: 把纸和笔放在
什么地方？

B: 请把纸和笔放在
桌子上。

Bǎ zhǐ hé bǐ fàng zài

shénme dìfang?

Qǐng bǎ zhǐ hé bǐ fàng zài

zhuōzi shang.

1.   →

2.   →

3. →

4. →

D. Recap and Narrate

Working with a partner, recap the content of Dialogue I:

1. 高文中为什么
   去医院看病？

2. 高文中昨天吃
   什么了？

3. 他是什么时候吃的
   蛋糕，什么时候
   开始生病的？

4. 高文中把蛋糕
   放在哪儿了？放了
   几天了？

5. 高文中发烧吗？

6. 医生说高文中
   怎么了？

7. 医生说高文中
   得打针吗？

8. 医生说一天吃
   几次药？每次几片？

1. Gāo Wénzhōng wèishénme
   qù yīyuàn kàn bìng?

2. Gāo Wénzhōng zuótiān chī
   shénme le?

3. Tā shì shénme shíhou chī de
   dàngāo, shénme shíhou
   kāishǐ shēng bìng de?

4. **Gāo Wénzhō**ng bǎ dàngāo
   fàng zài nǎr le? Fàng le
   jǐ tiān le?

5. Gāo Wénzhōng fā shāo ma?

6. Yīshēng shuō Gāo Wénzhōng
   zěnme le?

7. Yīshēng shuō Gāo Wénzhōng
   děi dǎ zhēn ma?

8. Yīshēng shuō yì tiān chī
   jǐ cì yào? Měi cì jǐ piàn?

9. 医生说高文中
   最好怎么样？

10. 高文中觉得这个
    办法好吗？

9. Yīshēng shuō Gāo Wénzhōng
   zuìhǎo zěnmeyàng?

10. Gāo Wénzhōng juéde zhè ge
    bànfǎ hǎo ma?

Using the words and phrases in blue as prompts, connect your answers above to form a narrative like this example:

高文中的姐姐上个星期
过生日，高文中把没吃
完的蛋糕放在冰箱里。
蛋糕放了五六天了，昨
天晚上他吃了几口，夜
里肚子就疼起来，今天
早上上了好几次厕所，
他肚子疼极了，就去医
院看病。医生给他检
查，说他是吃蛋糕把肚
子吃坏了。高文中不希
望打针，医生说不用打
针，吃药就可以。那种
药一天吃三次，一次两
片，饭前吃饭后吃都可
以。医生还说最好二十
四小时不吃饭。高文中
觉得这个办法不好。

Gāo Wénzhōng de jiějie shàng
ge xīngqī guò shēngrì, Gāo
Wénzhōng bǎ méi chī wán de
dàngāo fàng zài bīngxiāng li.
Dàngāo fàng le wǔ liù tiān le,
zuótiān wǎnshang tā chī le jǐ
kǒu, yèli dùzi jiù téng qi lai,
jīntiān zǎoshang shàng le hǎo
jǐ cì cèsuǒ, tā dùzi téng jí le, jiù
qù yīyuàn kàn bìng. Yīshēng
gěi tā jiǎnchá, shuō tā shì chī
dàngāo bǎ dùzi chī huài le. Gāo
Wénzhōng bù xīwàng dǎ zhēn,
yīshēng shuō búyòng dǎ zhēn,
chī yào jiù kěyǐ. Nà zhǒng yào yì
tiān chī sān cì, yí cì liǎng piàn,
fàn qián chī fàn hòu chī dōu
kěyǐ. Yīshēng hái shuō zuìhǎo
èrshí sì xiǎoshí bù chī fàn. Gāo
Wénzhōng juéde zhè ge bànfǎ bù
hǎo.

Dialogue II: Allergies

 王朋，你怎么了？眼睛怎么红红的，感冒了吗？

 没感冒。我也不知道怎么了，最近这几天身体很不舒服。眼睛又红又痒。

 你一定是对⑤什么过敏了。

 我想也是，所以去药店买了一些药。已经吃了四、五种了，花了不少钱，都没有用。

 把你买的药拿出来给我看看。

 这些就是。

 这些药没有用。为什么不去看医生？你没有健康保险吗？

 我有保险。可是我这个学期功课很多，看医生太花时间。

那你也得赶快去看医生❶。
要不然病会越来越⑥重。

我想再吃点儿别的药试试❷。
我上次生病，没去看医生，
休息两天，最后也好了。

不行，不行，你太懒了。
再说⑦，你不能自己乱吃药。
走，我跟你看病去。

LANGUAGE NOTES

❶ The two phrases 看医生 (kàn yīshēng) and 看病 (kàn bìng) are interchangeable, although in northern China 看病 (kàn bìng) is much more common than 看医生 (kàn yīshēng).

❷ When tasting or trying the flavor of a food or drink, one says 我尝尝 (Wǒ cháng chang, Let me taste it) instead of 我试试 (Wǒ shì shi, Let me try), although one says 试试 (shì shi) when trying most other things.

Wáng Péng, nǐ zěnme le? Yǎnjing zěnme hóng hóng de, gǎnmào le ma?

Méi gǎnmào. Wǒ yě bù zhīdào zěnme le, zuìjìn zhè jǐ tiān shēntǐ hěn bù shūfu. Yǎnjing yòu hóng yòu yǎng.

Nǐ yídìng shì duì⑤ shénme guòmǐn le.

Wǒ xiǎng yě shì, suǒyǐ qù yàodiàn mǎi le yì xiē yào. Yǐjīng chī le sì, wǔ zhǒng le, huā le bù shǎo qián, dōu méiyǒu yòng.

Bǎ nǐ mǎi de yào ná chu lai gěi wǒ kàn kan.

Zhè xiē jiù shì.

Zhè xiē yào méiyǒu yòng. Wèishénme bú qù kàn yīshēng? Nǐ méiyou jiànkāng bǎoxiǎn ma?

Wǒ yǒu bǎoxiǎn. Kěshì wǒ zhè ge xuéqī gōngkè hěn duō. Kàn yīshēng tài huā shíjiān.

Nà nǐ yě děi gǎnkuài qù kàn yīshēng❹. Yàobùrán bìng huì yuè lái yuè⑥ zhòng.

Wǒ xiǎng zài chī diǎnr bié de yào shì shi. Wǒ shàng cì shēng bìng, méi qù kàn yīshēng, xiūxi liǎng tiān, zuìhòu yě hǎo le.

Bù xíng, bù xíng, nǐ tài lǎn le. Zàishuō⑦, nǐ bù néng zìjǐ luàn chī yào. Zǒu, wǒ gēn nǐ kàn bìng qu.

VOCABULARY

1.	感冒	gǎnmào	v	to have a cold
2.	生病	shēng bìng	vo	to get sick
3.	身体	shēntǐ	n	body; health
4.	痒	yǎng	adj	itchy
5.	过敏	guòmǐn	v	to be allergic to
6.	药店	yàodiàn	n	pharmacy
7.	健康	jiànkāng	adj/n	healthy; health
8.	保险	bǎoxiǎn	n	insurance
9.	赶快	gǎnkuài	adv	right away; quickly; in a hurry
10.	要不然	yàobùrán	conj	otherwise
11.	越来越	yuè lái yuè	adv	more and more [See Grammar 6.]
12.	上次	shàng cì		last time
13.	休息	xiūxi	v	to take a break; to rest
14.	懒	lǎn	adj	lazy
15.	再说	zàishuō	conj	moreover [See Grammar 7.]
16.	乱	luàn	adv	randomly; arbitrarily; messily

These are signs you may see in clinics and hospitals in China. Can you guess what the rooms are for? Can you read the sign on the right in the correct tones?

Grammar

5. The Preposition 对 (duì)

The preposition 对 (duì) introduces the person or thing that receives a certain effect from someone or something else. Its English translation varies depending on the context.

❶ 这种药对感冒很有用。

Zhè zhǒng yào duì gǎnmào hěn yǒu yòng.

(This medicine is very effective for colds.)

❷ 他的电脑对他练习发音很有用。

Tā de diànnǎo duì tā liànxí fāyīn hěn yǒu yòng.

(His computer is very useful for his pronunciation practice.)

❸ 你一定对什么东西过敏了。

Nǐ yídìng duì shénme dōngxi guòmǐn le.

(You must be allergic to something.)

6. 越来越··· (yuè lái yuè...)

The structure 越来越··· (yuè lái yuè...) denotes a progressive change over time.

❶ 李友的中文越来越好。

Lǐ Yǒu de Zhōngwén yuè lái yuè hǎo.

(Li You's Chinese is getting better and better.)

❷ 天气越来越暖和了。

Tiānqì yuè lái yuè nuǎnhuo le.

(The weather is becoming warmer and warmer.)

❸ 表姐考试考得越来越糟糕。

Biǎojiě kǎo shì kǎo de yuè lái yuè zāogāo.

(My cousin is doing worse and worse on her exams.)

---

7. 再说 (zàishuō)

The expression 再说 (zàishuō) introduces an additional reason for an action that has been taken or decision that has been made. It is different from 再 + 说 (zài + shuō, to say again).

❶ A: 你为什么不去纽约？

Nǐ wèishénme bú qù Niǔyuē?

(Why aren't you going to New York?)

B: 我没有时间，再说，也没有钱。

Wǒ méiyǒu shíjiān, zàishuō, yě méiyǒu qián.

(I don't have the time, and besides, I don't have the money.)

❷ 我不喜欢今天晚上的舞会，音乐不好，再说人也太少。

Wǒ bù xǐhuan jīntiān wǎnshang de wǔhuì, yīnyuè bù hǎo, zàishuō rén yě tài shǎo.

(I didn't like the dance party tonight. The music was lousy. Besides, there were too few people there.)

Like 再说 (zàishuō), 而且 (érqiě, moreover; in addition) also conveys the idea of "furthermore, additionally," etc., but the clause that follows it may or may not be explanatory in nature. Compare the following sentences:

❸ A: 你为什么不去纽约？

Nǐ wèishénme bú qù Niǔyuē?

(Why aren't you going to New York?)

B: 我没有时间，而且，也没有钱。

Wǒ méiyǒu shíjiān, érqiě, yě méiyǒu qián.

(I don't have the time. Besides, I don't have the money.)

Note: In (3), 而且 (érqiě) can be replaced with 再说 (zàishuō).

❹ 这是王先生，他不但是我的老师，而且也是
我的朋友。

Zhè shì Wáng xiānsheng, tā búdàn shì wǒ de lǎoshī, érqiě yě shì wǒ de

péngyou.

(This is Mr. Wang. He is not only my teacher but also my friend.)

Note: In (4), 而且 (érqiě) cannot be replaced with 再说 (zàishuō):

4a *这是王先生，他不但是我的老师，再说也是
我的朋友。

*Zhè shì Wáng xiānsheng, tā búdàn shì wǒ de lǎoshī, zàishuō yě shì wǒ de

péngyou.

Language Practice

E. Allergy! Allergy! Allergy!

Go around the class and ask your classmates if they are allergic to the following items.

EXAMPLE:

→ **A:** Joe, 你对味精
过敏吗？

Joe, nǐ duì wèijīng

guòmǐn ma?

B: 我对味精过敏。/
我对味精不过敏。

Wǒ duì wèijīng guòmǐn./

Wǒ duì wèijīng bú guòmǐn.

1.

2. →

3. →

Then tally who's allergic to what:

Joe, Maya,…, 对味精过敏。
…

Joe, Maya,…, duì wèijīng guòmǐn.
…

| F. Role-Play |

1. Pretend you are a teacher, and use 要不然 (yàobùrán) to advise your students not to fall into bad study habits.

> EXAMPLE:
>
> 你得多写汉字，要不然
> 你的中文不会好。
>
> Nǐ děi duō xiě Hànzì, yàobùrán
> nǐ de Zhōngwén bú huì hǎo.

1st piece of advice:

2nd piece of advice:

3rd piece of advice:

2. Pretend you are a parent, and use 要不然 (yàobùrán) to advise your child to take care of himself/herself at college.

> EXAMPLE:
>
> 如果身体不舒服，
> 你得去看医生，
> 要不然病会越来
> 越重。
>
> Rúguǒ shēntǐ bù shūfu,
> nǐ děi qù kàn yīshēng,
> yàobùrán bìng huì yuè lái
> yuè zhòng.

1st piece of advice:

2nd piece of advice:

3rd piece of advice:

G. Agree or Disagree?

Work with a partner to find out if you both share the same sentiments about how your Chinese study is progressing.

EXAMPLE:　生词　　多 vs. 少

→ A: 你觉得生词越来越多还是越来越少？

Nǐ juéde shēngcí yuè lái yuè duō háishi yuè lái yuè shǎo?

B: 我觉得生词越来越多/少。

Wǒ juéde shēngcí yuè lái yuè duō/shǎo.

1. 功课　　多 vs. 少　　　　gōngkè　　　duō vs. shǎo

2. 课文　　长 vs. 短　　　　kèwén　　　cháng vs. duǎn

3. 考试　　难 vs. 容易　　　kǎoshì　　　nán vs. róngyì

4. 语法　　难 vs. 容易　　　yǔfǎ　　　　nán vs. róngyì

H. Reasons and Excuses

EXAMPLE:

A: 你为什么不吃早饭？

Nǐ wèishénme bù chī zǎofàn?

B: 我没时间，再说我不饿。

Wǒ méi shíjiān, zàishuō wǒ bú è.

1. A: 你为什么不听录音？

A: Nǐ wèishénme bù tīng lùyīn?

B: _____

2. A: 你为什么不运动？   A: Nǐ wèishénme bú yùndòng?

   B: _____

3. A: 你为什么寒假没回   A: Nǐ wèishénme hánjià méi huí
      家看爸爸妈妈？   jiā kàn bàba māma?

   B: _____

4. A: 你为什么学中文？   A: Nǐ wèishénme xué Zhōngwén?

   B: _____

5. A: 你为什么上   A: Nǐ wèishénme shàng
      这个学校？   zhè ge xuéxiào?

   B: _____

I. Recap and Narrate

Working with a partner, recap the content of Dialogue II:

1. 王朋的眼睛
   为什么红了？
   感冒了吗？

   1. Wáng Péng de yǎnjing
      wèishénme hóng le?
      Gǎnmào le ma?

2. 王朋说他怎么了？

   2. Wáng Péng shuō tā zěnme le?

3. 李友说王朋生了
   什么病？

   3. Lǐ Yǒu shuō Wáng Péng shēng le
      shénme bìng?

4. 王朋吃药了吗？

   4. Wáng Péng chī yào le ma?

5. 李友说王朋得
   做什么？

   5. Lǐ Yǒu shuō Wáng Péng děi
      zuò shénme?

6. 王朋有健康
   保险吗？

   6. Wáng Péng yǒu jiànkāng
      bǎoxiǎn ma?

7. 他为什么不去看病？

8. 李友说不看医生病会越来越重，王朋说什么？

9. 李友觉得王朋的话对吗？

7. Tā wèishénme bú qù kàn bìng?

8. Lǐ Yǒu shuō bú kàn yīshēng bìng huì yuè lái yuè zhòng, Wáng Péng shuō shénme?

9. Lǐ Yǒu juéde Wáng Péng de huà duì ma?

Using the words and phrases in blue as prompts, connect your answers above to form a narrative like this example:

王朋最近觉得很不舒服，眼睛又红又痒，不知道生了什么病。李友说他可能是对什么过敏。王朋也觉得是对什么过敏，所以吃了四、五种药，可是都没用。李友看了王朋吃的药，告诉他那些药没有用，得去看医生。王朋说这学期功课太多，看医生太花时间。李友问王朋是不是没有健康保险，王朋说他有。李友让王朋赶快去看病，要不然病会越来越重。王朋说他上次生病，没看医生，休息几天，最后病也好了。李友说王朋太懒，再说也不能自己乱吃药，所以她要跟王朋一起去看医生。

Wáng Péng zuìjìn juéde hěn bù shūfu, yǎnjing yòu hóng yòu yǎng, bù zhīdào shēng le shénme bìng. Lǐ Yǒu shuō tā kěnéng shì duì shénme guòmǐn. Wáng Péng yě juéde shì duì shénme guòmǐn, suǒyǐ chī le sì, wǔ zhǒng yào, kěshì dōu méi yòng. Lǐ Yǒu kàn le Wáng Péng chī de yào, gàosù tā nà xiē yào méiyǒu yòng, děi qù kàn yīshēng. Wáng Péng shuō zhè xuéqī gōngkè tài duō, kàn yīshēng tài huā shíjiān. Lǐ Yǒu wèn Wáng Péng shì bú shì méiyǒu jiànkāng bǎoxiǎn, Wáng Péng shuō tā yǒu. Lǐ Yǒu ràng Wáng Péng gǎnkuài qù kàn bìng, yàobùrán bìng huì yuè lái yuè zhòng. Wáng Péng shuō tā shàng cì shēng bìng, méi kàn yīshēng, xiūxi jǐ tiān, zuìhòu bìng yě hǎo le. Lǐ Yǒu shuō Wáng Péng tài lǎn, zàishuō yě bù néng zìjǐ luàn chī yào, suǒyǐ tā yào gēn Wáng Péng yìqǐ qù kàn yīshēng.

HOW ABOUT YOU?

What Are You Allergic To?

1.	花粉	huāfěn	n	pollen
2.	花生	huāshēng	n	peanuts
3.	猫	māo	n	cats
4.	灰尘	huīchén	n	dust

If the source of your allergy is not listed, please ask your teacher and make a note here:

_____

What Allergy Symptoms Do You Have?

1.	头疼	tóu téng		to have a headache
2.	咳嗽	késòu	v	to cough
3.	打喷嚏	dǎ pēnti	vo	to sneeze
4.	流鼻涕	liú bítì	vo	to have a runny nose

If there are other symptoms you would like to know how to say, please ask your teacher and make a note here:

_____

Culture Highlights

❶ Before Western medicine 西医 (Xīyī) was first introduced to China during the seventeenth century by European missionaries, the Chinese had relied exclusively on traditional Chinese medicine 中医 (Zhōngyī), a system including acupuncture, herbal medicine, massage, and other therapies. Even now, these indigenous ways of medical treatment remain a well-respected option. Many Chinese people choose to use traditional Chinese medicine for various ailments along with or instead of Western medicine. Although by no means a panacea, traditional Chinese medicine can be surprisingly effective. Many of the reasons for the effectiveness of therapies such as acupuncture and cupping are not fully understood by modern science.

Traditional Chinese herbal medicine being provided at a medical clinic.

❷ To see a doctor, a Chinese outpatient has to pay a registration fee
(挂号费 guàhào fèi). The fee is typically equivalent to no more than
one US dollar, but could be considerably higher if one wants to consult
an esteemed specialist (专家 zhuānjiā). For prescribed tests, outpatients usually have to pay up front.

According to the sign, what do people do here?

❸ While injections (打针 dǎ zhēn) and intravenous infusion (打点滴
dǎ diǎndī in Taiwan and 输液 shū yè in mainland China) are
seldom used in American hospitals for outpatients, they are much
more common treatments for outpatients in Chinese hospitals, clinics
and doctors' offices, even for common ailments like a cold.

❹ An outpatient in China would usually pick up his or her prescription
from a pharmacy within the hospital itself. One can, however, get
medicines from independent pharmacies.

❺ Until the 1980s, employees in all state-owned enterprises and
institutions in China were offered free medical care, which became
a huge financial burden for the government. That practice was
discontinued in the 1990s. The cities in China are currently in a
transitional period toward a better-regulated system of medical
insurance, while most people in the rural areas are still without any
insurance coverage for their health care.

English Text

Dialogue I

(A patient is going to a hospital for treatment)

Gao Wenzhong: Doctor, my stomachache is killing me!

Doctor: What did you have to eat yesterday?

Gao Wenzhong: It was my sister's birthday last week. We didn't finish the cake. Last night I had a few bites. My stomach began to hurt at night, and this morning I went to the bathroom several times.

Doctor: Where did you put the cake?

Gao Wenzhong: In the refrigerator.

Doctor: How long had it been there?

Gao Wenzhong: About five or six days.

Doctor: Do you have a fever?

Gao Wenzhong: No, I don't.

Doctor: Please lie down. Let me check.

*   *   *

Doctor: You upset your stomach by eating that cake.

Gao Wenzhong: Do I need an injection?

Doctor: No, you don't need an injection. Just take this medicine, three times a day, two pills at a time.

Gao Wenzhong: Doctor, how many times a day? Could you please repeat that?

Doctor: Three times a day, two pills at a time.

Gao Wenzhong: All right. Before or after meals?

Doctor: Either before or after meals is fine, but you'd better not eat anything for twenty-four hours.

Gao Wenzhong: Then I'll be starving. That's not a good idea. That's not a good remedy!

Dialogue II

Li You: Wang Peng, what's the matter? How come your eyes are red? Did you catch a cold?

Wang Peng: No, I didn't catch a cold. I don't know what's wrong with me. I haven't been feeling well the last few days. My eyes are red and itchy.

Li You: You must be allergic to something.

Wang Peng: I think so, too. That's why I went to the pharmacy and got some medicine. I've taken four or five kinds and spent quite a bit of money, but none of them has been effective.

Li You: Take out the medicines you bought. Let me take a look.

Wang Peng: Here you are.

Li You: These medicines are useless. Why didn't you go to the doctor? Don't you have health insurance?

Wang Peng: I do have health insurance. I have too much homework this semester. Going to the doctor takes too much time.

Li You: Even so, you still need to go see a doctor as soon as possible. Otherwise, you'll get sicker and sicker.

Wang Peng: I'd like to try some other medicines first. Last time I was sick I didn't go to the doctor. After a couple days' rest, I was fine.

Li You: No way, no way, you're too lazy. Besides, you can't just randomly take medicine by yourself. Let's go. I'll go to the doctor with you.

This clinic specializes in the seven health problems listed. Do you recognize any of them?

PROGRESS CHECKLIST

Before proceeding to Lesson 16, be sure you can complete the following tasks in Chinese:

I am able to—

☑ Tell the doctor about my symptoms;

☐ Ask the doctor if a shot or medicine is needed for treatment;

☐ Follow and repeat the doctor's instructions on when and how often to take the medicine;

☐ Tell people about my allergies and briefly describe my allergy symptoms.

That's How the Chinese Say It!

A Review of Functional Expressions from Lessons 11–15

After gauging your progress and before moving on to the next phase, let's take a break and see how some of the functional expressions that you have encountered in the previous lessons really work!

I. 在 (zài, to exist)

When you think someone else might have something of yours, you should ask "我的…在你那儿吗？ (Wǒ de…zài nǐ nàr ma?)" instead of "你有我的…吗？ (Nǐ yǒu wǒ de…ma?)"

❶ A: 老师，我的功课在您那儿吗？

Lǎoshī, wǒ de gōngkè zài nín nàr ma?

(Teacher, do you have my homework?)

B: 我已经还给你了。

Wǒ yǐjīng huán gěi nǐ le.

(I gave it to you already.)

(还给, huán gěi: to return something [to someone])

A: 是吗？对不起，我再找找。

Shì ma? Duìbuqǐ, wǒ zài zhǎo zhao.

(Oh, you did? Sorry, I'll look for it again.)

❷ A: 妈妈，我的护照在您那儿吗？

Māma, wǒ de hùzhào zài nín nàr ma?

(Mom, do you have my passport?)

B: 在我这儿。给你吧。

Zài wǒ zhèr. Gěi nǐ ba.

(Yes, I have it. Here you are.)

❸ A: 我的手机还在你那儿吗？
     昨天你拿去用了。

   Wǒ de shǒujī hái zài nǐ nàr ma?

   Zuótiān nǐ ná qù yòng le.

   (Do you still have my cell phone?

   You took it yesterday.)

   B: 哦，还在我这儿，
      我忘了还给你了。

   Ò, hái zài wǒ zhèr, wǒ wàng le huán gěi nǐ le.

   (Oh yeah, I still have it. I forgot to return it to you.)

II. Complimentary Expressions

Note the different expressions for men, women, and children.

❶ 那个小孩真可爱。

   Nà ge xiǎohái zhēn kě'ài.

   (That little kid is really cute.)

❷ 她长得真好看！

   Tā zhǎng de zhēn hǎokàn!

   (She's really beautiful!)

❸ 李友长得很漂亮。

   Lǐ Yǒu zhǎng de hěn piàoliang.

   (Li You looks very pretty.)

❹ 王朋真帅。

   Wáng Péng zhēn shuài.

   (Wang Peng is really handsome.)

❺ 那个班的学生都很酷。

   Nà ge bān de xuésheng dōu hěn kù.

   (The students in that class are all very cool.)

III. 怎么了？ (Zěnme le? What's the matter? What's wrong?)

One can ask "你怎么了？" (Nǐ zěnme le?) upon finding someone under unusual circumstances or showing signs of concern, anxiety, or pain.

❶ A: 你怎么了？怎么这么不高兴？

Nǐ zěnme le? Zěnme zhème bù gāoxìng?

(What's the matter? Why are you so unhappy?)

B: 我的女朋友不爱我了。

Wǒ de nǚpéngyou bú ài wǒ le.

(My girlfriend doesn't love me anymore.)

❷ A: 怎么了？眼睛怎么这么红？

Zěnme le? Yǎnjing zěnme zhème hóng?

(What's wrong? Why are your eyes so red?)

B: 没什么。我可能对什么东西过敏了。

Méi shénme. Wǒ kěnéng duì shénme dōngxi guòmǐn le.

(It's nothing. I may be allergic to something.)

IV. 糟糕 (zāogāo, [It's] awful/What a mess)

This formula is often used when one suddenly realizes that something important has been forgotten or something of consequence has gone wrong.

❶ A: 糟糕，我的信用卡不见了。

Zāogāo, wǒ de xìnyòngkǎ bú jiàn le.

(Shoot! My credit card has disappeared.)

B: 快给你爸爸打电话吧。

Kuài gěi nǐ bàba dǎ diànhuà ba.

(Hurry, call your dad.)

❷ A: 糟糕，快要考试了，我还没准备好。

Zāogāo, kuài yào kǎo shì le, wǒ hái méi zhǔnbèi hǎo.

(Darn it. It's almost time for the test. I am not ready yet.)

B: 你没听说吗？老师病了，今天不考试了。

Nǐ méi tīngshuō ma? Lǎoshī bìng le, jīntiān bù kǎo shì le.

(Didn't you hear? The teacher is sick. We don't have the test today!)

A: 是吗？那太好了！

Shì ma? Nà tài hǎo le!

(Really? That's great!)

Any other useful expressions you would like to learn?

Please ask your teacher and make a note here:

_____

_____

_____

LESSON 16

第十六课

Dì shíliù kè

Dating
约会
Yuēhuì

 LEARNING OBJECTIVES

In this lesson, you will learn to use Chinese to

- Describe how long you've known someone;
- Invite someone to go on a date;
- Make the necessary arrangements to go out with friends;
- Accept a date courteously;
- Decline a date politely;
- End a phone conversation without hurting the other person's feelings.

 RELATE AND GET READY

In your own culture/community—

1. How can you get tickets for a popular event?

2. Is it socially acceptable to call a person you have only met once and whose phone number you obtained indirectly?

3. Is it impolite to directly say "no" to decline a date?

4. How can you end an unwanted phone conversation without being rude?

Dialogue I: Seeing a Movie

王朋跟李友在同一个学校学习，他们认识已经快半年了。王朋常常帮李友练习说中文。他们也常常一起出去玩儿，每次都玩儿得^①很高兴。李友对王朋的印象^❶很好，王朋也很喜欢李友，他们成了好朋友。

*　　*　　*

这个周末学校演^❷一个中国电影，我们一起去看，好吗？

LANGUAGE NOTES

❶ For the use of the word 印象 (yìnxiàng, impression), compare these two sentences:

李友对王朋的印象很好。 (Lǐ Yǒu duì Wáng Péng de yìnxiàng hěn hǎo, Li You has a very good impression of Wang Peng.)

李友给王朋的印象很好。 (Lǐ Yǒu gěi Wáng Péng de yìnxiàng hěn hǎo, Li You made a very good impression on Wang Peng.)

❷ The phrase 演电影 (yǎn diànyǐng, to show a film) in this lesson is interchangeable with 放电影 (fàng diànyǐng), but in addition, 演电影 (yǎn diànyǐng) can also mean "to act in a film."

好啊！不过，听说看电影的人很多，买得到^②票吗？

票已经买好了，我费了很大的力气才买到。

好极了！我早^③就想看中国电影了。还有别人跟我们一起去吗？

没有，就^③我们俩^④。

好。什么时候？

后天晚上八点。

看电影以前，我请你吃晚饭。

太好了！一言为定^⑤。

❸ The primary meaning of 早 (zǎo) is "early," but in an extended sense it can also mean "a long time ago," or "early on."

❹ 俩 (liǎ) stands for 两个 (liǎng ge).

❺ 一言为定 (yì yán wéi dìng), which literally means "achieving certainty with one word," is one of the numerous four-character idioms that have their origins in Classical Chinese but continue to be on the lips of almost every native speaker of the language.

Wáng Péng gēn Lǐ Yǒu zài tóng yí ge xuéxiào xuéxí, tāmen rènshi yǐjīng kuài bàn nián le. Wáng Péng chángcháng bāng Lǐ Yǒu liànxí shuō Zhōngwén. Tāmen yě chángcháng yìqǐ chū qu wánr, měi cì dōu wánr de^① hěn gāoxìng. Lǐ Yǒu duì Wáng Péng de yìnxiàng❶ hěn hǎo, Wáng Péng yě hěn xǐhuan Lǐ Yǒu, tāmen chéng le hǎo péngyou.

*   *   *

Zhè ge zhōumò xuéxiào yǎn❷ yí ge Zhōngguó diànyǐng, wǒmen yìqǐ qù kàn, hǎo ma?

Hǎo a! Búguò, tīngshuō kàn diànyǐng de rén hěn duō, mǎi de dào^② piào ma?

Piào yǐjīng mǎi hǎo le, wǒ fèi le hěn dà de lìqi cái mǎi dào.

Hǎo jí le! Wǒ zǎo^③ jiù xiǎng kàn Zhōngguó diànyǐng le. Hái yǒu bié rén gēn wǒmen yìqǐ qù ma?

Méiyǒu, jiù^③ wǒmen liǎ^④.

Hǎo. Shénme shíhou?

Hòutiān wǎnshang bā diǎn.

Kàn diànyǐng yǐqián, wǒ qǐng nǐ chī wǎnfàn.

Tài hǎo le! Yì yán wéi dìng❺.

VOCABULARY

1.	同	tóng	adj	same; alike
2.	印象	yìnxiàng	n	impression
3.	成	chéng	v	to become
4.	演	yǎn	v	to show (a film); to perform
5.	费	fèi	v	to spend; to take (effort)
6.	力气	lìqi	n	strength; effort
7.	就	jiù	adv	just; only (indicating a small number)
8.	俩	liǎ	nu+m	(coll.) two
9.	后天	hòutiān	t	the day after tomorrow
10.	一言为定	yì yán wéi dìng		that settles it; that's settled; it's decided

Grammar

1. Descriptive Complements (II)

The subject of a sentence can be described by a complement following 得 (de).

❶　我们玩儿得很高兴。

Wǒmen wánr de hěn gāoxìng.

(We had a happy time playing.)

[We played. We were very happy.]

❷　孩子笑得很可爱。

Háizi xiào de hěn kě'ài.

(The kid gave a very cute smile.)

[The child smiled, and the child looked cute.]

3 他打球打得很累。

Tā dǎ qiú dǎ de hěn lèi.

(He was worn out from playing ball.)

[He played ball, and he was worn out.]

4 他高兴得又唱又跳。

Tā gāoxìng de yòu chàng yòu tiào.

(He was so happy that he ended up singing and dancing.)

[He was happy, and he was singing and dancing.]

In the sentences above, the verbs 玩 (wán), 笑 (xiào), and 打球 (dǎ qiú) and the adjective 高兴 (gāoxìng) give the causes, while the complements 高兴 (gāoxìng), 可爱 (kě'ài), 累 (lèi) and 又唱又跳 (yòu chàng yòu tiào) describe the effects on the subject.

As shown in (1), (2), and (3), when an adjective serves as a descriptive complement, it is often preceded by the adverb 很 (hěn), just like a predicate adjective.

A complement describing the subject seldom appears in the negative.

(4a) *他高兴得没有又唱又跳。

*Tā gāoxìng de méiyǒu yòu chàng yòu tiào.

2. Potential Complements

得 (de) or 不 (bu) is placed between a verb and a resultative or directional complement to indicate whether a certain result can be realized or not.

1 跳舞太难，我学不会。

Tiàowǔ tài nán, wǒ xué bu huì.

(Dancing is too difficult. I can't learn it.)

2 A: 你晚上六点半点能回来吗？我等你吃晚饭。

Nǐ wǎnshang liù diǎn bàn néng huí lai ma? Wǒ děng nǐ chī wǎnfàn.

(Can you be back by 6:30 p.m.? I will wait for you for dinner.)

B: 我得开会，六点半回不来。

Wǒ děi kāi huì, liù diǎn bàn huí bu lái.

(I have a meeting, and can't make it back by 6:30 p.m.)

❸ 这张碟我今天看不完。

Zhè zhāng dié wǒ jīntiān kàn bu wán.

(I can't finish watching this DVD today.)

❹ 那个字怎么写，我想不起来了。

Nà ge zì zěnme xiě, wǒ xiǎng bu qǐ lái le.

(I can't remember how to write that character.)

[See Dialogue 2 for 想不起来 (xiǎng bu qǐ lái).]

❺ 健康保险太贵，我买不起。

Jiànkāng bǎoxiǎn tài guì, wǒ mǎi bu qǐ.

(Health insurance is too expensive. I can't afford it.)

❻ **A:** 这封中文信你看得懂吗？

Zhè fēng Zhōngwén xìn nǐ kàn de dǒng ma?

(Can you understand this Chinese letter?)

B: 我看得懂。

Wǒ kàn de dǒng.

(Yes, I can understand it.)

Potential complements usually appear in negative sentences. They are used in affirmative sentences much less often, mainly in answering questions that contain a potential complement, as in (6).

The affirmative form and the negative form of a potential complement can be put together to form a question.

❼ 五十个饺子你吃得完吃不完？

Wǔ shí ge jiǎozi nǐ chī de wán chī bu wán?

(Can you eat fifty dumplings or not?)

Potential complements are an important feature of Chinese. They are often the only way to convey the idea that the absence of certain conditions prevents a result from being achieved. Potential complements have a unique function that cannot be fulfilled by the "不能 (bù néng) + verb + resultative/directional complement" construction. For example, 做不完 (zuò bu wán) means "not able to finish," while 不能做完 (bù néng zuò wán) conveys the idea of "not allowed to finish."

⑧   老师说得太快，我听不清楚。

Lǎoshī shuō de tài kuài, wǒ tīng bu qīngchu.

(The teacher speaks too fast. I can't hear [him] clearly.)

(8a)   *老师说得太快，我不能听清楚。

*Lǎoshī shuō de tài kuài, wǒ bù néng tīng qīngchu.

⑨   今天的功课太多，我做不完。

Jīntiān de gōngkè tài duō, wǒ zuò bu wán.

(There is too much homework today. I can't finish it.)

(9a)   *今天的功课太多，我不能做完。

*Jīntiān de gōngkè tài duō, wǒ bù néng zuò wán.

A potential complement cannot be used in a 把 (bǎ) sentence, either.

(9b)   *我把今天的功课做不完。

*Wǒ bǎ jīntiān de gōngkè zuò bu wán.

3. 就 (jiù)

When used before a noun or pronoun, 就 (jiù) means "only." Often the noun or pronoun is modified by a numeral-measure word combination.

❶   我们班人很少，就七个学生。

Wǒmen bān rén hěn shǎo, jiù qī ge xuésheng.

(Our class is small, with just seven students.)

❷   今天功课很少，就五个汉字。

Jīntiān gōngkè hěn shǎo, jiù wǔ ge Hànzì.

(There's little homework today. Only five Chinese characters.)

❸   我们一家五口，就你对味精过敏。

Wǒmen yì jiā wǔ kǒu, jiù nǐ duì wèijīng guòmǐn.

(There are five people in our family. Only you are allergic to MSG.)

4 三个房间我打扫了两个，就一个房间还没
整理。

Sān ge fángjiān wǒ dǎsǎo le liǎng ge, jiù yí ge fángjiān hái méi zhěnglǐ.

(I have cleaned two of the three rooms. Only one room hasn't been tidied up yet.)

Language Practice

A. **Your Comments, Please**

Work with your partner and ask each other the following questions:

EXAMPLE:

A: 你昨天晚上写汉字
写得累不累？

A: Nǐ zuótiān wǎnshang xiě Hànzì xiě de lèi bú lèi?

B: 我昨天晚上写汉字写
得很累/不累。你呢？

B: Wǒ zuótiān wǎnshang xiě Hànzì xiě de hěn lèi/bú lèi. Nǐ ne?

1. A: 你每天上课上得
累不累？

Nǐ měi tiān shàng kè shàng de lèi bú lèi?

2. A: 你昨天晚上睡觉睡
得舒服不舒服？

Nǐ zuótiān wǎnshang shuì jiào shuì de shūfu bù shūfu?

3. A: 你上个周末玩儿得
高兴不高兴？

Nǐ shàng ge zhōumò wánr de gāoxìng bù gāoxìng?

B. First Day of School!

Find out about your practice partner's first day of school.

EXAMPLE:

A: 你找得到找不到你的教室？

A: Nǐ zhǎo de dào zhǎo bu dào nǐ de jiàoshì?

B: 我找得到我的教室。／我找不到我的教室。

B: Wǒ zhǎo de dào wǒ de jiàoshì./ Wǒ zhǎo bu dào wǒ de jiàoshì.

1. A: 你买得到买不到你要的书？

A: Nǐ mǎi de dào mǎi bu dào nǐ yào de shū?

2. A: 你听得懂听不懂中文老师说的话？

A: Nǐ tīng de dǒng tīng bu dǒng Zhōngwén lǎoshī shuō de huà?

3. A: 你看得清楚看不清楚老师写的字？

A: Nǐ kàn de qīngchu kàn bu qīngchu lǎoshī xiě de zì?

C. Are You a Competitive Hot Dog Eater?

Do you think you and your partner would be up to the challenge of competing in a hot-dog-eating competition? How about some other competitions? Let's find out.

EXAMPLE:

 x 30

→ **A:** 你吃得完三十个热狗吗？

Nǐ chī de wán sānshí ge règǒu ma?

B: 我吃得完三十个热狗。／我吃不完三十个热狗。

Wǒ chī de wán sānshí ge règǒu. Wǒ chī bu wán sānshí ge règǒu.

1. 　x 100

2. 　x 10

3. 　x 15

4. 　x 20

5. 　x 25

D. How Well Do You Know the Integrated Chinese Cast?

EXAMPLE:

A: 他们都有弟弟吗？　　Tāmen dōu yǒu dìdi ma?

B: 不，就高小音一个人
有弟弟。

Bù, jiù Gāo Xiǎoyīn yí ge rén

yǒu dìdi.

1. A: 他们都会滑冰吗？　　**1. A:** Tāmen dōu huì huá bīng ma?

2. A: 他们都吃素吗？

2. A: Tāmen dōu chī sù ma?

3. A: 他们都爱吃蛋糕吗？

3. A: Tāmen dōu ài chī dàngāo ma?

4. A: 他们都不会说
英文吗？

4. A: Tāmen dōu bú huì shuō
Yīngwén ma?

E. Recap and Narrate

Working with a partner, recap the content of Dialogue I:

1. 王朋和李友认识
多长时间了？

1. Wáng Péng hé Lǐ Yǒu rènshi
duō cháng shíjiān le?

2. 王朋常常帮李友
做什么？

2. Wáng Péng chángcháng bāng Lǐ
Yǒu zuò shénme?

3. 王朋和李友一起玩儿
的时候，高兴吗？

3. Wáng Péng hé Lǐ Yǒu yīqǐ wánr
de shíhou, gāoxìng ma?

4. 王朋和李友为什么
成了好朋友？

4. Wáng Péng hé Lǐ Yǒu wèishénme
chéng le hǎo péngyou?

5. 王朋这个周末请
李友做什么？

5. Wáng Péng zhè ge zhōumò qǐng
Lǐ Yǒu zuò shénme?

6. 王朋买到电影
   票了吗？

6. Wáng Péng mǎi dào diànyǐng
   piào le ma?

7. 几个人去看电影？

7. Jǐ ge rén qù kàn diànyǐng?

8. 李友说看电影以前要
   做什么？

8. Lǐ Yǒu shuō kàn diànyǐng
   yǐqián yào zuò shénme?

Using the words and phrases in blue as prompts, connect your answers above to form a narrative like this example:

王朋和李友在同一个学校学习快半年了。王朋常常帮李友学中文，他们常常一起玩儿，每次都玩儿得很高兴。李友对王朋的印象很好，王朋也很喜欢李友，他们成了好朋友。

这个周末学校演一个中国电影，看电影的人很多，王朋费了很大力气才买到票。他请李友去看电影，李友说好极了。她问王朋还有别人跟他们一起看电影吗，王朋说就他们俩。李友很高兴，说看电影以前她请王朋吃晚饭。

Wáng Péng hé Lǐ Yǒu zài tóng yí ge xuéxiào xuéxí kuài bàn nián le. Wáng Péng chángcháng bāng Lǐ Yǒu xué Zhōngwén, tāmen chángcháng yìqǐ wánr, měi cì dōu wánr de hěn gāoxìng. Lǐ Yǒu duì Wáng Péng de yìnxiàng hěn hǎo, Wáng Péng yě hěn xǐhuan Lǐ Yǒu, tāmen chéng le hǎo péngyou.

Zhè ge zhōumò xuéxiào yǎn yí ge Zhōngguó diànyǐng, kàn diànyǐng de rén hěn duō, Wáng Péng fèi le hěn dà lìqi cái mǎi dào piào. Tā qǐng Lǐ Yǒu qù kàn diànyǐng, Lǐ Yǒu shuō hǎo jí le. Tā wèn Wáng Péng hái yǒu bié rén gēn tāmen yìqǐ kàn diànyǐng ma, Wáng Péng shuō jiù tāmen liǎ. Lǐ Yǒu hěn gāoxìng, shuō kàn diànyǐng yǐqián tā qǐng Wáng Péng chī wǎnfàn.

Dialogue II: Turning Down an Invitation

  喂，请问李友小姐在吗？

我就是。请问你是哪一位？

 我姓费，你还记得❶我吗？

姓费？

 你还记得上个月高小音的生日舞会吗？我就是最后请你跳舞的那个人。你再想想。想起来了吗？

 对不起，我想不起来。

 我是高小音的中学同学。

LANGUAGE NOTES

❶ 记得 (jìde, to remember) vs. 想起来 (xiǎng qi lai, to remember; to recall): While 记得 (jìde) pertains to the continuous state of remembering, 想起来 (xiǎng qi lai) refers to the mental act of retrieving information from one's memory. Thus one can say: "我记得他上过我的课，可是我想不起来他叫什么名字。" (Wǒ jìde tā shàng guo wǒ de kè, kěshì wǒ xiǎng bu qǐ lái tā jiào shénme míngzi, I do remember he took my class, but I can't think of his name at the moment).

是吗？你是怎么知道我的电话号码的？

是小音告诉我的。

费先生，你有事吗？

这个周末你有空儿吗？我想请你去跳舞。

这个周末不行，下个星期我有三个考试。

没关系，下个周末怎么样？你考完试，我们好好儿玩儿玩儿。

下个周末也不行，我要从宿舍搬出去④，得打扫、整理房间。

你看下下个周末，好不好？

对不起，下下个周末更不行了，我要跟我的男朋友去纽约旅行。

…那…

费先生，对不起，我的手机没电了。再见！

喂…喂…

❷ 好好儿 (hǎohāor, all out; to one's heart's content) is a colloquial expression that often precedes a verb to serve as an adverbial, e.g. 考试以后我要去纽约好好儿玩儿玩儿 (Kǎo shì yǐhòu wǒ yào qù Niǔyuē hǎohāor wánr wanr. After the test I want to go to New York and have a great time). Note the different tone for the reduplicated syllable 好. For the rules on the pronunciation of reduplicated monosyllabic adjectives, see Grammar 6 in Lesson 12.

Wéi, qǐng wèn Lǐ Yǒu xiǎojiě zài ma?

Wǒ jiù shì. Qǐng wèn nǐ shì nǎ yí wèi?

Wǒ xìng Fèi, nǐ hái jìde❶ wǒ ma?

Xìng Fèi?

Nǐ hái jìde shàng ge yuè Gāo Xiǎoyīn de shēngrì wǔhuì ma? Wǒ jiù shì zuìhòu qǐng nǐ tiào wǔ de nà ge rén. Nǐ zài xiǎng xiang. Xiǎng qi lai le ma?

Duìbuqǐ, wǒ xiǎng bù qǐ lái.

Wǒ shì Gāo Xiǎoyīn de zhōngxué tóngxué.

Shì ma? Nǐ shì zěnme zhīdào wǒ de diànhuà hàomǎ de?

Shì Xiǎoyīn gàosu wǒ de.

Fèi xiānsheng, nǐ yǒu shì ma?

Zhè ge zhōumò nǐ yǒu kòngr ma? Wǒ xiǎng qǐng nǐ qù tiào wǔ.

Zhè ge zhōumò bù xíng, xià ge xīngqī wǒ yǒu sān ge kǎo shì.

Méi guānxi, xià gè zhōumò zěnmeyàng? Nǐ kǎo wán shì, wǒmen hǎohāor❷ wánr wanr.

Xià ge zhōumò yě bù xíng, wǒ yào cóng sùshè bān chu qu④, děi dǎsǎo, zhěnglǐ fángjiān.

Nǐ kàn xià xià ge zhōumò, hǎo bù hǎo?

Duìbuqǐ, xià xià ge zhōumò gèng bù xíng le, wǒ yào gēn wǒ de nánpéngyou qù Niǔyuē lǚxíng.

…Nà…

Fèi xiānsheng, duìbuqǐ, wǒ de shǒujī méi diàn le. Zàijiàn!

Wéi …wéi …

VOCABULARY

1.	记得	jìde	v	to remember
2.	想起来	xiǎng qi lai	vc	to remember; to recall
3.	号码	hàomǎ	n	number
4.	搬	bān	v	to move
5.	打扫	dǎsǎo	v	to clean up (a room, apartment or house)
	扫	sǎo	v	to sweep
6.	整理	zhěnglǐ	v	to put in order
7.	房间	fángjiān	n	room
8.	旅行	lǚxíng	v	to travel
9.	电	diàn	n	electricity

There are many parks in Taipei that you could take a date to. Circle four on the map. If you wish to have some coffee on your date, can you locate a coffee shop on the map?

Grammar

4. Directional Complements (II)

Directional complements indicate the direction in which a person or object moves. A directional verb such as 上 (shàng, to go up), 下 (xià, to go down), 进 (jìn, to go in), 出 (chū, to go out), 回 (huí, to return), 过 (guò, to go over), 起 (qǐ, to rise), 开 (kāi, to part from), 到 (dào, to arrive), 来 (lái, to come) or 去 (qù, to go) can be placed after another verb to become what is known as a "simple directional complement." When a simple directional complement such as 上, 下, 进, 出, 回, 过, 起, 开 or 到 (shang, xia, jin, chu, hui, guo, qi, kai or dao) is combined with 来 or 去 (lai or qu), we have what is called a "compound directional complement."

Simple Directional Complements:

Pattern I:

A. Subject + Verb + Place Word / Noun (Phrase) + 来/去

❶ 她　下　楼　　来。

subject + verb + place word + directional complement

Tā xià lóu lai.

(She is coming downstairs.)

❷ 她上楼去。

Tā shàng lóu qu.

(She is going upstairs.)

❸ 请　你　买　一些水果　来。

subject + verb + noun phrase + directional complement

Qǐng nǐ mǎi yì xiē shuǐguǒ lai.

(Please buy some fruit [and bring it] here.)

❹ 你给他送一点儿吃的东西去。

Nǐ gěi tā sòng yìdiǎnr chī de dōngxi qu.

(Take some food to him.)

When a verb is followed by a location word, that verb can only be a directional verb such as 上 (shàng), 下 (xià), 进 (jìn), 出 (chū), 回 (huí), 过 (guò), or 到 (dào), as shown in (1) and (2).

B. Subject + Verb + 来/去 + Noun

❺ 他买来了一些水果。

Tā mǎi lai le yì xiē shuǐguǒ.

(He bought some fruit and brought it here.)

When the object of the verb is a location word, the sentence can only appear in Pattern A, as in (1) and (2). When the object is a regular noun and the action is not completed, the sentence often appears in Pattern A as well, as in (3) and (4). If the action is completed, the sentence can appear either in Pattern A or in Pattern B. Pattern A should therefore be memorized as the essential form.

Pattern II:

A. Subject + Verb + 上/下··· + Place Word /Noun

❻ 他走上楼。

Tā zǒu shang lóu.

(He walked upstairs.)

[The sentence doesn't indicate whether the speaker is upstairs or downstairs.]

❼ 老师走进教室。

Lǎoshī zǒu jin jiàoshì.

(The teacher walked into the classroom.)

[The sentence doesn't indicate whether the speaker is in the classroom or not.]

❽ 他拿出一张纸。

Tā ná chu yì zhāng zhǐ.

(He took out a piece of paper.)

Compound Directional Complements

A. Subject + Verb + 上/下··· + Place Word / Noun+ 来/去

⑨ 她走下楼来。

Tā zǒu xia lóu lai.

(She walked downstairs.)

[The speaker is downstairs.]

⑩ 老师走进教室去/来。

Lǎoshī zǒu jin jiàoshì qu/lai.

(The teacher walked into the classroom.)

[With 去, the speaker is not in the classroom; with 来, the speaker is in the classroom.]

⑪ 弟弟跳上床来/去。

Dìdi tiào shang chuáng lai/qu.

(My little brother jumped onto the bed.)

[With 来, the speaker is on the bed; with 去, the speaker is not on the bed.]

⑫ 我的同学走进书店来/去。

Wǒ de tóngxué zǒu jin shūdiàn lai/qu.

(My classmate walked into the bookstore.)

[With 来, the speaker was in the bookstore; with 去, the speaker was not in the bookstore.]

⑬ 请你买回一些梨来。

Qǐng nǐ mǎi hui yì xiē lí lai.

(Please buy some pears and bring them back here.)

⑭ 他拿出一张纸来。

Tā ná chu yì zhāng zhǐ lai.

(He took out a piece of paper.)

⑮   请大家都拿起笔来。

Qǐng dàjiā dōu ná qi bǐ lai.

(Please pick up a pen, everyone.)

起 (qi), in the same way as 起来 (qi lai), signifies a movement from a lower point to a higher point.

However, 起 (qi) compounds only with 来 (lai), never with 去 (qu), in forming a directional complement combination.

The difference between 上 (shang) and 起 (qi) is that 上 (shang) is followed by a location word which indicates the end point of the movement, while 起 (qi) never precedes a location word.

⑯   走上楼

zǒu shang lóu

(to go upstairs)

(16a)   *走起楼

*zǒu qi lóu

B. Subject + Verb + 上／下… **+** 来／去 **+ Noun**

⑰   他买回来了一些水果。

Tā mǎi hui lai le yì xiē shuǐguǒ.

(He bought some fruit and brought it back here.)

As in the case of the simple directional compounds, when the object is a location word, the sentence appears only in Pattern A, as in (11) and (12). If the object is a regular noun and the action is not completed, the sentence often appears in Pattern A as well, as in (13), (14), and (15). If the action is completed, the sentence can appear either in Pattern A or in Pattern B. Again, Pattern A should be memorized as the essential form.

When the 把 (bǎ) construction is used with a directional complement, the sentence can appear in either of these two patterns:

I. Simple Directional Complement

Subject + 把 **+ Object + Verb +** 来／去

⑱   请把你的床搬来。

Qǐng bǎ nǐ de chuáng bān lai.

(Please move your bed here.)

⑲   把这杯冰茶拿去。

Bǎ zhè bēi bīngchá ná qu.

(Take this glass of iced tea [with you].)

II. Compound Directional Complement

Subject + 把 + Object + Verb + 上/下… (+ place word) + 来/去

⑳   我把书拿起来了。

Wǒ bǎ shū ná qi lai le.

(I picked up the book.)

㉑   快把车开回家去。

Kuài bǎ chē kāi hui jiā qu.

(Drive the car back home right away.)

Language Practice

F. Second Opinion

After you bought or did something, you want to get a second opinion from your friends.

EXAMPLE:

A: 这是我刚买的鞋，
你看看怎么样？

Zhè shì wǒ gāng mǎi de xié,
nǐ kàn kan zěnmeyàng?

1.

2.

3.   [See Language Note 2 from Dialogue II in Lesson 15.]

4. [See Language Note 2 from Dialogue II in Lesson 15.]

G. Ask Nicely!

Make these requests to your partner, and try to soften the tone by reduplicating the verb:

1. You would like to see your partner's family picture.

2. You want your partner to have a look at the characters you have written.

3. You wish to listen to your partner's MP3.

4. You want to use your partner's cell phone.

5. You want your partner to help you look for your book.

6. You hope your partner will practice Chinese with you.

H. The Big Move

You are moving into the second-floor apartment in the house shown in the picture on the left. You are standing with all your stuff on the first floor, while the previous tenant has left behind some of her stuff upstairs. Tell the movers how to finish the move.

Before

After

Hint: For things to be moved upstairs, you should say 把_____搬／拿上（楼）去 (Bǎ _____bān/ná shang lóu qu); for things to be placed downstairs, you should say 把_____搬／拿下（楼）来 (Bǎ_____bān/ná xia lóu lai).

1.

2.

3.

4.

5.

6.

7.

I. Recap and Narrate

Working with a partner, recap the content of Dialogue II:

1. 费先生是谁？

2. 费先生是怎么
   认识李友的？

3. 李友还记得
   费先生吗？

4. 费先生是怎么知道
   李友的电话号码的？

5. 费先生为什么给
   李友打电话？

6. 李友说这个周末她
   为什么不能去跳舞？

7. 下个周末呢？

8. 下下个周末呢？

9. 费先生还想约
   李友吗？

1. Fèi xiānsheng shì shéi?

2. Fèi xiānsheng shì zěnme
   rènshi Lǐ Yǒu de?

3. Lǐ Yǒu hái jìde
   Fèi xiānsheng ma?

4. Fèi xiānsheng shì zěnme zhīdào
   Lǐ Yǒu de diànhuà hàomǎ de?

5. Fèi xiānsheng wèishénme gěi
   Lǐ Yǒu dǎ diànhuà?

6. Lǐ Yǒu shuō zhè ge zhōumò tā
   wèishénme bù néng qù tiào wǔ?

7. Xià ge zhōumò ne?

8. Xià xià ge zhōumò ne?

9. Fèi xiānsheng hái xiǎng yuē
   Lǐ Yǒu ma?

Using the words and phrases in blue as prompts, connect your answers above to form a narrative like this example:

费先生是高小音的中学同学，在高小音的生日舞会上，他是最后一个请李友跳舞的人。今天他给李友打电话，约李友这个周末去跳舞。李友说下个星期有三个考试，所以这个周末不能去跳舞。费先生问下个周末行不行，李友说她下个周末要从宿舍搬出去，得打扫整理房间。费先生又问下下个周末行不行，李友说更不行，她要跟男朋友去纽约旅行。费先生可能还要约李友别的时间去跳舞，可是李友说她的手机没电了，费先生就不能再说什么了。

Fèi xiānsheng shì Gāo Xiǎoyīn de zhōngxué tóngxué, zài Gāo Xiǎoyīn de shēngrì wǔhuì shàng, tā shì zuìhòu yí ge qǐng Lǐ Yǒu tiào wǔ de rén. Jīntiān tā gěi Lǐ Yǒu dǎ diànhuà, yuē Lǐ Yǒu zhè ge zhōumò qù tiào wǔ. Lǐ Yǒu shuō xià ge xīngqī yǒu sān ge kǎo shì, suǒyǐ zhè ge zhōumò bù néng qù tiào wǔ. Fèi xiānsheng wèn xià ge zhōumò xíng bù xíng, Lǐ Yǒu shuō tā xià ge zhōumò yào cóng sùshè bān chu qu, děi dǎsǎo zhěnglǐ fángjiān. Fèi xiānsheng yòu wèn xià xià ge zhōumò xíng bù xíng, Lǐ Yǒu shuō gèng bù xíng, tā yào gēn nánpéngyou qù Niǔyuē lǚxíng. Fèi xiānsheng kěnéng hái yào yuē Lǐ Yǒu bié de shíjiān qù tiào wǔ, kěshì Lǐ Yǒu shuō tā de shǒujī méi diàn le, Fèi xiānsheng jiù bù néng zài shuō shénme le.

HOW ABOUT YOU?

What activity would you enjoy on a date?

1. 听音乐会	tīng yīnyuèhuì	vo	to go to a concert
2. 唱卡拉OK	chàng kǎlā'ōukēi	vo	to sing karaoke
3. 参观博物馆	cānguān bówùguǎn	vo	to visit a museum
4. 野餐	yěcān	v	to picnic
5. 兜风	dōu fēng	vo	to go for a drive

What other activities do you think would be good ideas for a date?

Please ask your teacher how to say them and make a note here:

_____

Culture Highlights

1 In premodern China, marriages were almost invariably arranged by the parents. Intimate contact between unmarried young men and women was strictly prohibited. Traditionally, Chinese people shied away from any public display of affection. Even as recently as the 1980s, one seldom saw a couple walking on the street hand-in-hand, but today people do not make much fuss about couples hugging and kissing each other in public.

2 Valentine's Day, a Western holiday, is becoming popular in China now, especially among young people in the cities. As in the West, it is commercially a big day for retailers and restaurants, and young people spend lavishly on roses, chocolates, and candlelight dinners. Meanwhile, some people have been pushing to make the seventh day of the seventh month on the lunar calendar the Chinese "Valentine's Day," or 情人节 (Qíngrénjié). According to a romantic legend that came into existence nearly two millennia ago, the seventh day of the seventh month is the only day of the year when the Cowherd and the Weaving Girl, a loving couple that was forcibly separated, are allowed to meet each other on a bridge of magpies over the Silver River (银河, Yínhé), the Chinese name for the Milky Way.

3 Chinese people are typically very concerned about "saving face," not only for themselves but for other people as well. That is the reason a Chinese person would usually try to find excuses when turning down a request or an offer, instead of rejecting it bluntly.

4 Seeing movies is part of the nightlife in Chinese cities, especially for people going out on dates. Meanwhile, Peking (Beijing) opera (京剧, jīngjù), a traditional form of entertainment that once flourished in many cities, especially those in the north, has been losing ground in competition with films, TV, karaoke clubs, and internet bars.

A theatrical scene from Beijing Opera

English Text

Dialogue I

Wang Peng and Li You go to the same school. They have known each other for almost six months now. Wang Peng often helps Li You practice speaking Chinese. They also often go out for fun, and they always have a good time. Li You has a very good impression of Wang Peng, and Wang Peng likes Li You very much, too. So they've become good friends.

*   *   *

Wang Peng: This weekend they're showing a Chinese film at school. Shall we go together?

Li You: Yes, but I hear that many people are going to see that film. Will we be able to get tickets?

Wang Peng: I already got the tickets. It took a lot of trying.

Li You: Fantastic. I've wanted to see a Chinese film for a long time. Anyone else going with us?

Wang Peng: No one else. Just the two of us.

Li You: OK. When?

Wang Peng: The day after tomorrow, eight o'clock.

Li You: Before the movie, I'll take you to dinner.

Wang Peng: Great! It's a deal.

Dialogue II

Mr. Fei: Hello, is Miss Li You there?

Li You: This is she. Who is this, please?

Mr. Fei: My name is Fei. Do you remember me?

Li You: Mr. Fei?

Mr. Fei: Do you still remember Gao Xiaoyin's birthday party last month? I was the last person who asked you to dance. Think again. Do you remember now?

Li You: I'm sorry. I can't recall.

Mr. Fei: I was Gao Xiaoyin's high school classmate.

Li You: Is that so? How did you get my number?

Mr. Fei: Xiaoyin gave it to me.

Li You: Mr. Fei, can I help you?

Mr. Fei: Are you free this weekend? I'd like to ask you out to dance.

Li You: This weekend won't do. Next week I have three tests.

Mr. Fei: No problem. What about the following weekend? After your tests are over, we'll go have a good time.

Li You: Next weekend won't work, either. I'm moving out of the dorm. I have to clean and tidy up my room.

Mr. Fei: How about two weeks from now?

Li You: I'm sorry, two weeks from now would be even more impossible. I'm going on a trip to New York with my boyfriend.

Mr. Fei: In that case...

Li You: Mr. Fei, I'm sorry, my cell phone is out of power. Bye.

Mr. Fei: Hello...hello...

PROGRESS CHECKLIST

Before proceeding to Lesson 17, be sure you can complete the following tasks in Chinese:

I am able to—

☑ Set up a movie date or another outing with friends;

☐ Comment on how much work it takes to make arrangements for a date;

☐ Invite someone to go on a date;

☐ Accept an invitation to go on a date;

☐ Courteously decline a date;

☐ End a phone conversation without being rude.

LESSON 17

Renting an Apartment

第十七课 租房子

Dì shíqī kè   **Zū fángzi**

 LEARNING OBJECTIVES

In this lesson, you will learn to use Chinese to

- Describe your current and ideal living quarters;
- Name common pieces of furniture;
- State how long you have been living at your current residence;
- Comment briefly on why a place is or isn't good for someone;
- Discuss and negotiate rent, utilities, and security deposits.

 RELATE AND GET READY

In your own culture/community—

1. What is the best way to find an apartment for rent?
2. What defines an "apartment"? What other living arrangements are available?
3. What are the advantages and disadvantages of living in a student dorm? How about living in an apartment?
4. Do people typically sign a lease for an apartment? Do leases include clauses for security deposits and pets? What other issues do leases cover?

Narrative: Finding a Better Place

王朋在学校的宿舍住了两个学期了①。他觉得宿舍太吵，睡不好觉，房间太小，连电脑都②放不下③，再说也没有地方可以做饭，很不方便，所以准备下个学期搬出去住。他找房子找了一个多④月了，可是还没有找到合适的。刚才他在报纸上看到了一个广告，说学校附近有一套公寓出租，离学校很近，走路只要五分钟，很方

便。公寓有一个卧
室，一个厨房，一
个卫生间❶，一个客
厅，还带家具。王朋
觉得这套公寓可能对
他很合适。

LANGUAGE NOTES

❶ While 洗澡间 (xǐzǎojiān) is often used in Taiwan to refer to a bathroom (with a toilet and shower or bathtub), 卫生间 (wèishēngjiān, lit., hygiene room) is the most frequently used term for bathrooms in mainland China. In public places 卫生间 (wèishēngjiān) simply means "restroom." Other Chinese terms for "bathroom" and "restroom" include:

浴室 (yùshì), bathroom for bathing, usually without a toilet, 厕所 (cèsuǒ), public restroom with no bathing facilities, 洗手间 (xǐshǒujiān), restroom or bathroom, and 化妆室 (huàzhuāngshì), restroom (mainly in Taiwan). Occasionally, some Chinese speakers refer to the restroom euphemistically as 一号 (yī hào), literally, number one.

Wáng Péng zài xuéxiào de sùshè zhù le liǎng ge xuéqī le①. Tā juéde sùshè tài chǎo, shuì bu hǎo jiào. Fángjiān tài xiǎo, lián diànnǎo dōu② fàng bu xià③, zàishuō yě méiyǒu dìfang kěyǐ zuò fàn, hěn bù fāngbiàn, suǒyǐ zhǔnbèi xià ge xuéqī bān chu qu zhù. Tā zhǎo fángzi zhǎo le yí ge duō④ yuè le, kěshì hái méiyǒu zhǎo dào héshì de. Gāngcái tā zài bàozhǐ shang kàn dào le yí ge guǎnggào, shuō xuéxiào fùjìn yǒu yí tào gōngyù chūzū, lí xuéxiào hěn jìn, zǒu lù zhǐ yào wǔ fēnzhōng, hěn fāngbiàn. Gōngyù yǒu yí ge wòshì, yí ge chúfáng, yí ge wèishēngjiān❶, yí ge kètīng, hái dài jiājù. Wáng Péng juéde zhè tào gōngyù kěnéng duì tā hěn héshì.

VOCABULARY

1.	吵	chǎo	v/adj	to quarrel; noisy
2.	连	lián	prep	even
3.	做饭	zuò fàn	vo	to cook; to prepare a meal
4.	报纸	bàozhǐ	n	newspaper
5.	广告	guǎnggào	n	advertisement
6.	附近	fùjìn	n	vicinity; neighborhood; nearby area
7.	套	tào	m	(measure word for suite or set)
8.	公寓	gōngyù	n	apartment
9.	出租	chūzū	v	to rent out
10.	走路	zǒu lù	vo	to walk
11.	分钟	fēnzhōng	n	minute
12.	卧室	wòshì	n	bedroom
13.	厨房	chúfáng	n	kitchen
14.	卫生间	wèishēngjiān	n	bathroom
15.	客厅	kètīng	n	living room
16.	家具	jiājù	n	furniture
17.	可能	kěnéng	mv/adj	maybe; possible

Grammar

> ## 1. Verb + 了 (le) + Numeral + Measure Word + Noun + 了 (le)

The sentence 王朋在学校的宿舍住了两个学期了。(Wáng Péng zài xuéxiào de sùshè zhù le liǎng ge xuéqī le.) means that Wang Peng has been living on campus for two semesters up to this moment. On its own, the sentence usually implies that the action has been continuing for some time and is expected to last into the future.

❶ A: 你开出租汽车开了几年了？

Nǐ kāi chūzū qìchē kāi le jǐ nián le?)

(How many years have you been driving a cab?)

B: 一年半了。

Yì nián bàn le.

(For a year and a half now.)

❷ 弟弟写电子邮件写了半个钟头了，不知道还要写多长时间。

Dìdi xiě diànzǐ yóujiàn xiě le bàn ge zhōngtóu le, bù zhīdào hái yào xiě duō cháng shíjiān.

(My younger brother has been writing e-mails for half an hour. Who knows how much longer he will be.)

The following two sentences are different in meaning:

❸ 他病了三天了。

Tā bìng le sān tiān le.

(He has been sick for three days.)

[The illness has continued for three days and he currently remains sick.)

❹ 他病了三天。

Tā bìng le sān tiān.

(He was sick for three days.)

[He recovered from the illness on the fourth day.]

If, however, a clause in this pattern is followed by another clause, it may suggest that the action may come to an end.

❺   我打扫房子打扫了一上午了，想休息一下。

Wǒ dǎsǎo fángzi dǎsǎo le yí shàngwǔ le, xiǎng xiūxi yí xià.

(I've been cleaning the house all morning. I'd like to take a break.)

This structure is not limited to temporal expressions. It can also be used to indicate quantity:

❻   衣服我已经买了三件了，够了。

Yīfu wǒ yǐjīng mǎi le sān jiàn le, gòu le.

(I have already bought three pieces of clothing. That's plenty.)

❼   这封信我已经看了两遍了，不想再看了。

Zhè fēng xìn wǒ yǐjīng kàn le liǎng biàn le, bù xiǎng zài kàn le.

(I've read this letter twice already and don't want to read it again.)

---

2. 连...都/也 (lián...dōu/yě)

连 (lián) is an intensifier which is always used in conjunction with 都/也 (dōu/yě).

❶   我姐姐的孩子很聪明，连日本话都会说。

Wǒ jiějie de háizi hěn cōngming, lián Rìběnhuà dōu huì shuō.

(My sister's child is really smart. She can even speak Japanese.)

❷   我弟弟学中文学了一年了，可是连"天"字都不会写。

Wǒ dìdi xué Zhōngwén xuéle yì nián le, kěshì lián "tiān" zì dōu bú huì xiě.

(My younger brother has been studying Chinese for a year now, but can't even write the character 天.)

❸   你怎么连药都忘了吃？

Nǐ zěnme lián yào dōu wàng le chī?

(How could you forget even to take your medicine?)

❹   昨天学的生词我连一个也不记得了。

Zuótiān xué de shēngcí wǒ lián yí ge yě bú jìde le.

(I can't recall even a single word we learned yesterday.)

What follows 连 (lián) usually represents an extreme case: the biggest or smallest, the best or worst, the most difficult or easiest, etc. (1), for instance, implies that Japanese is very difficult. If a child can speak such a difficult language as Japanese, then the child must be very intelligent. Similarly, 天 (tiān) is considered one of the easiest Chinese characters. If the younger brother in (2) does not know how to write 天 (tiān), it goes without saying that he can't write other more difficult characters.

3. Potential complements with Verb + 不下 (bu xià)

The V + 不下 (bu xià) structure suggests that a location or container in question does not have the capacity to hold something.

❶   这个客厅大是大，不过坐不下二十个人。

Zhè ge kètīng dà shì dà, búguò zuò bu xià èrshí ge rén.

(This living room is pretty spacious, but still not large enough to seat twenty people.)

❷   这张纸写不下八百个字。

Zhè zhāng zhǐ xiě bu xià bābǎi ge zì.

(This piece of paper isn't big enough to write 800 characters on.)

❸   这个冰箱放不下两个西瓜。

Zhè ge bīngxiāng fàng bu xià liǎng ge xīgua.

(This refrigerator won't fit two watermelons.)

4. 多 (duō) Indicating an Approximate Number

多 (duō) can be placed after a number to indicate an approximate number. The combination indicates not an exact number but a general numeric range, e.g., 十多个 (shí duō ge) means more than ten but fewer than twenty; it could be eleven, twelve, thirteen, etc.

If the concept represented by the noun is not divisible into smaller units, and the number is ten or a multiple of ten, 多 (duō) precedes the measure word, e.g., 二十多个人 (èrshí duō ge rén, more than twenty people), 三十多个学生 (sānshí duō ge xuésheng, more than thirty students), 一百多张纸 (yì bǎi duō zhāng zhǐ, over one hundred sheets of paper).

However, if the concept represented by the noun can be divided into smaller units (e.g., 一块钱 = 十毛, 一个星期 = 七天 [yí kuài qián = shí máo, yí ge xīngqī = qī tiān]), there are two possibilities. If the number is not ten or a multiple of ten, 多 (duō) should be used after the measure word, e.g., 七块多钱 (qī kuài duō qián, more than seven dollars but less than eight), 一个多星期 (yí ge duō xīngqī, more than one week but less than two). If the number is ten or a multiple of ten, 多 (duō) can be used either before the measure word, e.g., 十多块钱 (shí duō kuài qián, more than ten dollars but less than twenty), or after the measure word, e.g., 十块多钱 (shí kuài duō qián, more than ten dollars but less than eleven), but these two options represent different numeric ranges.

❶ 这支笔一块多钱。

Zhè zhī bǐ yí kuài duō qián.

(This pen is over one dollar.)

[The price is more than one dollar but less than two.]

❷ 我们班有二十多个学生。

Wǒmen bān yǒu èrshí duō ge xuésheng.

(There are over twenty students in our class.)

[There are more than twenty students but fewer than thirty.]

❸ 妹妹感冒十多天了。

Mèimei gǎnmào shí duō tiān le.

(My younger sister has had a cold for more than ten days.)

[The number of days is between ten and twenty.]

❹ 他昨天买了四十多个梨。

Tā zuótiān mǎi le sìshí duō ge lí.

(He bought over forty pears yesterday.)

[The number is between forty and fifty.]

❺   他昨天买礼物花了一百多块钱。

Tā zuótiān mǎi lǐwù huā le yìbǎi duō kuài qián.

(He bought over one hundred dollars' worth of gifts yesterday.)

[He spent more than one hundred dollars but less than two hundred.]

❻ A: 这双黑鞋十多块钱。

Zhè shuāng hēi xié shí duō kuài qián.

(This pair of black shoes is over ten dollars.)

[The price is more than ten dollars but less than twenty.]

B: 这双咖啡色的鞋十块多钱。

Zhè shuāng kāfēi sè de xié shí kuài duō qián.

(This pair of brown shoes is over ten dollars.)

[The price is more than ten dollars but less than eleven.]

❼ A: 这家饭馆儿的师傅和服务员认识十年多了。

Zhè jiā fànguǎnr de shīfu hé fúwùyuán rènshi shí nián duō le.

(The chef and the waiter in this restaurant have known each other for ten years and some months.)

[The length of time is longer than ten years but shorter than eleven.]

B: 我以为他们认识十多年了。

Wǒ yǐwéi tāmen rènshi shí duō nián le.

(I thought they had known each other for more than ten years.)

[The length of time is between ten and twenty years.]

Language Practice

A. Time Flies

Work with your partner and find out the following from each other.

1. 你学中文学了
   多长时间了?

   Nǐ xué Zhōngwén xué le

   duō cháng shíjiān le?

2. 你上(your school's name)上了
    多长时间了？

    Nǐ shàng (your school's name)
    shàng le duō cháng shíjiān le?

3. 你在你现在住的地方
    住了多长时间了？

    Nǐ zài nǐ xiànzài zhù de dìfang
    zhù le duō cháng shíjiān le?

Based on your partner's situation, you may also want to ask how long he/she has been working, involved in his/her hobbies, etc.

B. Can You Believe It?

A. Little Bai is absent-minded and often forgetful.

EXAMPLE:

He even forgot to bring a pen with him when he had to take a test.

→ 考试的时候，
  他连笔都/也忘了带了。

Kǎo shì de shíhòu,
tā lián bǐ dōu/yě wàng le dài le.

In addition:

1. He even forgot his girlfriend's birthday.

2. He didn't even remember his own phone number.

3. He even forgot to bring money when he was treating his friends to dinner.

B. Little Bai just moved into an apartment, and it already has so many problems.

EXAMPLE:

The apartment doesn't even have a kitchen.

→ 公寓连厨房都/
  也没有。

Gōngyù lián chúfáng dōu/
yě méi yǒu.

In addition:

1. His bathroom doesn't even have (running) water.

2. His bedroom is so tiny that even a bed cannot be placed in it.

3. His living room is so small that it cannot even seat five people.

C. Little Bai is also behind the times.

EXAMPLE:

He doesn't even know how to use a computer.

→ 小白连电脑都/
也不会用。

Xiǎo Bái lián diànnǎo dōu/
yě bú huì yòng.

In addition:

1. He doesn't know how to use a cell phone.

2. He doesn't know how to send email.

3. He doesn't know how to use a credit card.

C. Size-Wise

Take turns with your partner and find out the capacity of your apartment/room, living room, classroom, refrigerator, desk, etc. Use the proper verb for each question.

EXAMPLE:

apartment/room

→ A: 你的公寓/房间
住得下多少/几个人？

Nǐ de gōngyù/fángjiān
zhù de xià duōshao/jǐ ge rén?

B: 我的公寓/房间
住得下_____个人。

Wǒ de gōngyù/fángjiān
zhù de xià _____ ge rén.

1. living room

2. classroom

3. car

4. refrigerator

5. desk

D. Recap and Narrate

Working with a partner, recap the content of the Narrative:

1. 王朋在学校宿舍住了多长时间了？

2. 他为什么要搬出去？

3. 他找房子找了多长时间了？

4. 他找到合适的了吗？

5. 报纸的广告说有一个什么样的房子出租？

6. 王朋觉得这套公寓对他合适吗？

1. Wáng Péng zài xuéxiào sùshè zhù le duō cháng shíjiān le?

2. Tā wèishénme yào bān chu qu?

3. Tā zhǎo fángzi zhǎo le duō cháng shíjiān le?

4. Tā zhǎo dào héshì de le ma?

5. Bàozhǐ de guǎnggào shuō yǒu yí ge shénme yàng de fángzi chūzū?

6. Wáng Péng juéde zhè tào gōngyù duì tā héshì ma?

Using the words and phrases in blue as prompts, connect your answers above to form a narrative like this example:

王朋在学校的宿舍住了两个学期了。他觉得宿舍太吵，房间太小，再说也不能做饭，很不方便，所以准备下个学期搬出去。他找房子找了一个多月，也没有找到合适的。刚才他在报纸上看到了一个广告，说学校附近有一套公寓出租，那套公寓离学校很近，有一个卧室，一个厨房，一个卫生间，一个客厅，还带家具。王朋觉得这套公寓可能对他很合适。

Wáng Péng zài xuéxiào de sùshè zhù le liǎng ge xuéqī le. Tā juéde sùshè tài chǎo, fángjiān tài xiǎo, zàishuō yě bù néng zuò fàn, hěn bù fāngbiàn, suǒyǐ zhǔnbèi xià ge xuéqī bān chu qu. Tā zhǎo fángzi zhǎo le yí ge duō yuè, yě méiyǒu zhǎo dào héshì de. Gāngcái tā zài bàozhǐ shang kàn dào le yí ge guǎnggào, shuō xuéxiào fùjìn yǒu yí tào gōngyù chūzū, nà tào gōngyù lí xuéxiào hěn jìn, yǒu yí ge wòshì, yí ge chúfáng, yí ge wèishēngjiān, yí ge kètīng, hái dài jiājù. Wáng Péng juéde zhè tào gōngyù kěnéng duì tā hěn héshì.

Dialogue: Calling about an Apartment for Rent

 喂，请问你们是不是有
公寓出租？

有啊，一房一厅，非常
干净，还带家具。

有什么家具？

 客厅里有一套沙发、一
张饭桌跟四把椅子。卧
室里有一张床、一张书
桌和一个书架。

 你们那里安静不安静？

 非常安静。

LANGUAGE NOTES

❶ Instead of 一房一厅 (yì fáng yì tīng), one can also say 一室一厅 (yí shì yì tīng). Both expressions refer to an apartment with one bedroom and one living room. By the same token, one may refer to a two-bedroom apartment with a living room as 两房一厅 (liǎng fáng yì tīng) or 两室

每个月房租多少钱？

 八百五十元。

 八百五十美元？人民币差不多是…有一点儿贵，能不能便宜点儿？

 那你不用付水电费。

 要不要付押金？

 要多付一个月的房租当押金，搬出去的时候还给你。另外，我们公寓不准养宠物。

 没关系，我对养宠物没有兴趣❷，什么宠物都⑤不养。

 那太好了。你今天下午来看看吧。

 好。

一厅 (liǎng shì yì tīng).

❷ One should not mix up 有兴趣 (yǒu xìngqù) with 有意思 (yǒu yìsi). While 有兴趣 (yǒu xìngqù) is a verb that pertains to a person who is *interested* (in something), 有意思 (yǒu yìsi) is an adjective describing someone or something that is *interesting*.

 Wéi, qǐng wèn nǐmen shì bú shì yǒu gōngyù chūzū?

 Yǒu a, yì fáng yì tīng❶, fēicháng gānjìng, hái dài jiājù.

 Yǒu shénme jiājù?

 Kètīng li yǒu yí tào shāfā, yì zhāng fànzhuō gēn sì bǎ yǐzi. Wòshì li yǒu yì zhāng chuáng, yì zhāng shūzhuō hé yí ge shūjià.

 Nǐmen nàli ānjìng bù ānjìng?

 Fēicháng ānjìng.

 Měi ge yuè fángzū duōshao qián?

Bābǎi wǔshí yuán.

Bābǎi wǔshí Měiyuán? Rénmínbì chàbuduō shì... Yǒu yì diǎnr guì, néng bù néng piányi diǎnr?

Nà nǐ búyòng fù shuǐ diàn fèi.

Yào bú yào fù yājīn?

Yào duō fù yí ge yuè de fángzū dāng yājīn, bān chu qu de shíhou huán gěi nǐ. Lìngwài, wǒmen gōngyù bù zhǔn yǎng chǒngwù.

Méi guānxi, wǒ duì yǎng chǒngwù méi yǒu xìngqù②, shénme chǒngwù dōu⑤ bù yǎng.

Nà tài hǎo le. Nǐ jīntiān xiàwǔ lái kàn kan ba.

Hǎo.

VOCABULARY

1.	一房一厅	yì fáng yì tīng		one bedroom and one living room
2.	干净	gānjìng	adj	clean
3.	沙发	shāfā	n	sofa
4.	饭桌	fànzhuō	n	dining table
5.	椅子	yǐzi	n	chair
6.	书桌	shūzhuō	n	desk
7.	书架	shūjià	n	bookcase; bookshelf
8.	那里	nàli	pr	there
9.	安静	ānjìng	adj	quiet
10.	房租	fángzū	n	rent
11.	元	yuán	m	(measure word for the basic Chinese monetary unit); yuan
12.	美元	Měiyuán	n	U.S. currency

VOCABULARY

13.	人民币	Rénmínbì	n	renminbi (RMB, Chinese currency)
	人民	rénmín	n	the people
	币	bì	n	currency
14.	差不多	chàbuduō	adv/adj	almost; nearly; similar
15.	费	fèi	n	fee; expenses
16.	押金	yājīn	n	security deposit
17.	当	dāng	v	to serve as; to be
18.	还	huán	v	to return (something)
19.	另外	lìngwài	conj	furthermore; in addition
20.	准	zhǔn	v	to allow; to be allowed
21.	养	yǎng	v	to raise
22.	宠物	chǒngwù	n	pet
23.	兴趣	xìngqù	n	interest

这个房间里有什么？
Zhè ge fángjiān li yǒu shénme?

Grammar

> ## 5. Question Pronouns with 都/也 (dōu/yě)

A question pronoun can appear in sentences other than questions. When a question pronoun is used in a statement with 都/也 (dōu/yě) appearing after it, it simply means "all" or "none" in the sense of being all-inclusive or all-exclusive.

❶ **A:** 你想喝点儿什么饮料？

Nǐ xiǎng hē diǎnr shénme yǐnliào?

(What beverage would you like to drink?)

B: 谢谢，我不渴，什么都不想喝。

Xièxie, wǒ bù kě, shénme dōu bù xiǎng hē.

(No, thanks. I am not thirsty. I don't feel like drinking anything.)

❷ 这些公寓我哪套都不租。

Zhè xiē gōngyù wǒ nǎ tào dōu bù zū.

(I am not renting any of these apartments.)

❸ 中国我什么地方都没去过。

Zhōngguó wǒ shénme dìfang dōu méi qù guo.

(I haven't been to any place in China.)

❹ 我什么宠物都不养。养宠物太麻烦了！

Wǒ shénme chǒngwù dōu bù yǎng. Yǎng chǒngwù tài máfan le!

(I don't keep any pets. Keeping pets is too much trouble!)

❺ 在这个城市，哪儿也吃不到糖醋鱼。

Zài zhè ge chéngshì, nǎr yě chī bu dào tángcùyú.

(You can't find sweet and sour fish anywhere in this city.)

6 **A:** 在舞会上你认识了谁？

Zài wǔhuì shang nǐ rènshi le shéi?

(Who did you get to know at the dance party?)

B: 我谁都没认识。

Wǒ shéi dōu méi rènshi.

(I didn't get to know anybody.)

7 你明天几点跟我见面都行。

Nǐ míngtiān jǐ diǎn gēn wǒ jiàn miàn dōu xíng.

(You can meet with me any time tomorrow.)

8 这些药我哪种都试过，对我的过敏都没有用。

Zhè xiē yào wǒ nǎ zhǒng dōu shì guo, duì wǒ de guòmǐn dōu méiyǒu yòng.

(I have tried all these medicines; none of them is effective for my allergies.)

According to the sign, what's not welcome here?

Language Practice

E. The Two Extremes

Aisha and Mona are twin sisters, but they could not be more different: Aisha is easygoing and Mona is difficult.

EXAMPLE 1:

Aisha likes all colors.   vs.   Mona hates all colors.

→ Aisha 什么颜色都喜欢。   Aisha shénme yánsè dōu xǐhuan.

Mona 什么颜色都
不喜欢。   Mona shénme yánsè dōu
bù xǐhuan.

EXAMPLE 2:

Aisha knows everyone.   vs.   Mona knows no one.

→ Aisha 谁都认识。   Aisha shéi dōu rènshi.

Mona 谁都不认识。   Mona shéi dōu bú rènshi.

1. Aisha eats all sorts of fruits and vegetables.   vs.   Mona eats no fruits and vegetables at all.

→

2. Aisha has been to all kinds of places.   vs.   Mona hasn't been anywhere.

→

3. Aisha is happy all the time.   vs.   Mona is unhappy all the time.

→

4. Everyone thinks Aisha is cool.   vs.   Everyone thinks Mona is no fun.

→

水池

F. A Floor Plan

Look at the floor plan of this apartment. Name the rooms and describe what's in each room.

G. Setting the Scene

Look at the picture and work with your partner to describe this room: what's in the room and how things are positioned. Don't forget the person and the dog.

H. To Move or Not to Move

Find out whether your partner likes the place he or she currently lives in. List the pros and cons of the place.

What suits him/her

1. _____
2. _____
3. _____
4. _____
5. _____

What doesn't suit him/her

1. _____
2. _____
3. _____
4. _____
5. _____

Then report to the class why your partner thinks he/she should stay or move out.

Carlos 觉得他的公寓/
宿舍对他很/不合适。
因为1 _____ ，2 _____ ，···
所以他不想/想搬出去。

Carlos juéde tā de gōngyù/

sùshè duì tā hěn/bù héshì

Yīnwèi 1 _____, 2 _____, ...

suǒyǐ tā bù xiǎng/xiǎng bān chu qu.

I. Recap and Narrate

Working with a partner, recap the content of the Dialogue:

1. 那个要出租的公寓
   租出去了吗？

2. 那个公寓有什么
   家具？

3. 那个公寓安静吗？

4. 房租是多少？

1. Nà ge yào chūzū de gōngyù
   zū chu qu le ma?

2. Nà ge gōngyù yǒu shénme
   jiājù?

3. Nà ge gōngyù ānjìng ma?

4. Fángzū shì duōshao?

5. 王朋问出租房子的
人能不能便宜一点儿，
那个人说什么？

6. 要不要付押金？

7. 这个公寓能养
宠物吗？

8. 王朋什么时候会
去看那个公寓？

5. Wáng Péng wèn chūzū fángzi de rén néng bù néng piányi yì diǎnr, nà ge rén shuō shénme?

6. Yào bú yào fù yājīn?

7. Zhè ge gōngyù néng yǎng chǒngwù ma?

8. Wáng Péng shénme shíhou huì qù kàn nà ge gōngyù?

Using the words and phrases in blue as prompts, connect your answers above to form a narrative like this example:

王朋看了报纸上的出租广告后，打电话给出租房子的人。出租房子的人说客厅里有一套沙发、一张饭桌跟四把椅子。卧室里有一张床、一张书桌和一个书架，还说那里非常安静。房租每个月是八百五十元，不用付水电费。那个人还说不准养宠物，得多付一个月的房租当押金，今天下午就可以去看房子。

Wáng Péng kàn le bàozhǐ shang de chūzū guǎnggào hòu, dǎ diànhuà gěi chūzū fángzi de rén. Chūzū fángzi de rén shuō kètīng li yǒu yí tào shāfā, yì zhāng fànzhuō gēn sì bǎ yǐzi. Wòshì li yǒu yì zhāng chuáng, yì zhāng shūzhuō hé yí ge shūjià, hái shuō nàli fēicháng ānjìng. Fángzū měi ge yuè shì bābǎi wǔshí yuán, búyòng fù shuǐ diàn fèi. Nà ge rén hái shuō bù zhǔn yǎng chǒngwù, děi duō fù yí ge yuè de fángzū dāng yājīn, jīntiān xiàwǔ jiù kěyǐ qù kàn fángzi.

HOW ABOUT YOU?

What's in your living quarters?

1.	音响	yīnxiǎng	n	stereo system
2.	灯	dēng	n	lamp; light
3.	柜子	guìzi	n	cabinet; cupboard
4.	植物	zhíwù	n	plant
5.	海报	hǎibào	n	poster

Any other household items in your room that you want to say in Chinese? Please ask your teacher and make a note here:

_____

房屋出租

三房兩廳
兩個廁所
有冰箱，洗衣機
月租：$1375
有意請電：425-754-
XXXX

房屋出租
$180-$350

電視CABLE，近公車站
有意者請電：206-
682-XXXX

报纸上出租房子的广告
Bàozhǐ shang chūzū fángzi de guǎnggào

Culture Highlights

❶ Until the late 1990s, college students in China were all required to live in dorms on campus, with six or seven of them sharing a room and possibly dozens sharing a bathroom. Because there was no place to cook in the dorms, everyone ate in the students' dining hall (学生餐厅 xuéshēng cāntīng) on campus. Since the early 1980s, foreign students have generally been segregated into designated dormitories, typically with two to a room. Living conditions for Chinese students, meanwhile, have improved substantially since the late 1990s. At some colleges, students now have the option of renting apartments off campus, if they can afford it.

❷ It is becoming increasingly convenient to rent an apartment in a Chinese city. One can look for listings online, in the local newspapers, or simply call or stop by one of the many 中介公司 (zhōngjiè gōngsī, intermediary companies), agencies that match apartment owners with potential tenants.

❸ Traditionally, the Chinese had a special love—many still do—for birds, especially parrots and canaries. Tropical fish also remain popular with many urbanites. Even crickets make good pets for some people. In the countryside, the most popular household pets are cats, at least partly for the practical purpose of keeping rats away. In recent decades, the population of dogs, especially in the cities, has increased dramatically. According to a report by *China News Week* in 2006, there were 550,000 "licensed" dogs in Beijing alone. By receiving the license, these animals became "legal residents" of the city.

English Text

Narrative

Wang Peng has been living in the school dorm for two semesters. He thinks that the dorm is too noisy, and he can't sleep well. His room is too small, and he can't even fit a computer there. Besides, he has nowhere to cook. It's really inconvenient, so he plans to move out next semester. He has been looking for a place for a month now, but he hasn't found anything suitable yet. He just saw an ad in the newspaper saying there's an apartment for rent. It's very close to school, only a five-minute walk—very convenient. The apartment includes a bedroom, a kitchen, a bathroom, and a living room, and it's furnished. Wang Peng thinks this apartment may be just right for him.

Dialogue

Wang Peng: Hi, do you have an apartment for rent?

Landlady: Yes, we do. One bedroom with a living room. It's very clean, and also furnished.

Wang Peng: What kind of furniture does it have?

Landlady: In the living room there is a sofa set, a dining table, and four chairs. The bedroom has a bed, a desk and a bookcase.

Wang Peng: Is it quiet over there?

Landlady: Extremely quiet.

Wang Peng: How much is the monthly rent?

Landlady: $850.

Wang Peng: 850 U.S. dollars? In renminbi that's almost...That's a little bit expensive. Could you come down a little bit?

Landlady: All right. You won't have to pay for the utilities.

Wang Peng: Do I have to pay a deposit?

Landlady: An extra month's rent as a security deposit, which will be returned to you when you move out. And another thing, no pets are allowed in our apartments.

Wang Peng: That doesn't matter. I'm not interested in keeping pets. I don't have pets of any kind.

Landlady: Great. Why don't you come over this afternoon and take a look?

Wang Peng: OK.

PROGRESS CHECKLIST

Before proceeding to Lesson 18, be sure you can complete the following tasks in Chinese:

I am able to—

- ☑ Describe my living quarters;
- ☐ Name common pieces of furniture;
- ☐ Discuss the suitability of various living arrangements;
- ☐ Ask about and negotiate rent, utilities, and security deposits.

出租公寓的广告
chūzū gōngyù de guǎnggào

LESSON 18
第十八课
Dì shíbā kè

Sports
运动
Yùndòng

 LEARNING OBJECTIVES

In this lesson, you will learn to use Chinese to

• Name some popular sports;
• Talk about your exercise habits;
• Discuss your feelings about various sports;
• Make a simple comparison between how soccer and American football are played.

 RELATE AND GET READY

In your own culture/community—

1. Do people exercise regularly?
2. Are most people sports fans? Which sports are most popular?
3. Are there many sports programs on TV?
4. Which is more popular, American football or soccer?

Dialogue I: My Gut Keeps Getting Bigger and Bigger!

  你看，我的肚子越来越大了。

你平常吃得那么多，又^①不运动，当然越来越胖了。

那怎么办呢？

如果怕胖，你一个星期运动两、三次，每次半个小时，肚子就会小了。

我两年没运动了^①，做什么运动呢？

最简单的运动是跑步。

冬天那么冷，夏天那么热，跑步太难受^②了。

LANGUAGE NOTES

❶ As mentioned before, 又 (yòu) can indicate repetition of an action over the course of time, e.g., 我昨天看了一个电影，今天又看了一个 (Wǒ zuótiān kàn le yí ge diànyǐng, jīntiān yòu kàn le yí ge, I watched a movie yesterday, and watched another one today). 又 (yòu) can also suggest augmentation or exacerbation of certain conditions or circumstances, as in the sentence 你平常吃得那么多，又不运动，当然越来越胖了。 (Nǐ píngcháng chī de nàme duō, yòu bú yùndòng, dāngrán yuè lái yuè pàng le. You usually eat so much, and on top of that you don't exercise. No wonder you're putting on more and more weight).

你打网球吧。

打网球得买网球拍、网球鞋，
你知道，网球拍、网球鞋贵极了！

找几个人打篮球吧。买个篮球很
便宜。

那每次都得打电话约人，麻烦死了。

你去游泳吧。不用找人，也不用花
很多钱，什么时候去都可以。

游泳？我怕水，太危险了，淹死了
怎么办？

我也没办法了。你不愿意运动，
那就胖下去③吧。

Nǐ kàn, wǒ de dùzi yuè lái yuè dà le.

Nǐ píngcháng chī de nàme duō, yòu❶ bú yùndòng, dāngrán yuè lái yuè pàng le.

Nà zěnme bàn ne?

Rúguǒ pà pàng, nǐ yí ge xīngqī yùndòng liǎng, sān cì, měi cì bàn ge xiǎoshí, dùzi jiù huì xiǎo
le.

Wǒ liǎng nián méi yùndòng le①, zuò shénme yùndòng ne?

Zuì jiǎndān de yùndòng shì pǎo bù.

Dōngtiān nàme lěng, xiàtiān nàme rè, pǎo bù tài nánshòu② le.

Nǐ dǎ wǎngqiú ba.

Dǎ wǎngqiú děi mǎi wǎngqiú pāi, wǎngqiú xié, nǐ zhīdao wǎngqiú pāi, wǎngqiú xié guì jí le!

Zhǎo jǐ ge rén dǎ lánqiú ba. Mǎi ge lánqiú hěn piányi.

Nà měi cì dōu děi dǎ diànhuà yuē rén, máfan sǐ le.

Nǐ qù yóu yǒng ba. Búyòng zhǎo rén, yě búyòng huā hěn duō qián, shénme shíhou qù dōu kěyǐ.

Yóu yǒng? Wǒ pà shuǐ, tài wēixiǎn le, yān sǐ le zěnme bàn?

Wǒ yě méi bànfǎ le. Nǐ bú yuànyì yùndòng, nà jiù pàng xia qu③ ba.

VOCABULARY

1.	当然	dāngrán	adv	of course
2.	胖	pàng	adj	fat
3.	怕	pà	v	to fear; to be afraid of
4.	简单	jiǎndān	adj	simple
5.	跑步	pǎo bù	vo	to jog
	跑	pǎo	v	to run
6.	难受	nánshòu	adj	hard to bear; uncomfortable [See Grammar 2.]
7.	网球	wǎngqiú	n	tennis
8.	拍	pāi	n	racket
9.	篮球	lánqiú	n	basketball
10.	游泳	yóu yǒng	vo	to swim
11.	危险	wēixiǎn	adj	dangerous
12.	淹死	yān sǐ	vc	to drown
13.	愿意	yuànyì	av	to be willing

北京语言大学
网球场

Grammar

1. **Duration of Non-Action**

Time Expression + 没 (méi) + **V** + (了)

This structure indicates that an action has not been or was not performed for a certain period of time.

❶   他三天没上网了。

Tā sān tiān méi shàng wǎng le.

(He hasn't gone online for three days.)

❷   我两年没检查身体了。

Wǒ liǎng nián méi jiǎnchá shēntǐ le.

(I haven't had a check-up in two years.)

❸   我的狗病了，一天没吃东西了。

Wǒ de gǒu bìng le, yì tiān méi chī dōngxi le.

(My dog is sick; she hasn't eaten anything for a day.)

❹   妹妹上个月特别忙，三个星期没回家。

Mèimei shàng ge yuè tèbié máng, sān ge xīngqī méi huí jiā.

(My younger sister was especially busy last month, and she didn't come home for three weeks.)

❺   去年寒假我去英国旅行，一个月没吃中国菜。

Qùnián hánjià wǒ qù Yīngguó lǚxíng, yí ge yuè méi chī Zhōngguó cài.

(I went on a trip to Britain during the winter break last year, and didn't eat any Chinese food for a month.)

Please note the difference between this construction and the one that indicates the duration of an action in an affirmative sentence. Compare:

❻ **A:** 我学了两年中文了。

Wǒ xué le liǎng nián Zhōngwén le.

(I have been studying Chinese for two years.)

B: 是吗？我两年没学中文了。

Shì ma? Wǒ liǎng nián méi xué Zhōngwén le.

(Really? I haven't studied Chinese for two years.)

---

2. 好/难 (hǎo/nán) + V

Some verbs can be preceded by 好 or 难 (hǎo or nán), and the resulting compounds become adjectives. In this case, 好 (hǎo) usually means "easy" while 难 (nán) means "difficult," e.g.: 好受/难受 (hǎoshòu/nánshòu, easy to bear/hard to bear), 好写/难写 (hǎoxiě/nánxiě, easy to write/hard to write), 好走/难走 (hǎozǒu/nánzǒu, easy to walk on/hard to walk on), 好说/难说 (hǎoshuō/nánshuō, easy to say/difficult to say), 好懂/难懂 (hǎodǒng/nándǒng, easy to understand/hard to understand), 好唱/难唱 (hǎochàng/nánchàng, easy to sing/hard to sing). In some other compounds, however, 好 (hǎo) suggests that the action represented by the verb is pleasant, while 难 (nán) means the opposite, e.g., 好吃/难吃 (hǎochī/nánchī, delicious/unappetizing), 好看/难看 (hǎokàn/nánkàn, pretty/ugly), 好听/难听 (hǎotīng/nántīng, pleasant to the ear/unpleasant to the ear), etc.

---

3. 下去 (xia qu) Indicating Continuation

下去 (xia qu) signifies the continuation of an action that is already in progress.

❶ 说下去。

Shuō xia qu.

(Go on speaking.)

❷ 你别念下去了，我一点儿也不喜欢听。

Nǐ bié niàn xia qu le, wǒ yì diǎnr yě bù xǐhuan tīng.

(Please stop reading. I don't like listening to it at all.)

❸   中文很有意思，我想学下去。

Zhōngwén hěn yǒu yìsi, wǒ xiǎng xué xia qu.

(Chinese is very interesting. I'd like to continue learning it.)

❹   你已经跑了一个多小时了，再跑下去，要累死了。

Nǐ yǐjǐng pǎo le yí ge duō xiǎoshí le, zài pǎo xia qu, yào lèi sǐ le.

(You've already been running for more than an hour; if you keep running, you'll be exhausted.)

Language Practice

A. What's the Matter?

Gao Wenzhong is not feeling well. Please help him describe his condition to his doctor.

EXAMPLE:

睡觉   ✗   三天   shuì jiào   ✗   sān tiān

→ 高文中三天没   Gāo Wénzhōng sān tiān méi
睡觉了。   shuì jiào le.

1. 吃东西 ✗   两天   chī dōngxi   ✗   liǎng tiān

2. 喝东西 ✗   一天   hē dōngxi   ✗   yì tiān

3. 上厕所 ✗   一个星期   shàng cèsuǒ   ✗   yí ge xīngqī

B. Why Hasn't She Called?

Wang Peng and Li You had a fight. They haven't seen each other, called, chatted online, or text-messaged for some time. With your partner, ask and answer questions about their strained relationship based on the visuals.

EXAMPLE:

  a week

→ **A:** 李友多长时间没
跟王朋见面了？

Lǐ Yǒu duō cháng shíjiān méi
gēn Wáng Péng jiàn miàn le?

B: 李友一个星期没
跟王朋见面了。

Lǐ Yǒu yí ge xīngqī méi
gēn Wáng Péng jiàn miàn le.

1. 5 days

2. 6 days

3. 7 days

C. Opinion Forum

By using the "好/难(hǎo/nán) + V" phrase, have a discussion with your partner and find out whether you have similar or different opinions of the listed items.

EXAMPLE:

A: 你觉得哪种茶好喝，
哪种茶难喝？

Nǐ juéde nǎ zhǒng chá hǎohē,

nǎ zhǒng chá nánhē?

B: 我觉得 (name of the tea)
很好喝。

Wǒ juéde (name of the tea)

hěn hǎohē.

我觉得 (name of the tea)
很难喝。

Wǒ juéde (name of the tea)

hěn nánhē.

1.

2.

3.

4.

Then report your findings to the class.

If you two share the same opinion, you can say:

Anya 跟我一样，
我们都觉得…

Anya gēn wǒ yíyàng,
wǒmen dōu juéde…

If you don't share the same opinion, then you can say:

Anya 跟我不一样，
她觉得…我觉得…

Anya gēn wǒ bù yíyàng,
tā juéde… wǒ juéde…

D. Recap and Narrate

Working with a partner, recap the content of Dialogue I:

1. 王朋说高文中
   的肚子为什么越来
   越大？

   1. Wáng Péng shuō Gāo Wénzhōng
      de dùzi wèishénme yuè lái
      yuè dà?

2. 王朋说高文中
   得怎么办？

   2. Wáng Péng shuō Gāo Wénzhōng
      děi zěnme bàn?

3. 高文中几年没
   运动了？

   3. Gāo Wénzhōng jǐ nián méi
      yùndòng le?

4. 王朋说最简单
   的运动是跑步，
   高文中说什么？

   4. Wáng Péng shuō zuì jiǎndān
      de yùndòng shì pǎo bù,
      Gāo Wénzhōng shuō shénme?

5. 高文中想打
   网球吗？为什么？

   5. Gāo Wénzhōng xiǎng dǎ
      wǎngqiú ma? Wèishénme?

6. 高文中想打
篮球吗？为什么？

7. 高文中想游泳
吗？为什么？

8. 王朋还有别的
办法吗？

6. Gāo Wénzhōng xiǎng dǎ
lánqiú ma? Wèishénme?

7. Gāo Wénzhōng xiǎng yóu yǒng
ma? Wèishénme?

8. Wáng Péng hái yǒu bié de
bànfǎ ma?

Using the words and phrases in blue as prompts, connect your answers above to form a narrative like this example:

高文中两年没运动了，平常又吃得很多，所以肚子越来越大，他问王朋怎么办。王朋说一个星期运动两、三次，每次半个小时，肚子就会小了。高文中不知道做什么运动好。王朋跟他说了几种运动，他都没有兴趣。跑步，他觉得冬天太冷，夏天太热，太难受；打网球，他觉得买网球拍、网球鞋太贵了；打篮球，他觉得每次约人太麻烦了；游泳，他觉得太危险，怕淹死。王朋也没有办法了，他告诉高文中如果不愿意运动，那就胖下去吧。

Gāo Wénzhōng liǎng nián méi yùndòng le, píngcháng yòu chī de hěn duō, suǒyǐ dùzi yuè lái yuè dà, tā wèn Wáng Péng zěnme bàn. Wáng Péng shuō yí ge xīngqī yùndòng liǎng, sān cì, měi cì bàn ge xiǎoshí, dùzi jiù huì xiǎo le. Gāo Wénzhōng bù zhīdào zuò shéme yùndòng hǎo. Wáng Péng gēn tā shuō le jǐ zhǒng yùndòng, tā dōu méiyǒu xìngqù. Pǎo bù, tā juéde dōngtiān tài lěng, xiàtiān tài rè, tài nánshòu; dǎ wǎngqiú, tā juéde mǎi wǎngqiú pāi, wǎngqiú xié tài guì le; dǎ lánqiú, tā juéde měi cì yuē rén tài máfan le; yóu yǒng, tā juéde tài wēixiǎn, pà yān sǐ. Wáng Péng yě méiyǒu bànfǎ le, tā gàosù Gāo Wénzhōng rúguǒ bú yuànyì yùndòng, nà jiù pàng xia qu ba.

Dialogue II: Watching American Football

王朋的妹妹王红刚从北京来，要在美国上大学①，现在住在高小音家里学英文。为了②提高英文水平，她每天都看两个小时的电视④。

LANGUAGE NOTES

① 上 (shàng) is a versatile verb. To board a car or plane is 上车/飞机 (shàng chē/fēijī), and to go to the bathroom is 上厕所 (shàng cèsuǒ). In this lesson, to go to school is 上学 (shàng xué) in colloquial Mandarin. So one can say 上小学/中学/大学 (shàng xiǎoxué/zhōngxué/dàxué) for attending elementary school/middle school/college.

② 为了 (wèile) usually appears in the first clause of a complex sentence, e.g., 为了学好中文，他每天听两个小时录音 (Wèile xué hǎo Zhōngwén, tā měitiān tīng liǎng ge xiǎoshí lùyīn. In order to learn Chinese well, he listens to the recording for two hours everyday).

＊　＊　＊

快把电视打开，足球比赛开始了。

是吗？我也喜欢看足球赛❸。…这是什么足球❹ 啊？怎么不是圆的？

这不是国际足球，这是美式足球。

足球应该用脚踢，为什么那个人用手抱着③ 跑呢？

美式足球可以用手。

你看，你看，那么多人都压在一起，下面的人不是要被⑥ 压坏了吗？

别担心，他们的身体都很棒，而且还穿特别的运动服，没问题。

我看了半天❺也看不懂。还是看别的吧。

你在美国住半年就会喜欢了。我男朋友看美式足球的时候，常常连饭都忘了吃。

❸ 赛 (sài) stands for 比赛 (bǐsài).

❹ Although the term 足球 (zúqiú) literally means "football," it refers to soccer, rather than American football. To avoid confusion, Chinese speakers refer to American football as 美式足球 (Měishì zúqiú, American-style football) or 橄榄球 (gǎnlǎn qiú, lit., "olive ball").

❺ 半天 (bàntiān) does not always mean exactly a "half day" as the word literally suggests. Rather, it often metaphorically denotes a comparatively long stretch of time.

Wáng Péng de mèimei Wáng Hóng gāng cóng Běijīng lái, yào zài Měiguó shàng dàxué❶,
xiànzài zhù zài Gāo Xiǎoyīn jiā li xué Yīngwén. Wèile❷ tígāo Yīngwén shuǐpíng, tā měi tiān
dōu kàn liǎng ge xiǎoshí de diànshì④.

*   *   *

 Kuài bǎ diànshì dǎ kāi, zúqiú bǐsài kāishǐ le.

 Shì ma? Wǒ yě xǐhuan kàn zúqiú sài❸...Zhè shì shénme zúqiú❹ a? Zěnme bú shì yuán de?

 Zhè bú shì guójì zúqiú, zhè shì Měishì zúqiú.

 Zúqiú yīnggāi yòng jiǎo tī, wèishénme nà ge rén yòng shǒu bào zhe⑤ pǎo ne?

 Měishì zúqiú kěyǐ yòng shǒu.

 Nǐ kàn, nǐ kàn, nàme duō rén dōu yā zài yìqǐ, xiàmian de rén bú shì yào bèi⑥ yā huài le ma?

Bié dān xīn, tāmen de shēntǐ dōu hěn bàng, érqiě hái chuān tèbié de yùndòngfú, méi wèntí.

Wǒ kàn le bàntiān❺ yě kàn bu dǒng. Háishi kàn bié de ba.

Nǐ zài Měiguó zhù bànnián jiù huì xǐhuan le. Wǒ nánpéngyou kàn Měishì zúqiú de shíhou,
chángcháng lián fàn dōu wàng le chī.

 VOCABULARY

1.	上大学	shàng dàxué	vo	to attend college/university
2.	为了	wèile	prep	for the sake of
3.	提高	tígāo	v	to improve; to raise; to heighten
4.	水平	shuǐpíng	n	level; standard
5.	足球	zúqiú	n	soccer; football
6.	比赛	bǐsài	n/v	game; match; competition; to compete
7.	国际	guójì	adj	international
8.	美式	Měishì	adj	American-style
9.	应该	yīnggāi	mv	should; ought to
10.	脚	jiǎo	n	foot

VOCABULARY

11.	踢	tī	v	to kick
12.	手	shǒu	n	hand
13.	抱	bào	v	to hold or carry in the arms
14.	压	yā	v	to press; to hold down; to weigh down
15.	被	bèi	prep	by [See Grammar 6.]
16.	担心	dān xīn	vo	to worry
17.	棒	bàng	adj	fantastic; super [colloq.]
18.	运动服	yùndòngfú	n	sportswear; athletic clothing
19.	半天	bàntiān		half a day; a long time

东亚足球四强赛

中国女足 0:2 负于韩国队

In this headline, what kind of sport event is reported?

Grammar

4. Duration of Actions

When a sentence contains both a time expression that indicates the duration of an action and an object, it needs to be formed in one of these two patterns:

A. Repetition of the verb

or

B. Time expression placed before the object, often with 的 (de).

1 **A.** 她每天听录音听一个小时。

Tā měitiān tīng lùyīn tīng yí ge xiǎoshí.

B.   她每天听一个小时(的)录音。

Tā měitiān tīng yí ge xiǎoshí (de) lùyīn.

(She listens to recordings for an hour every day.)

❷ A.   她每天下午游泳游四十分钟。

Tā měitiān xiàwǔ yóu yǒng yóu sìshí fēnzhōng.

B.   她每天下午游四十分钟(的)泳。

Tā měitiān xiàwǔ yóu sìshí fēnzhōng (de) yǒng.

(She swims for forty minutes every afternoon.)

❸ A.   她每天看英文报纸看两个小时，所以英文越来越好了。

Tā měitiān kàn Yīngwén bàozhǐ kàn liǎng ge xiǎoshí, suǒyǐ Yīngwén yuè lái yuè hǎo le.

B.   她每天看两个小时(的)英文报纸，所以英文越来越好了。

Tā měitiān kàn liǎng ge xiǎoshí (de) Yīngwén bàozhǐ, suǒyǐ Yīngwén yuè lái yuè hǎo le.

(She reads English newspapers for two hours every day, so her English is getting better and better.)

5. The Particle 着 (zhe)

着 (zhe) signifies the continuation of an action or a state. Its function is descriptive. When 着 (zhe) is used between two verbs, the one that precedes 着 (zhe) signifies the accompanying action, while the second verb signifies the main action.

❶   老师站着教课，学生坐着听课。

Lǎoshī zhàn zhe jiāo kè, xuésheng zuò zhe tīng kè.

(While the teacher stood lecturing, the students sat listening.)

❷ 我喜欢躺着听音乐。

Wǒ xǐhuan tǎng zhe tīng yīnyuè.

(I like to listen to music while lying down.)

❸ 美式足球可以抱着球跑。

Měishì zúqiú kěyǐ bào zhe qiú pǎo.

(In American football, you can run with the ball in your hands.)

着 (zhe) is normally used after a verb to indicate a continuing action or a state. 在 (zài) is normally used before a verb to indicate an ongoing action.

❹ **A:** 学生们在做什么呢？

Xuésheng men zài zuò shénme ne?

(What are the students doing?)

B: 在运动。

Zài yùndòng.

(They're exercising.)

在 (zài) in (4) above cannot be replaced with 着 (zhe). Likewise, 着 (zhe) in the earlier sentences cannot be replaced with 在 (zài), either.

---

6. 被/叫/让 (bèi/jiào/ràng) in Passive-Voice Sentences

A sentence in the passive voice can be constructed with 被 (bèi), 叫 (jiào), or 让 (ràng). Its structure is as follows:

receiver of the action + 被 (bèi)/ 叫 (jiào)/ 让 (ràng)
+ agent of the action + verb + other element (complement/ 了 {le}, etc.)

❶ 我的功课被/叫/让狗吃了。

Wǒ de gōngkè bèi/jiào/ràng gǒu chī le.

(My homework was eaten by my dog.)

❷   你买的那些书被/叫/让你的女朋友拿去了。

Nǐ mǎi de nà xiē shū bèi/jiào/ràng nǐ de nǚpéngyou ná qù le.

(The books that you bought were taken away by your girlfriend.)

❸   糟糕，你的网球拍被/叫/让我压坏了。

Zāogāo, nǐ de wǎngqiú pāi bèi/jiào/ràng wǒ yā huài le.

(Oh gosh, your tennis racket was crushed [by me].)

❹   你看，我的梨被/叫/让
你的西瓜压坏了。

Nǐ kàn, wǒ de lí bèi/jiào/ràng nǐ de xīgua yā huài le.

(Take a look. My pears were crushed by your watermelon.)

In Chinese, the passive voice is not used as often as it is in English. It often carries negative connotations and usually appears in situations that are unpleasant for the receiver of the action, or in situations where something is lost. As in the 把 (bǎ) structure (see Lesson 13), the verb is usually followed by another element, such as a complement or 了 (le).

In a passive-voice sentence with 被 (bèi)/叫 (jiào) /让 (ràng), the agent of the action does not always have to be specified. If the agent of the action is someone that is not identifiable or need not be identified, it can be referred to simply as 人 (rén, someone; people).

❺   我的信用卡被/叫/让人拿走了。

Wǒ de xìnyòngkǎ bèi/jiào/ràng rén ná zǒu le.)

(My credit card was taken away.)

With 被 (bèi), the agent of the action can be omitted from the sentence:

❻   同学们在教室里又唱又跳，他快
被吵死了。

Tóngxué men zài jiàoshì li yòu chàng yòu tiào, tā kuài

bèi chǎo sǐ le.

(His classmates are singing and dancing in the classroom.

The noise is driving him to distraction.)

被 (bèi) sometimes can be used in a positive sense, but we will not discuss it in detail here.

Language Practice

E. A Busy Day?

Take a look at the chart and summarize who did what for how long yesterday.

EXAMPLE	1.	2.	3.	4.	5.
8:00pm–11:00pm	7:00am–8:00am	7:30am–8:15am	11:00am–12:00pm	10:00am–12:30pm	4:00pm–6:30pm

EXAMPLE:

→ 费先生昨天跳舞跳了三个小时。   Fèi xiānsheng zuótiān tiào wǔ tiào le sān ge xiǎoshí.

or 费先生昨天跳了三个小时（的）舞。   Fèi xiānsheng zuótiān tiào le sān ge xiǎoshí (de) wǔ.

1.

2.

3.

4.

5.

F. Study Strategies

Wang Hong came to the United States to improve her English. To achieve her goal, she watches two hours of English-language TV every day. How can you improve your Chinese? Get together with a group of classmates and get everyone's suggestions by asking 怎么才能提高中文水平 (Zěnme cái néng tígāo Zhōngwén shuǐpíng?)

EXAMPLE:

→ 为了提高中文水平，你应该每天听两个小时（的）录音。

Wèile tígāo Zhōngwén shuǐpíng, nǐ yīnggāi měitiān tīng liǎng ge xiǎo shí (de) lùyīn.

1. Classmate #1

2. Classmate #2

3. Classmate #3

...

G. Describing What You See

Describe the persons in the pictures using "V + 着 (zhe)" structure.

EXAMPLE:

→ 王朋、高文中、
李友坐着聊天儿。

高小音站着聊天儿。

Wáng Péng, Gāo Wénzhōng,

Lǐ Yǒu zuò zhe liáo tiānr.

Gāo Xiǎoyīn zhàn zhe liáo tiānr.

1.

3.

2.

4.

H. Not His Lucky Day!

Use the 被 (bèi)/ 叫 (jiào)/ 让 (ràng) structure to describe what happened to Little Gao yesterday.

1. His homework was eaten by his dog.

→

2. His coffee was drunk by his sister.

→

3. His credit card was taken away from him by his mother.

→

4. His car was driven to school by his brother.

→

5. The birthday gift that he was going to give to his friend was crushed by the sofa.

→

Have any of these ever happened to you? Do you have any similar experiences that you could share with your class?

_____

_____

I. Workout Queen/King!

Go around the class and ask one another:

1. Do you exercise?

If so:

2. What sports do you play?

3. Why do you like them?

If not:

2. What sports do you dislike?

3. Why don't you like them?

4. How often do you exercise?

4. How long have you not been exercising?

5. How long do you exercise each time?

5. When do you plan to start exercising?

After gathering everyone's information, then tell the class who the workout king/queen is.

_____ 运动得最多，
是我们的运动天王！

_____ yùndòng de zuì duō,

shì wǒmen de yùndòng tiānwáng!

J. Recap and Narrate

Working with a partner, recap the content of Dialogue II:

1. 王红看过美式
   足球吗？

1. Wáng Hóng kàn guo Měishì
   zúqiú ma?

2. 国际足球和美式足球
   有什么不同？

2. Guójì zúqiú hé Měishì zúqiú
   yǒu shénme bù tóng?

3. 踢美式足球的人
   为什么不会被压坏？

3. Tī Měishì zúqiú de rén
   wèishénme bú huì bèi yā huài?

4. 王红看得懂美式
   足球吗？

4. Wáng Hóng kàn de dǒng Měishì
   zúqiú ma?

5. 怎么知道高小音的
   男朋友喜欢看美式
   足球？

5. Zěnme zhīdào Gāo Xiǎoyīn de
   nánpéngyou xǐhuan kàn Měishì
   zúqiú?

Using the words and phrases in blue as prompts, connect your answers above to form a narrative like this example:

王朋的妹妹王红刚从北京来，要在美国上大学，现在住在高小音家里学英文。为了练习英文，她每天都看两个小时的电视。这一天刚吃完晚饭，高小音就和王红看电视里的足球比赛。正在比赛的是美式足球，王红没看过美式足球，不知道球为什么不是圆的，踢球的人为什么用手抱着球跑。她看见那么多人都压在一起，担心下面的人会被压坏了。她看不懂，觉得没有意思。可是高小音说，在美国住半年就会喜欢了。

Wáng Péng de mèimei Wáng Hóng gāng cóng Běijīng lái, yào zài Měiguó shàng dàxué, xiànzài zhù zài Gāo Xiǎoyīn jiā li xué Yīngwén. Wèile liànxí Yīngwén, tā měi tiān dōu kàn liǎng ge xiǎoshí de diànshì. Zhè yì tiān gāng chī wán wǎnfàn, Gāo Xiǎoyīn jiù hé Wáng Hóng kàn diànshì li de zúqiú bǐsài. Zhèngzài bǐsài de shì Měishì zúqiú, Wáng Hóng méi kàn guo Měishì zúqiú, bù zhīdào qiú wèishénme bú shì yuán de, tī qiú de rén wèishénme yòng shǒu bào zhe qiú pǎo. Tā kàn jiàn nàme duō rén dōu yā zài yìqǐ, dān xīn xiàmian de rén huì bèi yā huài le. Tā kàn bù dǒng, juéde méiyǒu yìsi. Kěshì Gāo Xiǎoyīn shuō, zài Měiguó zhù bànnián jiù huì xǐhuan le.

HOW ABOUT YOU?

What's your favorite or least favorite sport?

1.	慢跑	mànpǎo	v/n	to jog; jogging
2.	打棒球	dǎ bàngqiú	vo	to play baseball
3.	打乒乓球	dǎ pīngpāngqiú	vo	to play table tennis
4.	做瑜伽	zuò yújiā	vo	to do yoga
5.	打太极拳	dǎ tàijíquán	vo	to do Tai Chi (a kind of traditional Chinese shadow boxing)

If the sports that you like and dislike are not listed above, ask your teacher and make a note here:

_____

Culture Highlights

❶ As living standards in China have improved in recent decades, the consumption of calorie-rich foods, especially meat, has been on the rise. Obesity has quietly become a problem for many people in urban areas, especially children. That change is reflected in sociolinguistic effects. Before the 1970s one could say "你胖了" (Nǐ pàng le, You've put on weight) and have it received as a compliment, but now one has to be really careful with that expression.

❷ In recent decades, China has consolidated its status as the leading sports power in Asia. In some sports events, such as table tennis and diving, China has enjoyed a dominant position in the world. By far the most popular sport in China, as in many other countries, is soccer, but ironically, China's national soccer team is second-rate even in Asia. What Chinese speakers call "football" (足球 zúqiú) is actually soccer in American English. American football, called 美式足球 (Měishì zúqiú) or 橄榄球 (gǎnlǎnqiú) in China, is not played there. Actually, not many people in China would understand the frenzy and exhilaration of American fans watching what can seem to be little more than a group scuffling on grass.

❸ One of the most spectacular scenes in a Chinese city is in the early morning, when hundreds or even thousands of men and women, most of them older people and retirees, gather in the parks to do Tai Chi boxing (太极拳 tàijíquán) and other forms of exercise.

4 In China, all television stations are state-owned. Apart from Chinese Central Television (CCTV), each province has its own TV stations. CCTV has a channel, CCTV 5, exclusively devoted to sports, where NBA games are regularly aired. It also offers an English channel, Channel 9, which can be received all over the world through satellite transmission.

●北京电视台—1
11:57 世界你好(午间版)
13:55 20集连续剧:崛起 2、3
●北京电视台—2
7:13 25集连续剧:似水浮生 23、24
16:03 东芝动物乐园
●北京电视台—3
16:14 20集连续剧:伴我同行 4、5
●北京电视台—4
7:14 30集连续剧:大马帮 12、13
9:18 28集连续剧:沈香 24、25
13:57 40集连续剧:风云争霸 37—40
●北京电视台—5
8:55 北京特快
9:57 连续剧:倚天屠龙记 14、15
●北京电视台—6
11:45 体育新闻
14:00 直播:2004 年喜力网球公开赛
●北京电视台—7
12:00 生活面对面
12:35 健康生活
12:48 专家门诊
14:05 魅力前线
15:35 神奇的地球
●北京电视台—8
12:00 开心一刻
12:36 30集连续剧:少年黄飞鸿 9、10
●北京电视台—9
9:06 连续剧:情定爱琴海 25—27
14:07 20集连续剧:坐庄 16—18
●中央电视台—1
9:25 20集连续剧:女子监狱 20
12:38 今日说法
16:00 天天饮食:干贝云丝豆腐羹
●中央电视台—新闻频道
11:30 法治在线
12:30 共同关注
13:30 体育报道
14:10 面对面
●中央电视台—2
11:00 健康之路:心慌心悸与房颤
11:50 天天饮食:培根奶油蘑菇汤
16:40 全球资讯榜
●中央电视台—3
10:19 曲苑杂坛精编版 23

●中央电视台—4
13:05 连续剧:将装修进行到底 14
●中央电视台—5
12:00 体坛快讯
●中央电视台—6
6:19 故事片:黑花杀手
8:04 故事片:乱世英雄乱世情
10:12 故事片:傅抱石
12:54 蓝天情感剧场:金色黄昏(美国)
14:47 故事片:约会阳光
16:38 故事片:走出硝烟的女神
●中央电视台—8
6:04 每日佳艺:你是我爸爸 27(葡萄牙)
6:53 20集连续剧:大案追踪 19
7:45 影视同期声
8:05 影视金曲
8:24 大剧场:神探狄仁杰 7—10
12:01 快乐剧场:室内剧:闲人马大姐 245、246
13:22 魅力100分:澡堂老板家的男人们(第一部)1—4(韩国)
●中央电视台—10
9:50 探索·发现:清宫秘档 22:光绪之死
16:43 探索·发现:清宫秘档案 18:皇帝的一天(上)
●中央电视台—11
14:35 九州大戏台:(京剧版)①京剧:初出茅庐②京剧:杨门女将·探谷选段
●中央电视台—12
14:15 动感剧场:过把瘾 7、8
●中国教育台—1
12:15 20集连续剧:嫂子 19、20
●上海东方卫视节目
12:40 律师视点
14:10 连续剧:半生缘 28、29
●天津电视台
15:20 警方报道
●天津电视台—1
12:10 连续剧:五月槐花香 31
●河北电视台—2
8:15 剧场:天下无双 13、14
●山西电视台
10:00 剧场:一个医生的故事 1、2
13:10 剧场:悲情红与黑 16—18

●内蒙古卫视节目
8:22 连续剧:国家公诉 20、21
13:27 法制专线
14:23 连续剧:危险旅程 5、6
●辽宁电视台
12:26 法制时空
●吉林电视台
16:18 警界纵横:家庭与社会
●江苏电视台
14:00 剧场:秋香 1—3
●浙江电视台
8:00 连续剧:追捕 18—20
●安徽电视台
12:50 连续剧:中国神探 4、5
●福建东南电视台
8:38 剧场:城市女人心 17—19
●江西电视台
7:41 连续剧:孝庄秘史 20
9:09 剧场:玉蜻蜓 2—4
●河南电视台
8:50 好剧回旋:当家的女人 17、18
●湖北电视台
13:20 快乐森林
●湖南电视台
7:40 剧场:封神榜 13—16
13:30 剧场:春去春又回 38—40
●广东电视台
16:08 连续剧:情满珠江 5、6
●旅游卫视节目
12:04 英达剧场:旅行社的故事 86
12:34 现在
16:00 玩转地球:旅游探险精选
●四川电视台
8:58 剧场:法网伊人 1—3
●贵州电视台
9:49 剧场:热血忠魂之独行侍卫 29—34
●云南电视台
13:10 连续剧:爱情宝典 11—13
●西藏电视台
13:07 连续剧:林则徐 9
●陕西电视台
8:10 连续剧:孝庄秘史 21—23
●甘肃电视台
8:00 连续剧:说出你的爱 5、6
14:35 连续剧:十三格格 30
●青海电视台
8:38 连续剧:保卫爱情 19、20
13:00 连续剧:保卫爱情 21、22
●宁夏电视台
13:42 影院:紧急追降
●新疆卫星节目
9:23 剧场:西厢记 1—3

(本版预告为各台昨日11:00公布的节目安排,临时调整请以当日电视台预告为准)

Is CCTV's Channel 9 listed? What other cities' TV listings can you recognize here?

English Text

Dialogue I

Gao Wenzhong: Look, my gut is getting bigger and bigger.

Wang Peng: You usually overeat, and on top of that you don't exercise; of course you're putting on more and more weight.

Gao Wenzhong: What should I do?

Wang Peng: If you're afraid of being overweight, you should exercise two or three times a week, for half an hour each time. Then your belly will get smaller.

Gao Wenzhong: I haven't exercised for two years. What kind of exercise should I do?

Wang Peng: The simplest exercise is jogging.

Gao Wenzhong: It's so cold in winter, and so hot in summer. Jogging is too uncomfortable.

Wang Peng: How about playing tennis?

Gao Wenzhong: Then I'd have to get a tennis racket and tennis shoes. You know tennis rackets and tennis shoes are very expensive!

Wang Peng: How about getting a few people together to play basketball? Buying a basketball is very inexpensive.

Gao Wenzhong: Then every time I'd have to call people and arrange to meet. That's way too much hassle.

Wang Peng: Then why don't you swim? There's no need to look for people, it wouldn't cost much money, and you could go any time.

Gao Wenzhong: Swimming? I'm afraid of water. That's too dangerous. What if I drown?

Wang Peng: There's nothing I can do [to help]. If you're not willing to exercise, then keep packing on the pounds.

Dialogue II

Wang Peng's younger sister, Wang Hong, just came from Beijing. She will be going to college in the United States. Right now she is staying at Gao Xiaoyin's place, studying English. To improve her English, she watches two hours of TV every day.

*   *   *

Gao Xiaoyin: Hurry, turn the TV on. The football game is starting.

Wang Hong: Really? I like watching football games too...What kind of football is this? How come it's not round?

Gao Xiaoyin: This is not international football, this is American football.

Wang Hong: To play football you should kick (the ball) with your feet. Why is that guy running with the ball in his hands?

Gao Xiaoyin: In American football you can use your hands.

Wang Hong: Look! All those people are piling on top of each other. Wouldn't the people underneath be crushed to pieces?

Gao Xiaoyin: Don't worry, they're really strong. Besides, they wear special sports clothing, so everything's fine.

Wang Hong: I've been watching for a while and I still don't get it. Let's watch something else.

Gao Xiaoyin: You only have to live in America for half a year before you will begin to like American football. When my boyfriend is watching a football game, often he will even forget to eat.

PROGRESS CHECKLIST

Before proceeding to Lesson 19, be sure you can complete the following tasks in Chinese:

I am able to—

☑ Explain briefly why certain sports are or are not appealing to me;

☐ Describe the frequency and duration of my exercise routine, or how long I haven't exercised;

☐ Make a simple comparison between how soccer and American football are played.

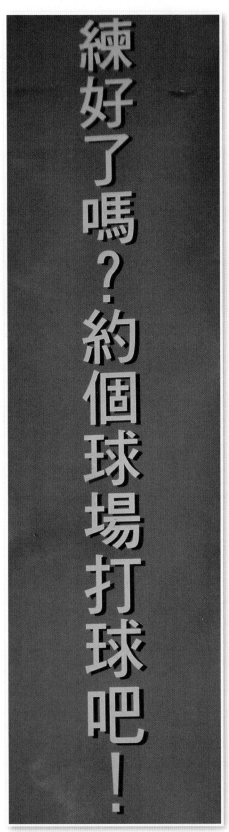

練好了嗎？約個球場打球吧！

What do you say?

LESSON 19   **Travel**

第十九课　旅行

Dì shíjiǔ kè　Lǚxíng

 LEARNING OBJECTIVES

In this lesson, you will learn to use Chinese to

- Talk about your plans for summer vacation;
- Describe what kind of city Beijing is;
- Describe your travel itinerary;
- Ask for discounts, compare airfares and routes, and book an airplane ticket;
- Ask about seat assignments and request meal accommodations based on your dietary restrictions or preferences.

 RELATE AND GET READY

In your own culture/community—

1. How do students normally spend the summer?
2. What town or city is the nearest cultural or political center? What are its special attractions?
3. Where can people get good deals on airline tickets?
4. What's a common expression for a commercial discount?

Dialogue I: Traveling to Beijing

李友，时间过得真快，马上就
要放假了，我们的同学，有的
去暑期班学习，有的去公司实
习，有的回家打工，你有什么
计划？

我还没有想好。你呢，王朋？

我暑假打算❶回北京去看父母。

是吗？我听说北京这个城市很
有意思。

当然。北京是中国的首都，也
是中国的政治、文化中心，有
很多名胜古迹。

LANGUAGE NOTES

❶ While the verbs 打算
(dǎsuàn) and 计划 (jìhuà)
are synonyms, the former is
more colloquial and the latter
more formal.

对啊，长城很有名。

 还有，北京的好饭馆多得
不得了①。

真的？我去过香港、台北，还没
去过北京，要是能去北京就好了。

那你跟我一起回去吧，我当你
的导游。

真的吗？那太好了！护照我已经
有了，我得赶快办签证②。

那我马上给旅行社打电话订
飞机票。

❷ To apply for a certificate or official documentation, one usually uses the verb 办 (bàn), especially in spoken Chinese, as in 办护照 (bàn hùzhào, to apply for a passport) and 办签证 (bàn qiānzhèng, to apply for a visa). More examples: 办学生证 (bàn xuéshēngzhèng, to apply for a student ID), 办手续 (bàn shǒuxù, to do the paperwork), and 办结婚证 (bàn jiéhūnzhèng, to apply for a marriage license).

Lǐ Yǒu, shíjiān guò de zhēn kuài, mǎshàng jiù yào fàng jià le, wǒmen de tóngxué, yǒude qù shǔqī bān xuéxí, yǒude qù gōngsī shíxí, yǒude huí jiā dǎ gōng, nǐ yǒu shénme jìhuà?

Wǒ hái méiyǒu xiǎng hǎo. Nǐ ne, Wáng Péng?

Wǒ shǔjià❶ dǎsuàn huí Běijīng qù kàn fùmǔ.

Shì ma? Wǒ tīngshuō Běijīng zhè ge chéngshì hěn yǒuyìsi.

Dāngrán. Běijīng shì Zhōngguó de shǒudū, yě shì Zhōngguó de zhèngzhì, wénhuà zhōngxīn, yǒu hěn duō míngshèng gǔjì.

Duì a, Chángchéng hěn yǒumíng.

Hái yǒu, Běijīng de hǎo fànguǎn duō de bù déliǎo①.

Zhēn de? Wǒ qù guo Xiānggǎng, Táiběi, hái méi qù guo Běijīng, yàoshi néng qù Běijīng jiù hǎo le.

Nà nǐ gēn wǒ yìqǐ huí qu ba, wǒ dāng nǐ de dǎoyóu.

Zhēn de ma? Nà tài hǎo le! Hùzhào wǒ yǐjīng yǒu le. Wǒ děi gǎnkuài bàn qiānzhèng❷.

Nà wǒ mǎshàng gěi lǚxíngshè dǎ diànhuà dìng fēijī piào.

VOCABULARY

1.	马上	mǎshàng	adv	immediately; right away
2.	放假	fàng jià	vo	go on vacation; have time off
	放	fàng	v	to let go; to set free
	假	jià	n	vacation; holiday
3.	公司	gōngsī	n	company
4.	实习	shíxí	v	to intern
5.	打工	dǎ gōng	vo	to work at a temporary job (often part time)
6.	计划	jìhuà	n/v	plan; to plan
7.	暑假	shǔjià	n	summer vacation
8.	打算	dǎsuàn	v/n	to plan; plan
9.	父母	fùmǔ	n	parents; father and mother
10.	首都	shǒudū	n	capital city
11.	政治	zhèngzhì	n	politics
12.	文化	wénhuà	n	culture
13.	名胜古迹	míngshèng gǔjì		famous scenic spots and historic sites
14.	有名	yǒumíng	adj	famous; well-known
15.	导游	dǎoyóu	n	tour guide
16.	护照	hùzhào	n	passport
17.	订	dìng	v	to reserve; to book (a ticket, a hotel room, etc.)
18.	签证	qiānzhèng	n	visa
19.	旅行社	lǚxíngshè	n	travel agency

VOCABULARY

Proper Nouns

20.	长城	Chángchéng	the Great Wall
21.	香港	Xiānggǎng	Hong Kong
22.	台北	Táiběi	Taipei

两张长城的照片
liǎng zhāng Chángchéng de zhàopiàn

你想去香港还是上海？
Nǐ xiǎng qù Xiānggǎng háishi Shànghǎi?

Grammar

1. 不得了 (bù déliǎo, **extremely**)

The expression 不得了 (bù déliǎo, extremely), which often follows the structure "adjective + 得 (de)," indicates a high degree, in the speaker's judgment, of the attribute signified by the adjective. For example, if one cannot stand the summer heat in a certain place, one can comment on it by saying:

❶   那个地方夏天热得不得了。

Nà ge dìfang xiàtiān rè de bù déliǎo.

(Summer is unbearably hot in that place.)

If the Great Wall is extremely crowded, one can describe the scene by saying:

❷   长城上的人多得不得了。

Chángchéng shàng de rén duō de bù déliǎo.

(There was an incredible number of people on the Great Wall.)

Language Practice

A. Planning Ahead

Ask your partner about his/her plans for tonight, 1) for the coming weekend, 2) for the summer break, 3) for next semester, and 4) for next year.

EXAMPLE:

你今天晚上打算做什么？   Nǐ jīntiān wǎnshang dǎsuàn zuò shénme?

1.

2.

3.

4.

B. Survey Your Class

Move around the classroom and interview your classmates to find out more about their opinions and experiences. Then report the results of your survey to the class by using "我的同学有的人···有的人··· (Wǒ de tóngxué yǒude rén…, yǒude rén…)." Possible topics include: your classmates' favorite beverages, cuisines, fruits, colors, or sports; their thoughts on Chinese pronunciation, Chinese grammar, or Chinese characters; their allergies, living arrangements, travel plans, etc. Each student should choose a different topic to ask about.

EXAMPLE: beverages

我的同学有的人喜欢喝可乐，有的人喜欢喝咖啡。

Wǒ de tóngxué yǒude rén xǐhuan hē kělè, yǒude rén xǐhuan hē kāfēi.

C. Name That Capital!

You have learned how to say "the capital of China is Beijing":

中国的首都是北京。   Zhōngguó de shǒudū shì Běijīng.

Now can you name the capitals of the following countries?

1. 美国   Měiguó
2. 英国   Yīngguó
3. 日本   Rìběn
4. 韩国   Hánguó   South Korea
5. 加拿大   Jiā'nádà   Canada
6. 墨西哥   Mòxīgē   Mexico
7. 澳大利亚   Àodàlìyà   Australia

...

D. World Cities

With your partner, recap what you know about Beijing, and then find one or two other cities in the world that are similar to Beijing in some ways. What do they have in common? If you could travel to any city in the world during your next vacation, where would you go? Why? What attractions would you especially want to see?

E. Name That Person! Name That Place!

You must know celebrities that you adore and ones that you dislike; you may have been to attractive places and repulsive ones. Share with the class your sentiments about those people and places by using the "adj + 得不得了 (de bù déliǎo)" formation.

Celebrities

EXAMPLE: 可爱   kě'ài

→ (name of the celebrity)   (name of the celebrity)
   可爱得不得了。   kě'ài de bù déliǎo.

1. 帅   shuài

2. 聪明   cōngming

3. 漂亮   piàoliang

4. 用功   yònggōng

5. 酷   kù

6. 坏   huài

7. 懒   lǎn

 ...

Places

1. 漂亮   piàoliang

2. 有意思   yǒu yìsi

3. 安静   ānjìng

4. 干净   gānjìng

5. 人多   rén duō

6. 热   rè

7. 冷   lěng

8. 危险   wēixiǎn

9. 吵   chǎo

. . .

F. What Do You Want to Be?

Survey your classmates to find out their aspirations for the future:

你以后想当什么？   Nǐ yǐhòu xiǎng dāng shénme?

老师、律师，还是医生？   Lǎoshī, lǜshī, háishi yīshēng?

G. Recap and Narrate

Working with a partner, recap the content of Dialogue I:

1. 快放暑假了，王朋   1. Kuài fàng shǔjià le, Wáng Péng
   的同学们想做   de tóngxué men xiǎng zuò
   什么？   shénme?

2. 李友暑假打算做
什么？

3. 王朋暑假打算做
什么？

4. 李友听说过北京吗？

5. 王朋说北京是一
个什么样的城市？

6. 李友想去北京吗？

7. 王朋为什么说去
北京他可以当李友的
导游？

8. 王朋和李友去
中国以前，得先
做什么？

2. Lǐ Yǒu shǔjià dǎsuàn zuò
shénme?

3. Wáng Péng shǔjià dǎsuàn zuò
shénme?

4. Lǐ Yǒu tīngshuō guo Běijīng ma?

5. Wáng Péng shuō Běijīng shì yí
ge shénme yàng de chéngshì?

6. Lǐ Yǒu xiǎng qù Běijīng ma?

7. Wáng Péng wèishénme shuō qù
Běijīng tā kěyǐ dāng Lǐ Yǒu de
dǎoyóu?

8. Wáng Péng hé Lǐ Yǒu qù
Zhōngguó yǐqián, děi xiān
zuò shénme?

Using the words and phrases in blue as prompts, connect your answers above to form a narrative like this example:

快放暑假了，王朋的同学有的去暑期班学习，有的去公司实习，有的回家去打工。李友还没想好暑假的计划。王朋要回北京看父母，他给李友介绍说北京是中国的首都，也是中国的政治、文化中心，有很多名胜古迹，北京的好饭馆儿多得不得了。李友去过台北和香港，但是没去过北京，听了王朋的介绍很想去北京。王朋让李友跟他一起回北京，他当李友的导游。李友听了很高兴。李友已经有护照了，得办签证。王朋说他赶快给旅行社打电话订飞机票。

Kuài fàng shǔjià le, Wáng Péng de tóngxué yǒude qù shǔqī bān xuéxí, yǒude qù gōngsī shíxí, yǒude huí jiā qù dǎ gōng. Lǐ Yǒu hái méi xiǎng hǎo shǔjià de jìhuà. Wáng Péng yào huí Běijīng kàn fùmǔ, tā gěi Lǐ Yǒu jièshào shuō Běijīng shì Zhōngguó de shǒudū, yě shì Zhōngguó de zhèngzhì, wénhuà zhōngxīn, yǒu hěn duō míngshèng gǔjì, Běijīng de hǎo fànguǎnr duō de bù déliǎo. Lǐ Yǒu qù guo Táiběi hé Xiānggǎng, dànshì méi qù guo Běijīng, tīng le Wáng Péng de jièshào hěn xiǎng qù Běijīng. Wáng Péng ràng Lǐ Yǒu gēn tā yìqǐ huí Běijīng, tā dāng Lǐ Yǒu de dǎoyóu. Lǐ Yǒu tīng le hěn gāoxìng. Lǐ Yǒu yǐjīng yǒu hùzhào le, děi bàn qiānzhèng. Wáng Péng shuō tā gǎnkuài gěi lǚxíngshè dǎ diànhuà dìng fēijī piào.

Dialogue II: Planning an Itinerary

 天一旅行社，你好。

你好。请问六月初❶到北京的机票多少钱？

您要买单程票还是往返票？

我要买两张往返票。

你想买哪家航空公司的？

哪家的便宜，就买哪②家的。

LANGUAGE NOTES

❶ 月初 (yuè chū) refers to the first few days of the month, typically from the 1st to the 5th or 6th. 月中 (yuè zhōng) is for the middle of the month, roughly from the 14th to 16th or 17th. 月底 (yuè dǐ) means the final days of the month, usually from the 27th or 28th. One can also say 年初 (nián chū, beginning of the year), 年中 (nián zhōng, middle of the year), and 年底 (nián dǐ, end of year). The words 初 (chū, beginning), 中 (zhōng, middle), and 底 (dǐ, end; bottom) usually compound with either 月 (yuè) or 年 (nián) and are never used with 星期 (xīngqī).

请等等，我查一下…好几家航空公司都有航班❷。中国国际航空公司，一千五③，直飞。西北航空公司正在打折③，差不多一千四百六十，可是要转机。

西北只比国航❹便宜四十几块钱❹，我还是买国航吧。

哪一天走❺？哪一天回来？

六月十号走，七月十五号回来。现在可以订位子吗？

可以。你们喜欢靠窗户的还是靠走道的？

靠走道的。对了❻，我朋友吃素，麻烦帮她订一份素餐。

没问题…您在北京要订旅馆、租车吗？

不用，谢谢！

❷ In Taiwan, people say 班机 (bānjī) instead of 航班 (hángbān).

❸ The approach to describing a discount in Chinese is different from that in English. In English the emphasis is on the amount that is given as a discount, e.g., 10% off, 20% off, etc. In Chinese, however, the emphasis is on the proportion of the original price that is actually paid. Therefore, 九折 (jiǔ zhé) means that the price is 90% of the original price, or 10% off; 七五折 (qī wǔ zhé) means 75% of the original price; and 对折 (duì zhé) 50% of the original price.

❹ 中国国际航空公司 (Zhōngguó Guójì Hángkōng Gōngsī, literally, "China International Airlines") is often shortened to 国航 (Guóháng). It's known in English as Air China.

❺ As introduced in Lesson 10, the basic meaning of 走 (zǒu) is "to walk." Here 走 (zǒu) means to leave or to depart.

❻ 对了 (duì le) is often used when one suddenly thinks of something. For instance, if a student is saying goodbye to his classmate, and all of a sudden it occurs to him that they need to study for a test the next day, he can say: 明天见。…对了，明天考试，别忘了复习。(Míngtiān jiàn....Duì le, míngtiān kǎo shì, bié wàng le fùxí, See you tomorrow. ...Oh yes, we have a test tomorrow. Don't forget to review.)

Tiān Yī lǚxíngshè, nǐ hǎo.

Nǐ hǎo. Qǐng wèn liùyuè chū❶ dào Běijīng de jīpiào duōshao qián?

Nín yào mǎi dānchéng piào háishi wǎngfǎn piào?

Wǒ yào mǎi liǎng zhāng wǎngfǎn piào.

Nǐ xiǎng mǎi nǎ jiā hángkōng gōngsī de?

Nǎ jiā de piányi, jiù mǎi nǎ② jiā de.

Qǐng děng deng, wǒ chá yí xià... Hǎo jǐ jiā hángkōng gōngsī dōu yǒu hángbān❷. Zhōngguó Guójì Hángkōng Gōngsī, yì qiān wǔ③, zhífēi. Xīběi Hángkōng Gōngsī zhèngzài dǎ zhé❸, chàbuduō yì qiān sì bǎi liùshí, kěshì yào zhuǎn jī.

Xīběi zhǐ bǐ Guóháng④ piányi sìshí jǐ kuài qián④, wǒ háishi mǎi Guóháng ba.

Nǎ yì tiān zǒu❺? Nǎ yì tiān huí lai?

Liùyuè shí hào zǒu, qīyuè shíwǔ hào huí lai. Xiànzài kěyǐ dìng wèizi ma?

Kěyǐ. Nǐmen xǐhuan kào chuānghu de háishi kào zǒudào de?

Kào zǒudào de. Duì le❻, wǒ péngyou chī sù, máfan bāng tā dìng yí fèn sùcān.

Méi wèntí...Nín zài Běijīng yào dìng lǚguǎn, zū chē ma?

Búyòng, xièxie!

这是去哪儿的车票？是单程票还是往返票？
Zhè shì qù nǎr de chēpiào? Shì dānchéng piào háishi wǎngfǎn piào?

VOCABULARY

1.	初	chū	n	beginning
2.	单程	dānchéng	n	one-way trip
3.	往返	wǎngfǎn	v	make a round trip; go there and back
4.	航空	hángkōng	n	aviation
5.	查	chá	v	to check; to look into
6.	航班	hángbān	n	scheduled flight
7.	千	qiān	nu	thousand
8.	直飞	zhí fēi		fly directly
9.	打折	dǎ zhé	vo	to sell at a discount; to give a discount
10.	转机	zhuǎn jī	vo	change planes
11.	靠	kào	v	to lean on; to lean against; to be next to
12.	窗户	chuānghu	n	window
13.	走道	zǒudào	n	aisle
14.	份	fèn	m	(measure word for meal order, job)
15.	素餐	sùcān	n	vegetarian meal
16.	旅馆	lǚguǎn	n	hotel
17.	租	zū	v	to rent

Proper Nouns

18.	中国国际航空公司	Zhōngguó Guójì Hángkōng Gōngsī	Air China
19.	西北航空公司	Xīběi Hángkōng Gōngsī	Northwest Airlines

国内4-8折

上海	深圳	广州	成都	重庆	昆明	西安
海口	厦门	桂林	三亚	福州	武汉	南京
贵阳	济南	青岛	大连	沈阳	长春	哈尔滨

去上海的机票最便宜能打几折？

Qù Shànghǎi de jīpiào zuì piányí néng dǎ jǐ zhé?

Grammar

2. Question Pronouns as Indefinite References (Whoever, Whatever, etc.)

A question pronoun repeated in two separate but related clauses of the same sentence forms the equivalent of the "question pronoun + -ever" expression in English. Its first occurrence refers to an indefinite person, object, time, place, etc. Its second occurrence then refers to that same person, object, time, place, etc.

❶ 谁想去，谁就去。

Shéi xiǎng qù, shéi jiù qù.

(Whoever wants to go can go.)

❷ 你吃什么，我就吃什么。

Nǐ chī shénme, wǒ jiù chī shénme.

(I'll have whatever you're having.)

❸ 哪双鞋便宜，就买哪双。

Nǎ shuāng xié piányi, jiù mǎi nǎ shuāng.)

(Buy whichever pair of shoes is the cheapest.)

❹ Taxi Driver: 您想怎么走？

Nín xiǎng zěnme zǒu?

(Which way do you want to take?)

Passenger: 怎么近，怎么走。

Zěnme jìn, zěnme zǒu.

(I'll take whichever is the shortest distance.)

In this kind of sentence, sometimes the two occurrences of the question pronoun play the same grammatical role, i.e, both are subjects, as in (1); or both are objects, as in (2). Sometimes the two occurrences of the question pronoun perform different grammatical functions. In (3), for example, the first 哪双 (nǎ shuāng) is the subject whereas the second 哪双 (nǎ shuāng) is the object. The adverb 就 (jiù) often precedes the verb in the second clause, but not always, as shown in (5) and (6) below.

❺   哪儿安静，我住哪儿。

Nǎr ānjìng, wǒ zhù nǎr.

(I'll live wherever it's quiet.)

❻ A: 他找谁帮他搬家具？

Tā zhǎo shéi bāng tā bān jiājù?

(Who is he going to ask to help him move his furniture?)

B: 谁身体棒，他找谁。

Shéi shēntǐ bàng, tā zhǎo shéi.

(He'll ask whoever is strong.)

3. Numbers over One Thousand

You have already learned how to count in Chinese up to a thousand.

Number	Chinese	Pinyin	English
1	一	yī	one
10	十	shí	ten
100	百	bǎi	hundred
1000	千	qiān	thousand

However, in Chinese the next larger unit after a thousand is not called *十千 (*shí qiān), but 万 (wàn). Even though the Chinese share the international practice of segmenting a long Arabic number into three-digit sets in writing or in print, they mentally divide the number into four-digit sets instead when they read it. Starting at the fifth digit from the right is the four-digit set of 万 (wàn), and the next four-digit set is that of 亿 (yì). In the examples below, we have artificially indicated such divisions as an aid.

English	Arabic Number	Chinese Mental Division	Chinese	Pinyin
thousand	1,000	1000	（一）千	(yì) qiān
ten thousand	10,000	1'0000	（一）万	(yí) wàn
hundred thousand	100,000	10'0000	十万	shí wàn
million	1,000,000	100'0000	（一）百万	(yì) bǎi wàn
ten million	10,000,000	1000'0000	（一）千万	(yì) qiān wàn
hundred million	100,000,000	1'0000'0000	（一）亿/ （一）万万	(yí) yì/ (yí) wànwàn
billion	1,000,000,000	10'0000'0000	十亿	shí yì

Examples of large numbers:

12,345 (1'2345)　　一万两千三百四十五
　　　　　　　　　　yí wàn liǎng qiān sān bǎi sìshíwǔ

25,000 (2'5000)　　两万五千
　　　　　　　　　　liǎng wàn wǔ qiān

340,876 (34'0876)　　三十四万零八百七十六
　　　　　　　　　　sānshísì wàn líng bā bǎi qīshíliù

1,000,900,000 (10'0090'0000)　　十亿零九十万
　　　　　　　　　　shí yì líng jiǔshí wàn

4. Comparative Sentences with 比 (bǐ) (II) [See also Grammar 1 in Lesson 11.]

In a sentence where 比 (bǐ) is used, a numeral + measure word combination can be placed after the adjective to indicate the disparity.

A + 比 (bǐ) + B + Adjective + Numeral + Measure Word + Noun

❶ 我们班比你们班多四个学生。

Wǒmen bān bǐ nǐmen bān duō sì ge xuésheng.

(Our class is larger than yours by four students.)

❷ 这件衬衫比那件衬衫贵二十块钱。

Zhè jiàn chènshān bǐ nà jiàn chènshān guì èrshí kuài qián.)

(This shirt is twenty dollars more expensive than that shirt.)

❸ 我的房租比你的便宜五百块。

Wǒ de fángzū bǐ nǐ de piányi wǔ bǎi kuài.

(My rent is five hundred dollars cheaper than yours.)

❹ 我表弟比我小三岁。

Wǒ biǎodì bǐ wǒ xiǎo sān suì.

(My cousin is three years younger than I.)

Language Practice

H. Big Sale

A furniture store is having a big sale. Compare the original prices and the sale prices, and figure out with a partner what discount the store is offering on each item.

EXAMPLE:

→   A: 这张床打几折？   Zhè zhāng chuáng dǎ jǐ zhé?

B: 这张床打八折。   Zhè zhāng chuáng dǎ bā zhé.

1.

2.

3.

4.

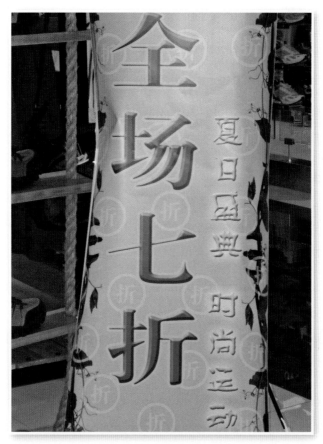

在这个商店买东西，可以打几折？
Zài zhè ge shāngdiàn mǎi dōngxi, kěyǐ dǎ jǐ zhé?

I. Being Flexible and Accommodating

Mr. Li has just started dating Ms. Wang. He tries to be very nice and asks Ms. Wang what she would like to do, where she would like to go, etc. Ms. Wang is trying to be nice, too, so she leaves it to Mr. Li to decide. Do a role play with a partner, and see if you two can settle on a day, time, place, and activity.

EXAMPLE: Pick a place to go.

→ 李先生：你想去
　　　　　哪儿玩儿？

　 王小姐：你想去哪儿
　　　　　玩儿，我就
　　　　　去哪儿玩儿。

Lǐ xiānsheng: Nǐ xiǎng qù
　　　　　　　nǎr wánr?

Wáng xiǎojiě: Nǐ xiǎng qù nǎr
　　　　　　　 wánr, wǒ jiù
　　　　　　　 qù nǎr wánr.

1. Find out what she is interested in.

2. Find out what cuisine she prefers.

3. Find out when she would like to see a movie.

4. Find out which city she would like to travel to.

J. I Almost Forgot!

1. You have just said goodbye to your friend, but suddenly it occurs to you that you need to borrow a Chinese book from him. What do you say?

2. You have been talking to your mom on the phone to ask for more money, and she has granted your request. You've just said "Thanks," but it occurs to you that you should mention your plan to travel to China for the summer and ask for your mom's opinion.

3. You are on the phone with your travel agency and have just booked your flight. Before you hang up the phone, it occurs to you that you should ask for a seat assignment.

K. Who Got a Better Deal?

Compare notes with your partner and find out the differences in what you pay for rent, security deposit, and utilities. Then report to the class.

1. 房租   fángzū

2. 押金   yājīn

3. 水电费   shuǐ diàn fèi

L. Don't Leave Any Questions Out!

Divide the class into two groups, one of travelers and the other of travel agents.

Travelers:

As an experienced traveler, what questions will you ask when you make a flight reservation? Make your list as detailed as possible.

1._____

2._____

3._____

4._____

5._____

…

Travel Agents:

As an experienced travel agent, what questions will you ask your customer when he/she books a flight? Make your list as detailed as possible.

1._____

2._____

3._____

4._____

5._____

…

After each group completes its list, the two groups should compare lists and see if any important questions have been left out. Then the whole class decides which list is more satisfactory.

M. Recap and Narrate

Working with a partner, ask and answer the following questions based on Dialogue II.

1. 王朋给哪个旅行社打电话？

   1. Wáng Péng gěi nǎ ge lǚxíngshè dǎ diànhuà?

2. 王朋要买什么时候、什么样的机票？

   2. Wáng Péng yào mǎi shénme shíhou, shénme yàng de jīpiào?

3. 王朋要买哪家航空公司的机票？

   3. Wáng Péng yào mǎi nǎ jiā hángkōng gōngsī de jīpiào?

4. 旅行社的人说机票
   多少钱？

   4. Lǚxíngshè de rén shuō jīpiào duōshao qián?

5. 王朋买了哪家
   航空公司的机票？

   5. Wáng Péng mǎi le nǎ jiā hángkōng gōngsī de jīpiào?

6. 王朋和李友哪天
   走，哪天回来？

   6. Wáng Péng hé Lǐ Yǒu nǎ tiān zǒu, nǎ tiān huí lai?

7. 王朋要什么样的
   位子？

   7. Wáng Péng yào shénme yàng de wèizi?

8. 王朋给李友订了
   什么？

   8. Wáng Péng gěi Lǐ Yǒu dìng le shénme?

Using the words and phrases in blue as prompts, connect your answers above to form a narrative like this example:

王朋打电话给旅行社订机票。他要买两张去北京的往返票，六月十号走，七月十五号回来。虽然西北航空公司在打折，但是得转机，中国国际航空公司只比西北航空公司贵四十块钱，可是不用转机，所以他买了国航的票。他订了靠走道的位子，还给李友订了一份素餐。

Wáng Péng dǎ diànhuà gěi lǚxíngshè dìng jīpiào. Tā yào mǎi liǎng zhāng qù Běijīng de wǎngfǎn piào, liùyuè shí hào zǒu, qīyuè shíwǔ hào huí lai. Suīrán Xīběi Hángkōng Gōngsī zài dǎ zhé, dànshì děi zhuǎn jī, Zhōngguó Guójì Hángkōng Gōngsī zhǐ bǐ Xīběi Hángkōng Gōngsī guì sìshí kuài qián, kěshì búyòng zhuǎn jī, suǒyǐ tā mǎi le Guóháng de piào. Tā dìng le kào zǒudào de wèizi, hái gěi Lǐ Yǒu dìng le yí fèn sùcān.

HOW ABOUT YOU?

What are the "must haves" when you travel?

1.	现金	xiànjīn	n	cash
2.	证件	zhèngjiàn	n	ID; document
3.	照相机	zhàoxiàngjī	n	camera

Is there anything else you must have when you travel? Please ask your teacher and make a note here:

_____

What would make your flight more comfortable?

1.	头等舱	tóuděngcāng	n	first class
2.	商务舱	shāngwùcāng	n	business class
3.	阿司匹林	āsīpīlín	n	aspirin
4.	枕头	zhěntou	n	pillow
5.	毯子	tǎnzi	n	blanket

公务舱就是商务舱。
Gōngwùcāng jiùshì shāngwùcāng.

Any other things that would make your flight more comfortable? Please ask your teacher and make a note here:

_____

Culture Highlights

❶ Most travel agencies in China belong to three travel agency groups targeting different types of tourists: International Travel Agencies (国际旅行社 Guójì Lǚxíngshè) or 国旅 (Guó Lǚ); China Travel Agencies (中国旅行社 Zhōngguó Lǚxíngshè) or 中旅 (Zhōng Lǚ); and Youth Travel Agencies (青年旅行社 Qīngnián Lǚxíngshè), also known as 青旅 (Qīng Lǚ). While 国旅 (Guó Lǚ) and 中旅 (Zhōng Lǚ) mainly serve foreign tourists and overseas Chinese respectively, 青旅 (Qīng Lǚ) is primarily oriented toward Chinese citizens.

北京青旅股份有限公司

中国旅行社总社 控股 中旅体育

❷ The busiest travel season in China is January and February, when millions upon millions of people travel to join their families or friends for the Chinese New Year. Railroad remains the major means of domestic travel. During the Chinese New Year period, all the railroad stations across the country are overcrowded with travelers awaiting their trains or seeking tickets. There are four different classes of train tickets: for carriages with hard seats (硬座 yìng zuò), cushioned seats (软座 ruǎn zuò), hard sleeping berths (硬卧 yìng wò), or cushioned sleeping berths (软卧 ruǎn wò). In recent decades, in the wake of the rapid growth of China's aviation industry, airplane travel has become an increasingly competitive option for domestic travelers.

English Text

Dialogue I

Wang Peng: Li You, time flies. It'll be break soon. Some of our classmates are going to summer school; some of them are going to intern at different companies. Some will go home and work. What are your plans?

Li You: I haven't decided. What about you, Wang Peng?

Wang Peng: I plan to go back to Beijing to see my parents.

Li You: Really? I hear that Beijing is a really interesting city.

Wang Peng: Of course. Beijing is China's capital, and it's also China's political and cultural center with lots of famous historic sites.

Li You: That's right. The Great Wall is very famous.

Wang Peng: And there are tons of great restaurants in Beijing.

Li You: Really? I've been to Hong Kong and Taipei, but I've never been to Beijing. I wish I could go to Beijing.

Wang Peng: Why don't you go with me? I could be your guide.

Li You: Really? That would be great! I already have a passport. I'll have to apply for a visa at once.

Wang Peng: I'll give the travel agency a call right away and get the plane tickets.

Dialogue II

Travel Agent: Tianyi Travel Agency, good morning.

Wang Peng: Good morning. How much is a ticket to Beijing for the beginning of June?

Travel Agent: One way or round trip?

Wang Peng: Two round trip tickets.

Travel Agent: Which airline?

Wang Peng: I'll get whichever airline is the least expensive.

Travel Agent: Please wait a moment. Let me check. Quite a few airlines fly there. Air China, $1,500, direct flight. Northwest is having a sale. About $1,460, but you have to change planes.

Wang Peng: Northwest is only $40 cheaper than China Airlines. I'll go with China Airlines.

Travel Agent: What are the dates for departure and return?

Wang Peng: Departing on June 10, returning on July 15. Can I reserve seats now?

Travel Agent: Yes, you can. Do you prefer window or aisle seats?

Wang Peng: Aisle seats. Oh, that's right, my friend is a vegetarian. Could you please order vegetarian meals for her?

Travel Agent: No problem. While in Beijing, do you need to make reservations for a hotel or car rental?

Wang Peng: No, thank you.

PROGRESS CHECKLIST

Before proceeding to Lesson 20, be sure you can complete the following tasks in Chinese:

I am able to—

- ☑ Describe my travel, study, and/or work plans for the summer;
- ☐ Give a basic description of Beijing;
- ☐ Make a travel reservation by giving my travel dates, asking for airfares, and comparing options;
- ☐ Inquire about seat assignments and special meal orders;
- ☐ Express a commercial discount.

这儿卖什么保险？
Zhèr mài shénme bǎoxiǎn?

LESSON 20

At the Airport

第二十课 在机场

Dì èrshí kè   Zài jīchǎng

 LEARNING OBJECTIVES

In this lesson, you will learn to use Chinese to

- Check in at the airport;
- Wish departing friends a safe journey and remind them to keep in touch;
- Greet guests at the airport;
- Compliment someone on his or her language ability;
- Ask about someone's health;
- Remind people to move on to the next event.

 RELATE AND GET READY

In your own culture/community—

1. What do people say when seeing someone off on a trip?
2. During the summer, do people prefer to fly or take road trips?
3. What do people say to their guests when greeting them at the airport, train, or bus station?
4. What are some local foods that your guests from elsewhere should try?

Dialogue I: Checking In at the Airport

（在国航的服务台）

 小姐，这是我们的^①
机票。

请把护照给我看看。
你们有几件行李要
托运？

两件。这个包不托
运，我们带上飞机。

麻烦您把箱子拿
上来。

小姐，没超重吧？

LANGUAGE NOTES

❶ When asking others for help, one polite way is to begin the request with 麻烦 (máfan).

没有。这是你们的护照、机票，这是登机牌。请到五号登机口上飞机。

谢谢。

*　*　*

哥哥，你们去北京了，就我一个人在这儿。

小红，别哭，我们几个星期就回来，你好好儿地学英文，别乱跑。

不是几个星期就回来，是几个星期以后才回来。

别担心，我姐姐小音会照顾你。

对，别担心。

飞机几点起飞？

中午十二点，还有两个多小时。

白英爱，你什么时候去纽约实习？

我不去纽约了。文中帮我在加州找了一份实习工作。

 The Chinese word for boarding pass is either 登机牌 (dēngjīpái, lit., boarding card) or 登机证 (dēngjīzhèng, lit., boarding certificate).

 In mainland China, boarding gates are called 登机口 (dēngjīkǒu). In Taiwan and Hong Kong, they are called 登机门 (dēngjīmén) and 闸口 (zhákǒu) respectively.

对，我们下个星期开车去加州。

 是吗？一边儿开车，一边儿玩儿，太好了。

 开车小心。祝你们玩儿得^① 高兴。

 祝你们一路平安。到了北京以后^②，别忘了给我们发个电子邮件。

 好，那我们秋天见。

 下个学期见。

 再见!

 (Zài Guóháng de fúwùtái)

 Xiǎojiě, zhè shì wǒmen de^① jīpiào.

 Qǐng bǎ hùzhào gěi wǒ kàn kan. Nǐmen yǒu jǐ jiàn xíngli yào tuōyùn?

 Liǎng jiàn. Zhè ge bāo bù tuōyùn, wǒmen dài shang fēijī.

 Máfan❶ nín bǎ xiāngzi ná shang lai.

 Xiǎojiě, méi chāozhòng ba?

 Méiyǒu. Zhè shì nǐmen de hùzhào, jīpiào, zhè shì dēngjīpái^②. Qǐng dào wǔ hào dēngjīkǒu^③ shàng fēijī.

  Xièxie.

* * *

 Gēge, nǐmen qù Běijīng le, jiù wǒ yí ge rén zài zhèr.

 Xiǎo Hóng, bié kū, wǒmen jǐ ge xīngqī jiù huí lai, nǐ hǎohāor de^① xué Yīngwén, bié luàn pǎo.

 Bú shì jǐ ge xīngqī jiù huí lai, shì jǐ ge xīngqī yǐhòu cái huí lai.

 Bié dān xīn, wǒ jiějie Xiǎoyīn huì zhàogu nǐ.

Duì, bié dān xīn.

Fēijī jǐ diǎn qǐfēi?

Zhōngwǔ shí'èr diǎn, hái yǒu liǎng ge duō xiǎoshí.

 Bái Yīng'ài, nǐ shénme shíhou qù Niǔyuē shíxí?

 Wǒ bú qù Niǔyuē le. Wénzhōng bāng wǒ zài Jiāzhōu zhǎo le yí fèn shíxí gōngzuò.

 Duì, wǒmen xià ge xīngqī kāi chē qù Jiāzhōu.

 Shì ma? Yìbiānr kāi chē, yìbiānr wánr, tài hǎo le.

 Kāi chē xiǎoxīn. Zhù nǐmen wánr de① gāoxìng.

 Zhù nǐmen yí lù píng'ān. Dào le Běijīng yǐhòu②, bié wàng le gěi wǒmen fā ge diànzǐ yóujiàn.

 Hǎo, nà wǒmen qiūtiān jiàn.

 Xià ge xuéqī jiàn.

 Zàijiàn!

这是一张登机牌。
Zhè shì yì zhāng dēngjīpái.

VOCABULARY

1.	行李	xíngli	n	luggage
2.	托运	tuōyùn	v	to check (luggage)
3.	包	bāo	n	bag; sack; bundle; package
4.	箱子	xiāngzi	n	suitcase; box
5.	超重	chāozhòng	v	to be overweight (of luggage, freight, etc.)
	超	chāo	v	to exceed; to surpass
6.	登机牌	dēngjīpái	n	boarding pass
	牌	pái	n	plate; tablet; card
7.	登机口	dēngjīkǒu	n	boarding gate
	口	kǒu	n	opening; entrance; mouth
8.	哭	kū	v	to cry; to weep
9.	地	de	p	(particle to link adverbial and verb) [See Grammar 1.]
10.	照顾	zhàogu	v	to look after; to care for; to attend to
11.	起飞	qǐfēi	v	(of airplanes) to take off
12.	小心	xiǎoxīn	v	to be careful
13.	一路平安	yí lù píng'ān		have a good trip; bon voyage

Grammar

1. 的 (de), 得 (de), 地 (de) Compared

A. 的 (de) usually follows an attributive but not an adverbial. The attributive can be formed by an adjective, a noun, or a verbal phrase.

❶ 漂亮的女孩子

piàoliang de nǚháizi

(pretty girl)

❷ 哥哥的公司

gēge de gōngsī

(older brother's company)

❸ 我的卧室

wǒ de wòshì

(my bedroom)

❹ 刚买的机票

gāng mǎi de jīpiào

(a recently purchased plane ticket)

❺ 妈妈给我们做的蛋糕

māma gěi wǒmen zuò de dàngāo

(the cake Mom made for us)

In most cases, 的 (de) is followed by a noun, as seen in (1) to (5), but it can also precede an adjective or verb if that adjective or verb serves as the subject or object in the sentence.

❻ 南京的热[是有名的]。

Nánjīng de rè [shì yǒumíng de].

(Nanjing's heat/That Nanjing is hot [is well-known].)

❼   他的死 [大家最近才听说]。

Tā de sǐ [dàjiā zuìjìn cái tīngshuō].

(His death/That he has died [became known to everyone only recently].)

B. 地 (de) links an adverb or adverbial to a following verb. An adjective, an adverb, or a set phrase can serve as an adverbial if followed by 地 (de).

❶   慢慢儿地吃

mànmānr de chī

(to eat slowly)

❷   很高兴地说

hěn gāoxìng de shuō

(to say happily)

❸   一直地走

yìzhí de zǒu

(to walk straight forward)

❹   好好儿地玩儿

hǎohāor de wánr

(to have some real fun)

C. 得 is used after a verb or an adjective to connect it with a descriptive complement or a complement of degree.

❶   跑得很快

pǎo de hěn kuài

(to run fast)

❷   做菜做得很好

zuò cài zuò de hěn hǎo

(to cook well)

❸   高兴得跳起來

gāoxìng de tiào qǐ lái

(to leap up with joy)

❹   危险得不得了

wēixiǎn de bù déliǎo

(unbelievably dangerous)

Compare the following two sentences:

❺   他高兴地唱着歌走回宿舍。

Tā gāoxìng de chàng zhe gē zǒu hui sùshè.

(He sang happily on his way back to the dorm.)

❻   他高兴得唱起歌来了。

Tā gāoxìng de chàng qi gē lai le.

(He was so happy that he started to sing.)

In (5) 高兴 (gāoxìng) is used to describe the manner of his singing. In (6) 高兴 (gāoxìng) is the cause of his singing.

A Quick Reference Table for 的，地，得 (de, de, de)

Attributive	+	的 (de)	+	Noun
Adverbial	+	地 (de)	+	Verb
Verb/Adj	+	得 (de)	+	Adj/Verb

2. ···的时候 (...de shíhou) **and** ···以后 (...yǐhòu) **Compared**

In a sentence of the pattern "V1 的时候 (de shíhou),V2...," the second action and the first action take place simultaneously.

❶   走的时候别忘了带些钱。

Zǒu de shíhou bié wàng le dài xiē qián.

(Don't forget to take some money with you when you leave.)

❷ 我看见他的时候，他正在打球。

Wǒ kàn jiàn tā de shíhou, tā zhèngzài dǎ qiú.

(When I saw him, he was playing ball.)

❸ 妹妹看短信的时候，一边看一边笑。

Mèimei kàn duǎnxìn de shíhou, yìbiān kàn yìbiān xiào.

(When my little sister was reading the text messages, she smiled as she read along.)

However, in a sentence of the pattern "V1 以后 (yǐhòu), V2...," the second action takes place after the first one.

❹ 他走了以后，才想起来忘了带钱。

Tā zǒu le yǐhòu, cái xiǎng qi lai wàng le dài qián.

(He didn't realize until after he had left that he had forgotten to take any money with him.)

The ⋯的时候 (de shíhou) structure describes two simultaneous actions. One may say in English, "When I get to China, I will eat Beijing roast duck," when one really means, "After I get to China, I'll eat Beijing roast duck." In Chinese, that idea has to be conveyed with 以后 (yǐhòu):

❺ 我到中国以后要吃北京烤鸭。

Wǒ dào Zhōngguó yǐhòu yào chī Běijīng kǎoyā.

(I will eat some Beijing roast duck after I arrive in China.)

[烤鸭 (kǎoyā, roast duck) See Dialogue II.]

(5a) *我到中国的时候要吃北京烤鸭。

*Wǒ dào Zhōngguó de shíhou yào chī Běijīng kǎoyā.

[This sentence is incorrect because you won't eat Beijing roast duck until *after* you arrive in China.]

Language Practice

A. Rules Are Rules

Parents and teachers always seem to have more rules for their children and students. Work with a partner and figure out what the rules are, based on the visuals.

EXAMPLE:

做功课的时候，

不准/不能看电视。

Zuò gōngkè de shíhou,

bù zhǔn/bù néng kàn diànshì.

1.

2.

3.

4.

B. Before or After

Work with a partner and find out when Wang Peng normally takes a shower, takes his medicine, goes online, and cleans his room.

EXAMPLE:

A: 王朋平常什么时候做功课？

Wáng Péng píngcháng shénme shíhou zuò gōngkè?

B: 他平常吃了晚饭以后做功课。

Wáng Péng píngcháng chī le wǎnfàn yǐhòu zuò gōngkè.

1.

2.

3.

4.

C. Heading to the Airport

Unlike Li You, you may not have a Chinese friend to accompany you on your trip to China and be your interpreter or tour guide. Work with a partner to make a list of questions and responses that may come in handy when you check in at a Chinese airline counter.

D. Before the School Break

Go around the classroom and ask each of your classmates about his/her summer plans, and how long the activities he/she has planned will last. Remind him/her to keep in touch, and give appropriate good wishes before moving on to the next person.

E. Recap and Narrate

Working with a partner, recap the content of the text:

1. 王朋和李友托运行李了吗？

   1. Wáng Péng hé Lǐ Yǒu tuōyùn xíngli le ma?

2. 他们在几号登机口上飞机？

   2. Tāmen zài jǐ hào dēngjīkǒu shàng fēijī?

3. 谁去机场送王朋和李友？

   3. Shéi qù jīchǎng sòng Wáng Péng hé Lǐ Yǒu?

4. 王红为什么哭了？

   4. Wáng Hóng wèishénme kū le?

5. 王朋让王红做什么？

   5. Wáng Péng ràng Wáng Hóng zuò shénme?

6. 王红觉得王朋和李友去北京的时间长吗？

   6. Wáng Hóng juéde Wáng Péng hé Lǐ Yǒu qù Běijīng de shíjiān cháng ma?

7. 飞机几点起飞？

   7. Fēijī jǐ diǎn qǐfēi?

8. 白英爱和高文中暑假做什么？

   8. Bái Yīng'ài hé Gāo Wénzhōng shǔjià zuò shénme?

9. 王朋和李友上飞机以前，大家都说了些什么？

9. Wáng Péng hé Lǐ Yǒu shàng fēijī yǐqián, dàjiā dōu shuō le xiē shéme?

Using the words and phrases in blue as prompts, connect your answers above to form a narrative like this example:

王朋和李友要去北京了，在机场他们托运了两件行李，要在五号登机口上飞机。王红、高文中和白英爱去送他们。王红哭了，因为她的父母在北京，哥哥也要去北京了。王朋让妹妹跟小音好好儿练习英文。高文中帮白英爱在加州找了一份工作，他们下个星期要开车去加州。王朋对他们俩说开车要小心，他们对王朋和李友说一路平安。大家说秋天见，下个学期见。

Wáng Péng hé Lǐ Yǒu yào qù Běijīng le, zài jīchǎng tāmen tuōyùn le liǎng jiàn xíngli, yào zài wǔ hào dēngjīkǒu shàng fēijī. Wáng Hóng, Gāo Wénzhōng hé Bái Yīng'ài qù sòng tāmen. Wáng Hóng kū le, yīnwèi tā de fùmǔ zài Běijīng, gēge yě yào qù Běijīng le. Wáng Péng ràng mèimei gēn Xiǎoyīn hǎohāor liànxí Yīngwén. Gāo Wénzhōng bāng Bái Yīng'ài zài Jiāzhōu zhǎo le yí fèn gōngzuò, tāmen xià ge xīngqī yào kāi chē qù Jiāzhōu. Wáng Péng duì tāmen liǎ shuō kāi chē yào xiǎoxīn, tāmen duì Wáng Péng hé Lǐ Yǒu shuō yí lù píng'ān. Dàjiā shuō qiūtiān jiàn, xià ge xuéqī jiàn.

Dialogue II: Arriving in Beijing

（在北京首都机场）

 小朋！

爸，妈！

累坏了吧?

还好③。爸，妈，我给
你们介绍一下，这是
我的同学李友。

叔叔，阿姨④❶，你们好。

欢迎你来北京。

李友，你的中文说得真好。

谢谢。是因为王朋教得好。

LANGUAGE NOTES

❶ One can address a person to
whom one is not related as 叔
叔 (shūshu, uncle) or 阿姨 (āyí,
aunt) if the person is about one's
parents' age. These respectful
forms of address can be applied
even to strangers.

哪里，是因为你聪明。

 哎，你们俩都聪明。

 小朋，你好像瘦了点儿。是不是打工太忙，没有时间吃饭？

 我没瘦。我常常运动，身体比以前棒多了。

 小红怎么样？

 她很好，英文水平提高了很多。

 走吧，我们上车以后，再慢慢儿地聊吧。爷爷、奶奶在烤鸭店等我们呢！

 烤鸭店？

(Zài Běijīng Shǒudū Jīchǎng)

 Xiǎo Péng!

 Bà, mā !

 Lèi huài le ba?

 Hái hǎo③. Bà, mā, wǒ gěi nǐmen jièshao yí xià, zhè shì wǒ de tóngxué Lǐ Yǒu.

 Shūshu, āyí④❶, nǐmen hǎo.

 Huānyíng nǐ lái Běijīng.

 Lǐ Yǒu, nǐ de Zhōngwén shuō de zhēn hǎo.

 Xièxie. Shì yīnwèi Wáng Péng jiāo de hǎo.

 Nǎli, shì yīnwèi nǐ cōngming.

 Āi, nǐmen liǎ dōu cōngming.

 Xiǎo Péng, nǐ hǎoxiàng shòu le diǎnr. Shì bu shì dǎ gōng tài máng, méiyǒu shíjiān chī fàn?

Wǒ méi shòu. Wǒ chángcháng yùndòng, shēntǐ bǐ yǐqián bàng duō le.

 Xiǎo Hóng zěnmeyàng?

 Tā hěn hǎo, Yīngwén shuǐpíng tígāo le hěn duō.

 Zǒu ba, wǒmen shàng chē yǐhòu, zài mànmānr de liáo ba. Yéye, nǎinai zài kǎoyā diàn děng wǒmen ne!

 Kǎoyā diàn?

VOCABULARY

1.	叔叔	shūshu	n	uncle [See Grammar 4.]
2.	阿姨	āyí	n	aunt [See Grammar 4.]
3.	欢迎	huānyíng	v	to welcome
4.	瘦	shòu	adj	thin, slim (usually of a person or animal); lean
5.	爷爷	yéye	n	paternal grandfather [See Grammar 4.]
6.	奶奶	nǎinai	n	paternal grandmother [See Grammar 4.]
7.	烤鸭	kǎoyā	n	roast duck

Proper Noun

8.	首都机场	Shǒudū Jīchǎng	the Capital Airport (in Beijing)

Grammar

---

3. 还 (hái) + Positive Adjective

还 (hái) when used before a commendatory adjective may indicate that something is acceptable if not truly outstanding.

1   **A:** 你对那家旅馆的印象怎么样?

Nǐ duì nà jiā lǚguǎn de yìnxiàng zěnmeyàng?

(What was your impression of that hotel?)

B: 还好。

Hái hǎo.

(It's okay.)

2   这个厨房还可以，挺干净的。

Zhè ge chúfáng hái kěyǐ, tǐng gānjìng de.

(This kitchen is all right. It's pretty clean.)

3   那套公寓还行，带家具。

Nà tào gōngyù hái xíng, dài jiājù.

(That apartment is not too bad. It's furnished.)

4   那个饭馆的红烧牛肉和家常豆腐还不错。

Nà ge fànguǎn de hóngshāo niúròu hé jiācháng dòufu hái búcuò.

(That restaurant's beef braised in soy sauce and family-style tofu are pretty good.)

4. Kinship Terms

The system of kinship terms in Chinese is rather complicated, especially because Chinese people make a distinction between paternal and maternal relatives, older and younger siblings, even among differently related uncles and aunts, etc. The following is a list of Chinese kinship terms: [f]: indicates a more formal way of address; [n]: northern Chinese usage; [s]: southern Chinese usage.

A. Parents:

father; dad	爸爸	(bàba)	
	父亲	(fùqin)	[f]
mother; mom	妈妈	(māma)	
	母亲	(mǔqin)	[f]

B. Grandparents:

[paternal] grandfather	爷爷	(yéye)	
	祖父	(zǔfù)	[f]
[paternal] grandmother	奶奶	(nǎinai)	
	祖母	(zǔmǔ)	[f]
[maternal] grandfather	姥爷	(lǎoye)	[n]
	外公	(wàigōng)	[s]
	外祖父	(wàizǔfù)	[f]
[maternal] grandmother	姥姥	(lǎolao)	[n]
	外婆	(wàipó)	[s]
	外祖母	(wàizǔmǔ)	[f]

C. Uncles and aunts:

father's older brother	大爷	(dàye)	[n]
	伯伯	(bóbo)	
	伯父	(bófù)	[f]
father's older brother's wife	大妈	(dàmā)	
	大娘	(dàniáng)	
	伯母	(bómǔ)	[f]
father's younger brother	叔叔	(shūshu)	
	叔父	(shūfù)	[f]
father's younger brother's wife	婶婶	(shěnshen)	
	婶儿	(shěnr)	
father's sister	姑姑	(gūgu)	
	姑妈	(gūmā)	
father's sister's husband	姑父	(gūfù)	
	姑丈	(gūzhàng)	
mother's brother	舅舅	(jiùjiu)	
mother's brother's wife	舅妈	(jiùmā)	

mother's sister	姨	(yí)	[n]
	阿姨	(āyí)	
	姨妈	(yímā)	
mother's sister's husband	姨父	(yífu)	
	姨丈	(yízhàng)	

D. Brothers, sisters and their spouses:

older brother	哥哥	(gēge)
older brother's wife	嫂嫂	(sǎosao)
	嫂子	(sǎozi)
older sister	姐姐	(jiějie)
older sister's husband	姐夫	(jiěfu)
younger brother	弟弟	(dìdi)
younger brother's wife	弟妹	(dìmèi)
younger sister	妹妹	(mèimei)
younger sister's husband	妹夫	(mèifu)

E. Cousins:

father's brother's son older than oneself	堂哥	(tánggē)
father's brother's son younger than oneself	堂弟	(tángdì)
father's brother's daughter older than oneself	堂姐	(tángjiě)
father's brother's daughter younger than oneself	堂妹	(tángmèi)
other male cousin older than oneself	表哥	(biǎogē)
other male cousin younger than oneself	表弟	(biǎodì)
other female cousin older than oneself	表姐	(biǎojiě)
other female cousin younger than oneself	表妹	(biǎomèi)

F. Children and their spouses:

son	儿子	(érzi)
son's wife	儿媳妇	(érxífu)
daughter	女儿	(nǚ'ér)
daughter's husband	女婿	(nǚxu)

H. Grandchildren:

son's son	孙子	(sūnzi)
son's daughter	孙女	(sūnnǚ)
daughter's son	外孙	(wàisūn)
daughter's daughter	外孙女	(wàisūnnǚ)

Language Practice

F. Being Diplomatic

This is your friend Ellen after a complete fashion makeover. She wants your opinion on her new look. You don't like her new style, but you don't want to hurt her feelings, so you try to be tactful.

EXAMPLE:

Ellen: 你觉得我的
大衣怎么样？

Nǐ juéde wǒ de

dàyī zěnmeyàng?

You: 我觉得你的大衣
还不错/还行。

Wǒ juéde nǐ de dàyī

hái búcuò/hái xíng.

1.   **2.**   **3.**

G. My Dear Puppy!

You and your friend just adopted a puppy and are very attentive to its every move. You are extremely careful, and often think the puppy is either losing weight, or gaining weight. You are also worried that the puppy might be 1) tired, 2) thirsty, 3) hungry, 4) having a cold, 5) having a fever, etc. By the way, the puppy's name is 毛毛 (Máomao).

EXAMPLE:

哎，我觉得毛毛
好像瘦了/胖了。

Āi, wǒ juéde Máomao

hǎoxiàng shòu le/pàng le.

What other things will you say when you look at the puppy?

1. _____

2. _____

3. _____

4. _____

5. _____

H. Seeing a Friend Off

Brainstorm with your partner and list the things that people say to each other when saying goodbye at the airport or train station, e.g. "safe journey," "give us a call when you get there," "I'll be back soon," "Don't worry, I'll be fine," etc.

_____

_____

_____

Put the phrases you listed in a logical order. Based on your list, do a role-play of a seeing-off scenario.

I. Greeting Newly Arrived Guests

Brainstorm with your partner and list the things that people say to each other when greeting guests at the airport/train station, e.g. "Welcome to …," "Thank you for picking me up," "You must be exhausted after a long trip," "I'm okay, not too tired," "Let me help you with your luggage," etc.

_____

_____

_____

Put the phrases you listed in a logical order. Based on you list, do a role-play between a guest and a person who comes to pick up the guest.

J. Recap and Narrate

Working with a partner, recap the content of Dialogue II:

1. 谁去北京首都机场接王朋和李友？

   Shéi qù Běijīng Shǒudū Jīchǎng jiē Wáng Péng hé Lǐ Yǒu?

2. 王朋说他累不累？

   Wáng Péng shuō tā lèi bu lèi?

3. 王朋的妈妈说李友的中文怎么样？

   Wáng Péng de māma shuō Lǐ Yǒu de Zhōngwén zěnmeyàng?

4. 李友和王朋说李友的中文为什么这么好？

   Lǐ Yǒu hé Wáng Péng shuō Lǐ Yǒu de Zhōngwén wèishénme zhème hǎo?

5. 王朋的妈妈觉得王朋的身体怎么样？

   Wáng Péng de māma juéde Wáng Péng de shēntǐ zěnmeyàng?

6. 王朋说他的身体怎么样？

   Wáng Péng shuō tā de shēntǐ zěnmeyàng?

7. 王朋说他妹妹在美国怎么样？

   Wáng Péng shuō tā mèimei zài Měiguó zěnmeyàng?

8. 王朋的爷爷、奶奶在哪儿等他们呢？

   Wáng Péng de yéye, nǎinai zài nǎr děng tāmen ne?

9. 李友听说要去烤鸭店以后，为什么说"烤鸭店？"

   Lǐ Yǒu tīngshuō yào qù kǎoyā diàn yǐhòu, wèishénme shuō "kǎoyā diàn?"

Using the words and phrases in blue as prompts, connect your answers above to form a narrative like this example:

王朋和李友到北京以后，在首都机场看见了王朋的爸爸妈妈，王朋把李友介绍给他的父母。王朋的妈妈说李友中文说得很好，李友说是因为王朋教得好，王朋说是因为李友聪明。王朋的妈妈觉得王朋瘦了，是不是打工太累了？王朋说他不但没瘦，而且因为常常运动，身体比以前棒多了。王朋还说妹妹在美国很好，英文水平提高了很多。王朋的爸爸让他们快上车，因为王朋的爷爷、奶奶在烤鸭店等他们呢。李友吃素，她去烤鸭店吃什么呢？

Wáng Péng hé Lǐ Yǒu dào Běijīng yǐhòu, zài Shǒudū Jīchǎng kàn jiàn le Wáng Péng de bàba māma, Wáng Péng bǎ Lǐ Yǒu jièshào gěi tā de fùmǔ. Wáng Péng de māma shuō Lǐ Yǒu Zhōngwén shuō de hěn hǎo, Lǐ Yǒu shuō shì yīnwèi Wáng Péng jiāo de hǎo, Wáng Péng shuō shì yīnwèi Lǐ Yǒu cōngming. Wáng Péng de māma juéde Wáng Péng shòu le, shì bú shì dǎ gōng tài lèi le? Wáng Péng shuō tā búdàn méi shòu, érqiě yīnwèi chángcháng yùndòng, shēntǐ bǐ yǐqián bàng duō le. Wáng Péng hái shuō mèimei zài Měiguó hěn hǎo, Yīngwén shuǐpíng tígāo le hěn duō. Wáng Péng de bàba ràng tāmen kuài shàng chē, yīnwèi Wáng Péng de yéye, nǎinai zài kǎoyā diàn děng tāmen ne. Lǐ Yǒu chī sù, tā qù kǎoyā diàn chī shénme ne?

以前的烤鸭师傅
yǐqián de kǎoyā shīfu

现在的烤鸭师傅
xiànzài de de kǎoyā shīfu

HOW ABOUT YOU?

What airport facility is important to you?

1.	饮水器	yǐnshuǐqì	n	water dispenser
2.	免税商店	miǎn shuì shāngdiàn	n	duty-free shop
3.	航站楼	hángzhànlóu	n	concourse (of airport)
4.	海关	hǎiguān	n	customs

Any other airport facilities you would like to know to say? Please ask your teacher and make a note here:

_____

这个商店卖北京烤鸭吗?
Zhè ge shāngdiàn mài Běijīng kǎoyā ma?

Culture Highlights

1 For domestic flights in China, each passenger is allowed to check only one piece of luggage. Snacks or meals are usually served on domestic flights.

2 Originally a delicacy on imperial menus, Beijing roast duck boasts a history several centuries long. Now it is arguably the food item most emblematic of the culinary culture of northern China. Indeed, its reputation is well reflected in the Chinese saying that no visit to Beijing is complete without a visit to the Great Wall and a meal at a roast duck restaurant. The most famous roast duck restaurant in Beijing is 全聚德 (Quánjùdé), which was established in 1864.

English Text

Dialogue I

(At the Air China Counter)

Wang Peng: Miss, these are our tickets.

Airline staff: Please show me your passports. How many pieces of checked luggage do you have?

Wang Peng: Two. We won't check this bag. We'll take it on board.

Airline staff: Please put the suitcases up here.

Li You: Miss, they are not over the weight limit, I hope.

Airline staff: No, they're not. Here are your passports and tickets. These are your boarding passes. Please go to Gate 5 to board the plane.

Wang Peng: Thank you.

        *   *   *

Wang Hong: You're both leaving for Beijing. I'll be all alone here.

Wang Peng: Xiao Hong, don't cry. We'll be back in just a few weeks. Work hard on your English. Don't go running around.

Wang Hong: Be back in a few weeks? Won't be back till a few weeks later!

Gao Wenzhong: Don't worry. My sister Xiaoyin will take good care of you.

Li You: That's right. Don't worry.

Bai Ying'ai: When does the plane leave?

Wang Peng: 12:00 noon. There are two hours left.

Li You: Bai Ying'ai, when are you going to New York for your internship?

Bai Ying'ai: I'm not going to New York anymore. Wenzhong helped me get an internship in California.

Gao Wenzhong: That's right. We're driving to California next week.

Li You: Really? Driving and sightseeing at the same time, that's really wonderful.

Wang Peng: Drive carefully. Have fun!

Bai Ying'ai: Have a safe trip. Don't forget to email us after you arrive in Beijing.

Wang Peng: OK. See you in the fall then.

Gao Wenzhong: See you next semester.

Bai Ying'ai and
Wang Hong: Goodbye!

Dialogue II

(At the Beijing Capital Airport)

Wang Peng's Dad: Xiao Peng!

Wang Peng: Dad, Mom!

Mom: You must be really tired.

Wang Peng: Not really. Dad, Mom, let me introduce you... This is my classmate Li You.

Li You: Uncle, Aunt, how do you do?

Dad: Welcome to Beijing.

Mom: Li You, you speak Chinese wonderfully.

Li You: Thank you. It's because Wang Peng is a good teacher.

Wang Peng: You flatter me. It's because you're smart.

Dad: Hey, you're both smart.

Mom: Xiao Peng, you seem to have lost some weight. Is it because you were too busy working and had no time to eat?

Wang Peng: Mom, I haven't lost any weight. I exercise a lot. I'm much stronger than before.

Mom: How is Xiao Hong?

Wang Peng: She's great. Her English has really improved.

Dad: Let's go. We'll talk at leisure after we get in the car. Grandpa and Grandma are waiting for us at the roast duck restaurant.

Li You: Roast duck restaurant?

PROGRESS CHECKLIST

Before proceeding to Level 2, be sure you can complete the following tasks in Chinese:

I am able to—

- ☑ Check in for a flight and check my luggage at the airport counter;
- ☐ Wish others a safe journey;
- ☐ Greet out-of-town guests at the airport;
- ☐ Compliment someone on his/her language ability;
- ☐ Express concern about someone's health;
- ☐ Remind people to move on to the next engagement.

That's How the Chinese Say It!

A Review of Functional Expressions from Lessons 16–20

After gauging your progress and before moving on to the next phase, let's take a break and see how some of the functional expressions that you have encountered in the previous lessons really work!

I. 一言为定(yì yán wéi dìng, it's a deal; it's decided)

You say "一言为定" (yì yán wéi dìng) when you and your friends or business partners have reached a decision. By saying it, you remind all the other parties that the decision should be remembered and honored.

❶ A: 明年我们去中国，怎么样？

Míngnián wǒmen qù Zhōngguó, zěnmeyàng?

(We'll go to China next year. How about it?)

B: 好啊！

Hǎo a!

(That's great.)

A: 一言为定。

Yì yán wéi dìng.

(That settles it.)

❷ A: 考完试我们出去玩儿，好吗？

Kǎo wán shì wǒmen chū qu wánr, hǎo ma?

(After the exam let's go out and have some fun, all right?)

B: 太好了。你开车？

Tài hǎo le. Nǐ kāi chē?

(Wonderful! Will you drive?)

A: 没问题。

Méi wèntí.

(No problem.)

B: 一言为定。

Yì yán wéi dìng.

(It's a deal.)

A: 一言为定。

Yì yán wéi dìng.

(Deal.)

II. "Good," "Very good," "Excellent," "Extraordinary"

Here are some expressions to convey varying degrees of approval, in progressive order of intensity:

❶   他的中文不错。

Tā de Zhōngwén búcuò.

(His Chinese is quite good.)

❷   他的中文很好。

Tā de Zhōngwén hěn hǎo.

(His Chinese is very good.)

❸   他的中文好得很。

Tā de Zhōngwén hǎo de hěn.

(His Chinese is very, very good.)

❹   他的中文非常好。

Tā de Zhōngwén fēicháng hǎo.

(His Chinese is unusually good.)

❺   他的中文好极了。

Tā de Zhōngwén hǎo jí le.

(His Chinese is fantastic.)

❻   他的中文好得不得了。

Tā de Zhōngwén hǎo de bù dé liǎo.

(His Chinese is extraordinary.)

III. Greetings and Farewells

Greetings

❶   你好，老师！

Nǐ hǎo, lǎoshī!

(Hello, professor!)

❷   王先生，早上好！

Wáng xiānsheng, zǎoshang hǎo!

(Good morning, Mr. Wang!)

❸   早安！

Zǎo'ān!

(Good morning!)

In daily life, however, a common way to greet a person is by asking a casual question about what that person is doing at the moment:

❶   老李，上课去呀？

Lǎo Lǐ, shàng kè qu ya?

(Lao Li, going to class?)

[It looks like Lao Li is going to class.]

❷   小王，回家呀？

Xiǎo Wáng, huí jiā ya?

(Little Wang, going home?)

[Upon seeing someone wrapping up his things and leaving the office, or someone on his way home, for instance.]

❸ 爸爸，回来了？

Bàba, huí lai le?

(Dad, you're home?)

[Upon seeing one's father walking in the door, for instance.]

Saying goodbye to guests

❶ 再见！

Zàijiàn!

(Bye!)

❷ 明天见！

Míngtiān jiàn!

(See you tomorrow!)

❸ 回头见！

Huí tóu jiàn!

(See you later!)

❹ 慢走！

Màn zǒu!

(Take care!) [Literally, walk carefully!]

Upon finishing a meal before others

❶ 慢吃！

Màn chī!

(Take your time [to enjoy the meal]!)

❷ 慢用！

Màn yòng!

(Enjoy the meal!)

Any other useful expressions you would like to learn?

Please ask your teacher and make a note here:

_____

_____

Vocabulary Index (Chinese-English)

The Chinese-English index is alphabetized according to *pinyin*. Words containing the same Chinese characters are first grouped together. Homonyms appear in the order of their tonal pronunciation (i.e., first tones first, second tones second, third tones third, fourth tones fourth, and neutral tones last). Proper nouns from the dialogues and readings are shown in green. Supplementary vocabulary from the "How About You?" section is shown in blue.

Simplified	Traditional	Pinyin	Part of Speech	English	Lesson
A					
啊	啊	a	p	(a sentence-final particle)	6
阿司匹林	阿司匹林	āsīpǐlín	n	aspirin	19
阿姨	阿姨	āyí	n	aunt	20
哎	哎	āi	excl	(exclamatory particle to express surprise or dissatisfaction)	13
爱	愛	ài	v	to love; to like; to be fond of	14
安静	安静	ānjìng	adj	quiet	17
B					
把	把	bǎ	m	(measure word for bunches of things, and chairs)	14
把	把	bǎ	prep	(indicating a thing is disposed of)	15
爸爸	爸爸	bàba	n	father, dad	2
吧	吧	ba	p	(a sentence-final particle)	5
白菜	白菜	báicài	n	bok choy	12
白英爱	白英愛	Bái Yīng'ài	pn	(a personal name)	2
百	百	bǎi	nu	hundred	9
百事可乐	百事可樂	Bǎishìkělè	pn	Pepsi-Cola	5
班	班	bān	n	class	14
搬	搬	bān	v	to move	16
斑马线	斑馬線	bānmǎxiàn	n	zebra crossing; pedestrian crosswalk	13
半	半	bàn	nu	half; half an hour	3
半天	半天	bàntiān		half a day; a long time	18
办	辦	bàn	v	to handle; to do	11
办法	辦法	bànfǎ	n	method; way (of doing something)	15

Simplified	Traditional	Pinyin	Part of Speech	English	Lesson
办公室	辦公室	bàngōngshì	n	office	6
帮	幫	bāng	v	to help	6
棒	棒	bàng	adj	fantastic; super [colloq.]	18
包	包	bāo	n	bag; sack; bundle; package	20
保险	保險	bǎoxiǎn	n	insurance	15
抱	抱	bào	v	to hold or carry in the arms	18
报纸	報紙	bàozhǐ	n	newspaper	17
杯	杯	bēi	m	(measure word for cup and glass)	5
北	北	běi	n	north	13
北京	北京	Běijīng	pn	Beijing	1
被	被	bèi	prep	by	18
本	本	běn	m	(measure word for books)	14
本子	本子	běnzi	n	notebook	7
鼻子	鼻子	bízi	n	nose	14
笔	筆	bǐ	n	pen	7
比	比	bǐ	prep/v	(comparison marker); to compare	11
比赛	比賽	bǐsài	n/v	game; match; competition; to compete	18
遍	遍	biàn	m	(measure word for complete courses of an action or instances of an action)	15
表姐	表姐	biǎojiě	n	older female cousin	14
别	別	bié	adv	don't	6
别人	別人	biérén	n	other people; another person	4
冰茶	冰茶	bīngchá	n	iced tea	12
冰箱	冰箱	bīngxiāng	n	refrigerator	15
饼干	餅乾	bǐnggān	n	cookies; crackers	14
病人	病人	bìngrén	n	patient	15
不	不	bù	adv	not; no	1
不错	不錯	(bùcuò) búcuò	adj	pretty good	4
不但…而且…	不但…而且…	(bùdàn) búdàn…, érqiě…	conj	not only..., but also...	11
不过	不過	(bùguò) búguò	conj	however; but	9
不好意思	不好意思	bù hǎoyìsi		to feel embarrassed	10
不用	不用	(bùyòng) búyòng		need not	9

Simplified	Traditional	Pinyin	Part of Speech	English	Lesson
C					
才	才	cái	adv	not until, only then	5
菜	菜	cài	n	dishes, cuisine	3
参观博物馆	參觀博物館	cānguān bówùguǎn	vo	to visit a museum	16
餐厅	餐廳	cāntīng	n	dining room, cafeteria	8
草莓	草莓	cǎoméi	n	strawberry	14
厕所	廁所	cèsuǒ	n	restroom, toilet	15
茶	茶	chá	n	tea	5
查	查	chá	v	to check; to look into	19
差不多	差不多	chàbuduō	adv/adj	almost; nearly; similar	17
常常	常常	chángcháng	adv	often	4
常老师	常老師	Cháng lǎoshī	pn	Teacher Chang	6
长城	長城	Chángchéng	pn	the Great Wall	19
长短	長短	chángduǎn	n	length	9
唱歌（儿）	唱歌（兒）	chàng gē(r)	vo	to sing (a song)	4
唱卡拉OK	唱卡拉OK	chàng kǎlā'ōukēi	vo	to sing karaoke	16
场	場	chǎng	n	field	13
超重	超重	chāozhòng	v	to be overweight (of luggage, freight, etc.)	20
潮湿	潮濕	cháoshī	adj	wet; humid	11
吵	吵	chǎo	v/adj	to quarrel; noisy	17
炒面	炒麵	chǎomiàn	n	stir-fried noodles	12
衬衫	襯衫	chènshān	n	shirt	9
成	成	chéng	v	to become	16
城市	城市	chéngshì	n	city	10
吃	吃	chī	v	to eat	3
吃坏	吃壞	chī huài	vc	to get sick because of bad food	15
宠物	寵物	chǒngwù	n	pet	17
初	初	chū	n	beginning	19
出去	出去	chū qu	vc	to go out	11
出租	出租	chūzū	v	to rent out	17
出租汽车	出租汽車	chūzū qìchē	n	taxi	10
厨房	廚房	chúfáng	n	kitchen	17

Simplified	Traditional	Pinyin	Part of Speech	English	Lesson
除了···以外	除了···以外	chúle...yǐwài	conj	in addition to; besides	8
春天	春天	chūntiān	n	spring	11
穿	穿	chuān	v	to wear; to put on	9
窗户	窗户	chuānghu	n	window	19
次	次	cì	m	(measure word for frequency)	13
聪明	聰明	cōngming	adj	smart; bright; clever	14
从	從	cóng	prep	from	13
错	錯	cuò	adj	wrong	12

D

Simplified	Traditional	Pinyin	Part of Speech	English	Lesson
打棒球	打棒球	dǎ bàngqiú	vo	to play baseball	18
打车	打車	dǎ chē	vo	to take a taxi	10
打电话	打電話	dǎ diànhuà	vo	to make a phone call	6
打工	打工	dǎ gōng	vo	to work at a temporary job (often part time)	19
打喷嚏	打噴嚏	dǎ pēnti	vo	to sneeze	15
打乒乓球	打乒乓球	dǎ pīngpāngqiú	vo	to play table tennis	18
打球	打球	dǎ qiú	vo	to play ball	4
打扫	打掃	dǎsǎo	v	to clean up (a room, apartment or house)	16
打算	打算	dǎsuàn	v/n	to plan; plan	19
打太极拳	打太極拳	dǎ tàijíquán	vo	to do Tai Chi (a kind of traditional Chinese shadow boxing)	18
打折	打折	dǎ zhé	vo	to sell at a discount; to give a discount	19
打针	打針	dǎ zhēn	vo	to get an injection	15
大	大	dà	adj	big; old	3
大哥	大哥	dàgē	n	eldest brother	2
大家	大家	dàjiā	pr	everybody	7
大姐	大姐	dàjiě	n	eldest sister	2
大小	大小	dàxiǎo	n	size	9
大学生	大學生	dàxuéshēng	n	college student	2
大衣	大衣	dàyī	n	overcoat	9
带	帶	dài	v	to bring; to take; to carry; to come with	12

Simplified	Traditional	Pinyin	Part of Speech	English	Lesson
单程	單程	dānchéng	n	one-way trip	19
单行道	單行道	dānxíngdào	n	one-way street	13
担心	擔心	dān xīn	vo	to worry	18
蛋	蛋	dàn	n	egg	12
蛋糕	蛋糕	dàngāo	n	cake	14
蛋花汤	蛋花湯	dànhuātāng	n	egg drop soup	12
但是	但是	dànshì	conj	but	6
当	當	dāng	v	to serve as; to be	17
当然	當然	dāngrán	adv	of course	18
导游	導遊	dǎoyóu	n	tour guide	19
到	到	dào	v	to go to; to arrive	6
德国	德國	Déguó	pn	Germany	1
德文	德文	Déwén	pn	the German language	6
地	地	de	p	(particle to link adverbial and verb)	20
的	的	de	p	(a possessive or descriptive particle)	2
得	得	de	p	(a structural particle)	7
得	得	děi	mv	must; to have to	6
灯	燈	dēng	n	lamp; light	17
登机口	登機口	dēngjīkǒu	n	boarding gate	20
登机牌	登機牌	dēngjīpái	n	boarding pass	20
等	等	děng	v	to wait; to wait for	6
第	第	dì	prefix	(prefix for ordinal numbers)	7
弟弟	弟弟	dìdi	n	younger brother	2
地方	地方	dìfang	n	place	13
地铁	地鐵	dìtiě	n	subway	10
地图	地圖	dìtú	n	map	13
地下(通)道	地下(通)道	dìxià (tōng)dào	n	pedestrian underpass	13
点	點	diǎn	m	o'clock (lit. dot, point, thus "points on the clock")	3
点菜	點菜	diǎn cài	vo	to order food	12
点(儿)	點(兒)	diǎn(r)	m	a little, a bit; some	5

Simplified	Traditional	Pinyin	Part of Speech	English	Lesson
电	電	diàn	n	electricity	16
电脑	電腦	diànnǎo	n	computer	8
电视	電視	diànshì	n	television	4
电影	電影	diànyǐng	n	movie	4
电子邮件	電子郵件	diànzǐ yóujiàn	n	email	10
碟	碟	dié	n	disc; small plate, dish, saucer	11
订	訂	dìng	v	to reserve; to book (a ticket, a hotel room, etc.)	19
东	東	dōng	n	east	13
东京	東京	Dōngjīng	pn	Tokyo	13
东西	東西	dōngxi	n	things; objects	9
冬天	冬天	dōngtiān	n	winter	11
懂	懂	dǒng	v	to understand	7
都	都	dōu	adv	both; all	2
兜风	兜風	dōu fēng	vo	to go for a drive	16
豆腐	豆腐	dòufu	n	tofu; bean curd	12
肚子	肚子	dùzi	n	belly; abdomen	15
对	對	duì	adj	right; correct	4
对不起	對不起	duìbuqǐ	v	sorry	5
多	多	duō	adv	how many/much; to what extent	3
多	多	duō	adj	many; much	7
多少	多少	duōshao	qpr	how much/many	9

E

Simplified	Traditional	Pinyin	Part of Speech	English	Lesson
俄文	俄文	Éwén	pn	the Russian language	6
饿	餓	è	adj	hungry	12
儿子	兒子	érzi	n	son	2
二姐	二姐	èrji	n	second oldest sister	2

F

Simplified	Traditional	Pinyin	Part of Speech	English	Lesson
发短信	發短信	fā duǎnxìn	vo	to send a text message; (lit.) to send a short message	10
发烧	發燒	fā shāo	vo	to have a fever	15
发音	發音	fāyīn	n	pronunciation	8

Simplified	Traditional	Pinyin	Part of Speech	English	Lesson
法国	法國	Fǎguó	pn	France	1
法文	法文	Fǎwén	pn	the French language	6
饭	飯	fàn	n	meal; (cooked) rice	3
饭馆(儿)	飯館(兒)	fànguǎn(r)	n	restaurant	12
饭卡	飯卡	fànkǎ	n	meal card	12
饭桌	飯桌	fànzhuō	n	dining table	17
方便	方便	fāngbiàn	adj	convenient	6
房间	房間	fángjiān	n	room	16
房租	房租	fángzū	n	rent	17
放	放	fàng	v	to put; to place	12
放假	放假	fàng jià	vo	go on vacation; have time off	19
非常	非常	fēicháng	adv	very, extremely, exceedingly	11
飞机	飛機	fēijī	n	airplane	10
(飞)机场	(飛)機場	(fēi)jīchǎng	n	airport	10
费	費	fèi	v	to spend; to take (effort)	16
费	費	fèi	n	fee; expenses	17
分	分	fēn	m	(measure word for 1/100 of a kuai, cent)	9
分钟	分鐘	fēnzhōng	n	minute	17
粉红色	粉紅色	fěnhóngsè	n	pink	9
份	份	fèn	m	(measure word for meal order, job)	19
风	風	fēng	n	wind	11
封	封	fēng	m	(measure word for letters)	8
服务员	服務員	fúwùyuán	n	waiter; attendant	12
附近	附近	fùjìn	n	vicinity; neighborhood; nearby area	17
父母	父母	fùmǔ	n	parents; father and mother	19
父亲节	父親節	Fùqīnjié	pn	Father's Day	3
付钱	付錢	fù qián	vo	to pay money	9
复习	復習	fùxí	v	to review	7

Simplified	Traditional	Pinyin	Part of Speech	English	Lesson
G					
干净	乾淨	gānjìng	adj	clean	17
感恩节	感恩節	Gǎn'ēnjié	pn	Thanksgiving	3
感冒	感冒	gǎnmào	v	to have a cold	15
赶快	趕快	gǎnkuài	adv	right away; quickly; in a hurry	15
刚	剛	gāng	adv	just	12
刚才	剛才	gāngcái	t	just now; a moment ago	11
钢笔	鋼筆	gāngbǐ	n	fountain pen	7
高速公路	高速公路	gāosù gōnglù	n	highway	10
高文中	高文中	Gāo Wénzhōng	pn	(a personal name)	2
高小音	高小音	Gāo Xiǎoyīn	pn	(a personal name)	5
高兴	高興	gāoxìng	adj	happy, pleased	5
告诉	告訴	gàosu	v	to tell	8
哥哥	哥哥	gēge	n	older brother	2
个	個	gè/ge	m	(a measure word for many common everyday objects)	2
给	給	gěi	v	to give	5
给	給	gěi	prep	to; for	6
跟	跟	gēn	prep	with	6
更	更	gèng	adv	even more	11
宫保鸡丁	宮保雞丁	gōngbǎo jīdīng	n	Kung Pao chicken	12
工程师	工程師	gōngchéngshī	n	engineer	2
工人	工人	gōngrén	n	worker	2
工商管理	工商管理	gōngshāng guǎnlǐ	n	business management	8
工作	工作	gōngzuò	n/v	job; to work	2
公共汽车	公共汽車	gōnggòng qìchē	n	bus	10
公司	公司	gōngsī	n	company	19
公寓	公寓	gōngyù	n	apartment	17
公园	公園	gōngyuán	n	park	11
功课	功課	gōngkè	n	homework; schoolwork	7
狗	狗	gǒu	n	dog	14
够	夠	gòu	adj	enough	12
拐	拐	guǎi	v	to turn	13
广告	廣告	guǎnggào	n	advertisement	17

Simplified	Traditional	Pinyin	Part of Speech	English	Lesson
逛街	逛街	guàng jiē	vo	to windowshop	4
贵	貴	guì	adj	honorable; expensive	1
柜子	櫃子	guìzi	n	cabinet; cupboard	17
国际	國際	guójì	adj	international	18
果汁	果汁	guǒzhī	n	fruit juice	5
过	過	guò	v	to pass	13
过敏	過敏	guòmǐn	v	to be allergic to	15
过	過	guo	p	(particle used after a verb to indicate a past experience)	13
H					
还	還	hái	adv	also; too; as well	3
还是	還是	háishi	conj	or	3
孩子	孩子	háizi	n	child	2
海报	海報	hǎibào	n	poster	17
海关	海關	hǎiguān	n	customs	20
海伦	海倫	Hǎilún	pn	Helen	14
韩国	韓國	Hánguó	pn	South Korea	1
韩文	韓文	Hánwén	pn	the Korean language	6
寒假	寒假	hánjià	n	winter vacation	10
汉字	漢字	Hànzì	n	Chinese characters	7
航班	航班	hángbān	n	scheduled flight	19
航空	航空	hángkōng	n	aviation	19
航站楼	航站樓	hángzhànlóu	n	concourse (of airport)	20
好	好	hǎo	adj	fine; good; nice; O.K.; it's settled	1
好吃	好吃	hǎochī	adj	delicious	12
好几	好幾	hǎo jǐ		quite a few	15
好久	好久	hǎo jiǔ		a long time	4
好玩儿	好玩兒	hǎowánr	adj	fun, amusing, interesting	11
好像	好像	hǎoxiàng	v	to seem; to be like	12
号	號	hào	m	(measure word for number in a series; day of the month)	3
号	號	hào	n	size	9
号码	號碼	hàomǎ	n	number	16
喝	喝	hē	v	to drink	5

Simplified	Traditional	Pinyin	Part of Speech	English	Lesson
和	和	hé	conj	and	2
合适	合適	héshì	adj	suitable	9
黑	黑	hēi	adj	black	9
很	很	hěn	adv	very	3
红	紅	hóng	adj	red	9
红绿灯	紅綠燈	hónglǜdēng	n	traffic light	13
红烧	紅燒	hóngshāo	v	to braise in soy sauce	12
后来	後來	hòulái	t	later	8
后天	後天	hòutiān	t	the day after tomorrow	16
胡萝卜	胡蘿蔔	húluóbo	n	carrot	12
护照	護照	hùzhào	n	passport	19
花	花	huā	v	to spend	10
花	花	huā	n	flower	14
花粉	花粉	huāfěn	n	pollen	15
花生	花生	huāshēng	n	peanuts	15
滑冰	滑冰	huá bīng	vo	to ice skate	11
画画儿	畫畫兒	huà huàr	vo	to draw; to paint	4
化学	化學	huàxué	n	chemistry	8
欢迎	歡迎	huānyíng	v	to welcome	20
还	還	huán	v	to return (something)	17
换	換	huàn	v	to exchange; to change	9
黄	黃	huáng	adj	yellow	9
黄瓜	黃瓜	huánggua	n	cucumber	12
灰尘	灰塵	huīchén	n	dust	15
灰色	灰色	huīsè	n	gray	9
回家	回家	huí jiā	vo	to go home	5
回来	回來	huí lai	vc	to come back	6
回去	回去	huí qu	vc	to go back; to return	11
会	會	huì	mv	can; know how to	8
会	會	huì	mv	will	11
活动	活動	huódòng	n	activity	13
或者	或者	huòzhě	conj	or	10
护士	護士	hùshi	n	nurse	2

Simplified	Traditional	Pinyin	Part of Speech	English	Lesson
J					
鸡	雞	jī	n	chicken	12
极	極	jí	adv	extremely	12
几	幾	jǐ	nu	how many; some; a few	2
记得	記得	jìde	v	to remember	16
计划	計劃	jìhuà	n/v	plan; to plan	19
家	家	jiā	n	family; home	2
家常	家常	jiācháng	n	home-style	12
家具	傢具	jiājù	n	furniture	17
加拿大	加拿大	Jiā'nádà	pn	Canada	1
加州	加州	Jiāzhōu	pn	California	1, 11
夹克	夾克	jiákè	n	jacket	9
检查	檢查	jiǎnchá	v	to examine	15
简单	簡單	jiǎndān	adj	simple	18
件	件	jiàn	m	(measure word for shirts, dresses, jackets, coats, etc.)	9
见	見	jiàn	v	to see	3
见面	見面	jiàn miàn	vo	to meet up; to meet with	6
健康	健康	jiànkāng	adj/n	healthy; health	15
教	教	jiāo	v	to teach	7
脚	腳	jiǎo	n	foot	18
饺子	餃子	jiǎozi	n	dumplings (with vegetable and/or meat filling)	12
叫	叫	jiào	v	to be called; to call	1
教室	教室	jiàoshì	n	classroom	8
教授	教授	jiàoshòu	n	professor	2
接	接	jiē	v	to catch; to meet; to welcome	14
节	節	jié	m	(measure word for class periods)	6
姐姐	姐姐	jiějie	n	older sister	2
介绍	介紹	jièshào	v	to introduce	5
今年	今年	jīnnián	t	this year	3
今天	今天	jīntiān	t	today	3
紧张	緊張	jǐnzhāng	adj	nervous, anxious	10
近	近	jìn	adj	near	13

Simplified	Traditional	Pinyin	Part of Speech	English	Lesson
进	進	jìn	v	to enter	5
进来	進來	jìn lai	vc	to come in	5
经济	經濟	jīngjì	n	economics	8
经理	經理	jīnglǐ	n	manager	2
九月	九月	jiǔyuè	n	September	3
就	就	jiù	adv	precisely; exactly	6
就	就	jiù	adv	just; only (indicating a small number)	16
橘子	橘子	júzi	n	tangerine	14
橘红色	橘紅色	júhóngsè	n	orange (color)	9
觉得	覺得	juéde	v	to feel; to think	4
军人	軍人	jūnrén	n	soldier; military officer	2

K

Simplified	Traditional	Pinyin	Part of Speech	English	Lesson
咖啡	咖啡	kāfēi	n	coffee	5
咖啡色	咖啡色	kāfēisè	n	brown; coffee color	9
卡片	卡片	kǎpiàn	n	card	14
开车	開車	kāi chē	vo	to drive a car	10
开会	開會	kāi huì	vo	to have a meeting	6
开始	開始	kāishǐ	v/n	to begin, to start; beginning	7
看	看	kàn	v	to watch; to look; to read	4
看病	看病	kàn bìng	vo	to see a doctor; (of a doctor) to see a patient	15
考试	考試	kǎo shì	vo/n	to give or take a test; test	6
烤鸭	烤鴨	kǎoyā	n	roast duck	20
靠	靠	kào	v	to lean on; to lean against; to be next to	19
咳嗽	咳嗽	késòu	v	to cough	15
渴	渴	kě	adj	thirsty	12
可爱	可愛	kě'ài	adj	cute; lovable	14
可口可乐	可口可樂	Kěkǒukělè	pn	Coca-Cola	5
可乐	可樂	kělè	n	[Coke or Pepsi] cola	5
可能	可能	kěnéng	mv/adj	maybe; possible	17
可是	可是	kěshì	conj	but	3
可以	可以	kěyǐ	mv	can; may	5
刻	刻	kè	m	quarter (of an hour)	3

Simplified	Traditional	Pinyin	Part of Speech	English	Lesson
课	課	kè	n	class; course; lesson	6
课本	課本	kèběn	n	textbook	7
课文	課文	kèwén	n	text of a lesson	7
客气	客氣	kèqi	adj	polite	6
客厅	客廳	kètīng	n	living room	17
空(儿)	空(兒)	kòng(r)	n	free time	6
口	口	kǒu	m	(measure word for number of family members)	2
哭	哭	kū	v	to cry; to weep	20
酷	酷	kù	adj	cool	7
裤子	褲子	kùzi	n	pants	9
快	快	kuài	adv/adj	quickly; fast, quick	5
快乐	快樂	kuàilè	adj	happy	10
块	塊	kuài	m	(measure word for the basic Chinese monetary unit)	9
矿泉水	礦泉水	kuàngquánshuǐ	n	mineral water	5

L

Simplified	Traditional	Pinyin	Part of Speech	English	Lesson
拉丁文	拉丁文	Lādīngwén	pn	the Latin language	6
来	來	lái	v	to come	5
蓝	藍	lán	adj	blue	10
篮球	籃球	lánqiú	n	basketball	18
懒	懶	lǎn	adj	lazy	15
老师	老師	lǎoshī	n	teacher	1
了	了	le	p	(a dynamic particle)	5
累	累	lèi	adj	tired	8
冷	冷	lěng	adj	cold	11
离	離	lí	prep	away from	13
梨	梨	lí	n	pear	14
里边	裏邊	lǐbian	n	inside	13
礼物	禮物	lǐwù	n	gift; present	14
李友	李友	Lǐ Yǒu	pn	(a personal name)	1
力气	力氣	lìqi	n	strength; effort	16
历史	歷史	lìshǐ	n	history	8

Simplified	Traditional	Pinyin	Part of Speech	English	Lesson
俩	倆	liǎ	nu+m	(coll.) two	16
连	連	lián	prep	even	17
脸	臉	liǎn	n	face	14
练习	練習	liànxí	v	to practice	6
练习本	練習本	liànxíběn	n	exercise book	7
凉拌	涼拌	liángbàn	v	(of food) cold "blended"; cold tossed	12
凉快	涼快	liángkuai	adj	pleasantly cool	11
两	兩	liǎng	nu	two; a couple of	2
聊天(儿)	聊天(兒)	liáo tiān(r)	vo	to chat	5
零食	零食	língshí	n	snacks	14
另外	另外	lìngwài	conj	furthermore; in addition	17
流鼻涕	流鼻涕	liú bítì	vo	to have a runny nose	15
楼	樓	lóu	n	multi-storied building; floor (of a multi-level building)	14
路口	路口	lùkǒu	n	intersection	13
录音	錄音	lùyīn	n/vo	sound recording; to record	7
旅馆	旅館	lǚguǎn	n	hotel	19
旅行	旅行	lǚxíng	v	to travel	16
旅行社	旅行社	lǚxíngshè	n	travel agency	19
绿	綠	lǜ	adj	green	10
律师	律師	lǜshī	n	lawyer	2
乱	亂	luàn	adv	randomly; arbitrarily; messily	15

M

Simplified	Traditional	Pinyin	Part of Speech	English	Lesson
妈妈	媽媽	māma	n	mother, mom	2
马上	馬上	mǎshàng	adv	immediately; right away	19
吗	嗎	ma	qp	(question particle)	1
麻烦	麻煩	máfan	adj	troublesome	10
麻婆豆腐	麻婆豆腐	mápó dòufu	n	Mapo tofu	12
买	買	mǎi	v	to buy	9
卖完	賣完	mài wán	vc	to be sold out	12
慢	慢	màn	adj	slow	7
慢跑	慢跑	mànpǎo	v/n	to jog; jogging	18
忙	忙	máng	adj	busy	3

Simplified	Traditional	Pinyin	Part of Speech	English	Lesson
猫	貓	māo	n	cats	15
毛	毛	máo	m	(measure word for 1/10 of a kuai, dime (for US money))	9
毛笔	毛筆	máobǐ	n	writing brush	7
毛衣	毛衣	máoyī	n	woolen sweater	9
帽子	帽子	màozi	n	hat; cap	9
没	没	méi	adv	not	2
没关系	没關係	méi guānxi		it doesn't matter	12
每	每	měi	pr	every; each	10
美国	美國	Měiguó	pn	America	1
美式	美式	Měishì	adj	American-style	18
美元	美元	Měiyuán	n	U.S. currency	17
妹妹	妹妹	mèimei	n	younger sister	2
闷热	悶熱	mēnrè	adj	hot and stifling	11
米饭	米飯	mǐfàn	n	cooked rice	12
免税商店	免税商店	miǎn shuì shāngdiàn	n	duty-free shop	20
面试	面試	miànshì	v/n	to interview; interview	11
明天	明天	míngtiān	t	tomorrow	3
名胜古迹	名勝古蹟	míngshèng gǔjì		famous scenic spots and historic sites	19
名字	名字	míngzi	n	name	1
墨西哥	墨西哥	Mòxīgē	pn	Mexico	1
母亲节	母親節	Mǔqīnjié	pn	Mother's Day	3

N

Simplified	Traditional	Pinyin	Part of Speech	English	Lesson
拿	拿	ná	v	to take; to get	13
哪	哪	nǎ/něi	qpr	which	6
哪里	哪裏	nǎli	pr	where	7
哪儿	哪兒	nǎr	qpr	where	5
那	那	nà	pr	that	2
那	那	nà	conj	in that case; then	4
那里	那裏	nàli	pr	there	17
那么	那麼	nàme	pr	(indicating degree) so, such	11
那儿	那兒	nàr	pr	there	8

Simplified	Traditional	Pinyin	Part of Speech	English	Lesson
奶奶	奶奶	nǎinai	n	paternal grandmother	20
男	男	nán	adj	male	2
南	南	nán	n	south	13
难	難	nán	adj	difficult	7
难受	難受	nánshòu	adj	hard to bear; uncomfortable	18
呢	呢	ne	qp	(question particle)	1
能	能	néng	mv	can; to be able to	8
你	你	nǐ	pr	you	1
年级	年級	niánjí	n	grade in school	6
念	念	niàn	v	to read aloud	7
您	您	nín	pr	you (honorific for 你)	6
牛肉	牛肉	niúròu	n	beef	12
纽约	紐約	Niǔyuē	pn	New York	1
农民	農民	nóngmín	n	farmer; peasant	2
暖和	暖和	nuǎnhuo	adj	warm	11
女	女	nǚ	adj	female	2
女儿	女兒	nǚ'ér	n	daughter	2

P

Simplified	Traditional	Pinyin	Part of Speech	English	Lesson
怕	怕	pà	v	to fear; to be afraid of	18
拍	拍	pāi	n	racket	18
盘	盤	pán	n	plate; dish	12
旁边	旁邊	pángbiān	n	side	13
胖	胖	pàng	adj	fat	18
跑步	跑步	pǎo bù	vo	to jog	18
朋友	朋友	péngyou	n	friend	3
篇	篇	piān	m	(measure word for essays, articles, etc.)	8
便宜	便宜	piányi	adj	cheap; inexpensive`	9
片	片	piàn	m	(measure word for tablet; slice)	15
票	票	piào	n	ticket	10
漂亮	漂亮	piàoliang	adj	pretty	5
瓶	瓶	píng	m/n	(measure word for bottles); bottle	5
平常	平常	píngcháng	adv	usually	7

Simplified	Traditional	Pinyin	Part of Speech	English	Lesson
苹果	蘋果	píngguǒ	n	apple	14
葡萄	葡萄	pútao	n	grape	14
葡萄牙文	葡萄牙文	Pútáoyáwén	pn	the Portuguese language	6
Q					
骑摩托车	騎摩托車	qí mótuōchē	vo	to ride a motorcycle	10
骑自行车	騎自行車	qí zìxíngchē	vo	to ride a bicycle	10
起床	起床	qǐ chuáng	vo	to get up	8
起飞	起飛	qǐfēi	v	(of airplanes) to take off	20
气球	氣球	qìqiú	n	balloons	14
汽水(儿)	汽水(兒)	qìshuǐ(r)	n	soft drink; soda pop	5, 14
千	千	qiān	nu	thousand	19
铅笔	鉛筆	qiānbǐ	n	pencil	7
签证	簽證	qiānzhèng	n	visa	19
钱	錢	qián	n	money	9
前	前	qián	n	forward; ahead	13
前面	前面	qiánmian	n	ahead; in front of	13
青菜	青菜	qīngcài	n	green/leafy vegetable	12
清楚	清楚	qīngchu	adj	clear	12
情人节	情人節	Qíngrénjié	pn	Valentine's Day	3
晴天	晴天	qíngtiān	n	sunny day	11
请	請	qǐng	v	please (polite form of request); to treat or to invite (somebody)	1
请客	請客	qǐng kè	vo	to invite someone (to dinner, coffee, etc.); to play the host	4
秋天	秋天	qiūtiān	n	autumn; fall	11
去	去	qù	v	to go	4
去年	去年	qùnián	t	last year	14
裙子	裙子	qúnzi	n	skirt	9
R					
然后	然後	ránhòu	adv	then	10
让	讓	ràng	v	to allow or cause (somebody to do something)	10
热	熱	rè	adj	hot	11

Simplified	Traditional	Pinyin	Part of Speech	English	Lesson
人	人	rén	n	people; person	1
人民币	人民幣	rénmínbì	n	renminbi (RMB, Chinese currency)	17
认识	認識	rènshi	v	to be acquainted with; recognize	3
日本	日本	Rìběn	pn	Japan	1, 13
日记	日記	rìjì	n	diary	8
日文	日文	Rìwén	pn	the Japanese language	6, 13
容易	容易	róngyì	adj	easy	7
肉	肉	ròu	n	meat	12
如果…的话	如果…的話	rúguǒ… de huà	conj	if	9

S

Simplified	Traditional	Pinyin	Part of Speech	English	Lesson
沙发	沙發	shāfā	n	sofa	17
商店	商店	shāngdiàn	n	store; shop	9
商人	商人	shāngrén	n	merchant; businessperson	2
商务舱	商務艙	shāngwùcāng	n	business class	19
上	上	shàng	v	to go [colloq.]	13
上菜	上菜	shàng cài	vo	to serve food	12
上次	上次	shàng cì		last time	15
上大学	上大學	shàng dàxué	vo	to attend college/university	18
上个	上個	shàng ge		the previous one	7
上海	上海	Shànghǎi	pn	Shanghai	1, 12
上课	上課	shàng kè	vo	to go to a class; to start a class; to be in class	7
上网	上網	shàng wǎng	vo	to go online; to surf the internet	8
上午	上午	shàngwǔ	t	morning	6
上衣	上衣	shàngyī	n	upper garment	9
谁	誰	shéi	qpr	who	2
身体	身體	shēntǐ	n	body; health	15
什么	什麼	shénme	qpr	what	1
生病	生病	shēng bìng	vo	to get sick	15
生词	生詞	shēngcí	n	new words; vocabulary	7
生日	生日	shēngrì	n	birthday	3
师傅	師傅	shīfu	n	master worker	12

Simplified	Traditional	Pinyin	Part of Speech	English	Lesson
十八	十八	shíbā	nu	eighteen	3
十二	十二	shí'èr	nu	twelve	3
时候	時候	shíhou	n	(a point in) time; moment; (a duration of) time	4
时间	時間	shíjiān	n	time	6
实习	實習	shíxí	v	to intern	19
试	試	shì	v	to try	9
是	是	shì	v	to be	1
事(儿)	事(兒)	shì(r)	n	matter; affair; event	3
收	收	shōu	v	to receive; to accept	9
手	手	shǒu	n	hand	18
手机	手機	shǒujī	n	cell phone	10
首都	首都	shǒudū	n	capital city	19
首都机场	首都機場	Shǒudū Jīchǎng	pn	the Capital Airport (in Beijing)	20
瘦	瘦	shòu	adj	thin, slim (usually of a person or animal); lean	20
售货员	售貨員	shòuhuòyuán	n	shop assistant; salesclerk	9
书	書	shū	n	book	4
书店	書店	shūdiàn	n	bookstore	13
书架	書架	shūjià	n	bookcase; bookshelf	17
书桌	書桌	shūzhuō	n	desk	17
舒服	舒服	shūfu	adj	comfortable	11
叔叔	叔叔	shūshu	n	uncle	20
属	屬	shǔ	v	to belong to	14
暑假	暑假	shǔjià	n	summer vacation	19
暑期	暑期	shǔqī	n	summer term	14
数学	數學	shùxué	n	mathematics	8
刷卡	刷卡	shuā kǎ	vo	to pay with a credit card	9
帅	帥	shuài	adj	handsome	7
双	雙	shuāng	m	(measure word for a pair)	9
水	水	shuǐ	n	water	5
水果	水果	shuǐguǒ	n	fruit	14
水平	水平	shuǐpíng	n	level; standard	18
睡觉	睡覺	shuì jiào	vo	to sleep	4
说	說	shuō	v	to say; to speak	6

Simplified	Traditional	Pinyin	Part of Speech	English	Lesson
说话	說話	shuō huà	vo	to talk	7
送	送	sòng	v	to see off or out; to take (someone somewhere)	10
送	送	sòng	v	to give as a gift	14
素	素	sù	adj	vegetarian; made from vegetables	12
素餐	素餐	sùcān	n	vegetarian meal	19
宿舍	宿舍	sùshè	n	dormitory	8
酸	酸	suān	adj	sour	12
酸辣汤	酸辣湯	suānlàtāng	n	hot and sour soup	12
算了	算了	suàn le		forget it; never mind	4
虽然	雖然	suīrán	conj	although	9
岁	歲	suì	n	year (of age)	3
所以	所以	suǒyǐ	conj	so	4

T

Simplified	Traditional	Pinyin	Part of Speech	English	Lesson
T恤衫	T恤衫	T-xùshān	n	T-shirt	9
他	他	tā	pr	he; him	2
她	她	tā	pr	she; her	2
它	它	tā	pr	it	9
台北	台北	Táiběi	pn	Taipei	19
太…了	太…了	tài…le		too; extremely	3
毯子	毯子	tǎnzi	n	blanket	19
汤姆	湯姆	Tāngmǔ	pn	Tom	14
糖醋鱼	糖醋魚	tángcùyú	n	fish in sweet and sour sauce	12
糖（果）	糖（果）	táng (guǒ)	n	candy	14
躺下	躺下	tǎng xia	vc	to lie down	15
桃儿	桃兒	táor	n	peach	14
套	套	tào	m	(measure word for suite or set)	17
特别	特別	tèbié	adv	especially	10
疼死	疼死	téng sǐ	adj+c	really painful	15
踢	踢	tī	v	to kick	18
提高	提高	tígāo	v	to improve; to raise; to heighten	18
天	天	tiān	n	day	3
天气	天氣	tiānqì	n	weather	11

Simplified	Traditional	Pinyin	Part of Speech	English	Lesson
天桥	天橋	tiānqiáo	n	pedestrian overpass	13
甜	甜	tián	adj	sweet	12
条	條	tiáo	m	(measure word for pants and long, thin objects)	9
跳舞	跳舞	tiào wǔ	vo	to dance	4
听	聽	tīng	v	to listen	4
听说	聽説	tīngshuō	v	to be told; to hear of	13
听音乐会	聽音樂會	tīng yīnyuèhuì	vo	to go to a concert	16
挺	挺	tǐng	adv	very; rather	9
同	同	tóng	adj	same; alike	16
同学	同學	tóngxué	n	classmate	3
头等舱	頭等艙	tóuděngcāng	n	first class	19
头疼	頭疼	tóu téng		to have a headache	15
图书馆	圖書館	túshūguǎn	n	library	5
托运	托運	tuōyùn	v	to check (luggage)	20

W

Simplified	Traditional	Pinyin	Part of Speech	English	Lesson
袜子	襪子	wàzi	n	socks	9
外国	外國	wàiguó	n	foreign country	4
外套	外套	wàitào	n	outer garment; coat; jacket	9
玩(儿)	玩(兒)	wán(r)	v	to have fun; to play	5
玩游戏机	玩遊戲機	wán yóuxìjī	vo	to play videogames	4
碗	碗	wǎn	n	bowl	12
晚	晚	wǎn	adj	late	7
晚饭	晚飯	wǎnfàn	n	dinner; supper	3
晚上	晚上	wǎnshang	t/n	evening; night	3
王红	王紅	Wáng Hóng	pn	(a personal name)	14
王朋	王朋	Wáng Péng	pn	(a personal name)	1
往	往	wǎng	prep	towards	13
往返	往返	wǎngfǎn	v	make a round trip; go there and back	19
网球	網球	wǎngqiú	n	tennis	18
网上	網上	wǎng shang		on the internet	11
忘	忘	wàng	v	to forget	12

Simplified	Traditional	Pinyin	Part of Speech	English	Lesson
危险	危險	wēixiǎn	adj	dangerous	18
喂	喂	wéi/wèi	interj	(on telephone) Hello!; Hey!	6
位	位	wèi	m	(polite measure word for people)	6
位子	位子	wèizi	n	seat	12
味精	味精	wèijīng	n	monosodium glutamate (MSG)	12
为了	為了	wèile	prep	for the sake of	18
为什么	為什麽	wèishénme	qpr	why	3
卫生间	衛生間	wèishēngjiān	n	bathroom	17
文化	文化	wénhuà	n	culture	19
问	問	wèn	v	to ask (a question)	1
问题	問題	wèntí	n	question; problem	6
我	我	wǒ	pr	I; me	1
我们	我們	wǒmen	pr	we	3
卧室	臥室	wòshì	n	bedroom	17
午饭	午飯	wǔfàn	n	lunch, midday meal	8
舞会	舞會	wǔhuì	n	dance party; ball	14
物理	物理	wùlǐ	n	physics	8

X

Simplified	Traditional	Pinyin	Part of Speech	English	Lesson
西	西	xī	n	west	13
西班牙文	西班牙文	Xībānyáwén	pn	the Spanish language	6
西北航空公司	西北航空公司	Xīběi Hángkōng Gōngsī	pn	Northwest Airlines	19
西瓜	西瓜	xīgua	n	watermelon	14
西装	西裝	xīzhuāng	n	(western-style) suit	9
希腊文	希臘文	Xīlàwén	pn	the Greek language	6
希望	希望	xīwàng	v/n	to hope; hope	8
喜欢	喜歡	xǐhuan	v	to like	3
洗澡	洗澡	xǐ zǎo	vo	to take a bath/shower	8
虾	蝦	xiā	n	shrimp	12
下车	下車	xià chē	vo	to get off (a bus, train, etc.)	10
下个	下個	xià ge		next one	6
下棋	下棋	xià qí	vo	to play chess	4
下午	下午	xiàwǔ	t	afternoon	6

Simplified	Traditional	Pinyin	Part of Speech	English	Lesson
下雪	下雪	xià xuě	vo	to snow	11
下雨	下雨	xià yǔ	vo	to rain	11
夏天	夏天	xiàtiān	n	summer	11
夏威夷	夏威夷	Xiàwēiyí	pn	Hawaii	1
先	先	xiān	adv	first	10
先生	先生	xiānsheng	n	Mr.; husband; teacher	1
线	線	xiàn	n	line	10
现金	現金	xiànjīn	n	cash	19
现在	現在	xiànzài	t	now	3
香港	香港	Xiānggǎng	pn	Hong Kong	19
香蕉	香蕉	xiāngjiāo	n	banana	14
箱子	箱子	xiāngzi	n	suitcase; box	20
想	想	xiǎng	mv	to want to; would like to; to think	4
想起来	想起來	xiǎng qi lai	vc	to remember; to recall	16
像	像	xiàng	v	to be like; to look like; to take after	14
小	小	xiǎo	adj	small; little	4
小姐	小姐	xiǎojiě	n	Miss; young lady	1
小时	小時	xiǎoshí	n	hour	15
小心	小心	xiǎoxīn	v	to be careful	20
笑	笑	xiào	v	to laugh at; to laugh; to smile	8
些	些	xiē	m	(measure word for an indefinite amount); some	12
鞋	鞋	xié	n	shoes	9
写	寫	xiě	v	to write	7
谢谢	謝謝	xièxie	v	to thank	3
新	新	xīn	adj	new	8
新年	新年	xīnnián	n	new year	10
信	信	xìn	n	letter (correspondence)	8
信用卡	信用卡	xìnyòngkǎ	n	credit card	9
星期	星期	xīngqī	n	week	3
星期四	星期四	xīngqīsì	n	Thursday	3
行	行	xíng	v	all right; O.K.	6

Simplified	Traditional	Pinyin	Part of Speech	English	Lesson
行李	行李	xíngli	n	luggage	20
姓	姓	xìng	v/n	(one's) surname is...; to be surnamed; surname	1
兴趣	興趣	xìngqù	n	interest	17
休息	休息	xiūxi	v	to take a break; to rest	15
学	學	xué	v	to study; to learn	7
学期	學期	xuéqī	n	school term; semester/quarter	8
学生	學生	xuésheng	n	student	1
学习	學習	xuéxí	v	to study; to learn	7
学校	學校	xuéxiào	n	school	5
雪碧	雪碧	Xuěbì	pn	Sprite	5

Y

Simplified	Traditional	Pinyin	Part of Speech	English	Lesson
压	壓	yā	v	to press; to hold down; to weigh down	18
押金	押金	yājīn	n	security deposit	17
亚洲研究	亞洲研究	Yàzhōu yánjiū	n	Asian studies	8
呀	呀	ya	p	(interjectory particle used to soften a question)	5
淹死	淹死	yān sǐ	vc	to drown	18
盐	鹽	yán	n	salt	12
颜色	顏色	yánsè	n	color	9
演	演	yǎn	v	to show (a film); to perform	16
眼睛	眼睛	yǎnjing	n	eye	14
洋葱	洋葱	yángcōng	n	onion	12
羊肉	羊肉	yángròu	n	lamb; mutton	12
养	養	yǎng	v	to raise	17
痒	癢	yǎng	adj	itchy	15
样子	樣子	yàngzi	n	style	9
药	藥	yào	n	medicine	15
药店	藥店	yàodiàn	n	pharmacy	15
要	要	yào	v	to want	5
要	要	yào	mv	will, to be going to; to want to, to have a desire to	6
要不然	要不然	yàobùrán	conj	otherwise	15
要是	要是	yàoshi	conj	if	6

Simplified	Traditional	Pinyin	Part of Speech	English	Lesson
爷爷	爺爺	yéye	n	paternal grandfather	20
也	也	yě	adv	too; also	1
野餐	野餐	yěcān	v	to picnic	16
夜里	夜裏	yèli	n	at night	15
一边	一邊	(yībiān) yìbiān	adv	simultaneously; at the same time	8
一定	一定	(yīdìng) yídìng	adj/adv	certain(ly); definite(ly)	14
一房一厅	一房一廳	(yī fáng yī tīng) yì fáng yì tīng		one bedroom and one living room	17
一共	一共	(yīgòng) yígòng	adv	altogether	9
一路平安	一路平安	(yī lù píng'ān) yí lù píng'ān		have a good trip; bon voyage	20
一起	一起	(yīqǐ) yìqǐ	adv	together	5
一下	一下	(yī xià) yí xià	n+m	once; a bit	5
一言为定	一言為定	(yī yán wéi dìng) yì yán wéi dìng		it's a deal, that settles it; it's decided	16
一样	一樣	(yīyàng) yíyàng	adj	same; alike	9
一直	一直	(yīzhí) yìzhí	adv	straight; continuously	13
衣服	衣服	yīfu	n	clothes	9
医生	醫生	yīshēng	n	doctor; physician	2
医院	醫院	yīyuàn	n	hospital	15
以后	以後	yǐhòu	t	after	6
以前	以前	yǐqián	t	before	8
以为	以為	yǐwéi	v	to assume erroneously	14
已经	已經	yǐjīng	adv	already	8
椅子	椅子	yǐzi	n	chair	17
意大利文	意大利文	Yìdàlìwén	pn	the Italian language	6
阴天	陰天	yīntiān	n	overcast day	11
因为	因為	yīnwèi	conj	because	3
音响	音響	yīnxiǎng	n	stereo system	17
音乐	音樂	yīnyuè	n	music	4
音乐会	音樂會	yīnyuèhuì	n	concert	8
饮料	飲料	yǐnliào	n	beverage	14
饮水器	飲水器	yǐnshuǐqì	n	water dispenser	20
印度	印度	Yìndù	pn	India	1
印象	印象	yìnxiàng	n	impression	16
应该	應該	yīnggāi	mv	should; ought to	18

Simplified	Traditional	Pinyin	Part of Speech	English	Lesson
英国	英國	Yīngguó	pn	Britain; England	3
英文	英文	Yīngwén	pn	English (language)	2
用	用	yòng	v	to use	8
用功	用功	yònggōng	adj	hard-working; diligent; studious	14
游泳	游泳	yóu yǒng	vo	to swim	18
有	有	yǒu	v	to have; to exist	2
有的	有的	yǒude	pr	some	4
有名	有名	yǒumíng	adj	famous; well-known	19
有意思	有意思	yǒu yìsi	adj	interesting	4
又	又	yòu	adv	again	11
右	右	yòu	n	right	13
鱼	魚	yú	n	fish	12
语法	語法	yǔfǎ	n	grammar	7
语言学	語言學	yǔyánxué	n	linguistics	8
预报	預報	yùbào	v	to forecast	11
预习	預習	yùxí	v	to preview	7
元	元	yuán	m	(measure word for the basic Chinese monetary unit); *yuan*	17
圆	圓	yuán	adj	round	14
圆珠笔	圓珠筆	yuánzhūbǐ	n	ballpoint pen	7
远	遠	yuǎn	adj	far	13
愿意	願意	yuànyì	av	to be willing	18
约	約	yuē	v	to make an appointment	11
月	月	yuè	n	month	3
越来越	越來越	yuè lái yuè	adv	more and more	15
越南	越南	Yuènán	pn	Vietnam	1
运动	運動	yùndòng	n	sports	13
运动服	運動服	yùndòngfú	n	sportswear; athletic clothing	18

Z

Simplified	Traditional	Pinyin	Part of Speech	English	Lesson
在	在	zài	prep	at; in; on	5
在	在	zài	v	to be present; to be at (a place)	6
再	再	zài	adv	again	9
再见	再見	zàijiàn	v	goodbye; see you again	3

Simplified	Traditional	Pinyin	Part of Speech	English	Lesson
再说	再說	zàishuō	conj	moreover	15
糟糕	糟糕	zāogāo	adj	in a terrible mess; how terrible	11
早	早	zǎo	adj	early	7
早饭	早飯	zǎofàn	n	breakfast	8
早上	早上	zǎoshang	t	morning	7
怎么	怎麼	zěnme	qpr	how; how come	7
怎么样	怎麼樣	zěnmeyàng	qpr	Is it O.K.? How is that? How does that sound?	3
站	站	zhàn	m	(measure word for stops of bus, train, etc.)	10
张	張	zhāng	m	(measure word for flat objects, paper, pictures, etc.)	7
长	長	zhǎng	v	to grow; to appear	14
长大	長大	zhǎng dà	vc	to grow up	14
找	找	zhǎo	v	to look for	4
找(钱)	找(錢)	zhǎo (qián)	v(o)	to give change	9
照顾	照顧	zhàogu	v	to look after; to care for; to attend to	20
照片	照片	zhàopiàn	n	picture; photo	2
照相机	照相機	zhàoxiàngjī	n	camera	19
这	這	zhè	pr	this	2
这么	這麼	zhème	pr	so; such	7
这儿	這兒	zhèr	pr	here	9
真	真	zhēn	adv	really	7
枕头	枕頭	zhěntou	n	pillow	19
整理	整理	zhěnglǐ	v	to put in order	16
证件	證件	zhèngjiàn	n	ID; document	19
正在	正在	zhèngzài	adv	in the middle of (doing something)	8
政治	政治	zhèngzhì	n	politics	19
枝	枝	zhī	m	(measure word for long, thin, inflexible objects, pens, rifles, etc.)	7
知道	知道	zhīdào	v	to know	8
直飞	直飛	zhí fēi		fly directly	19

Simplified	Traditional	Pinyin	Part of Speech	English	Lesson
植物	植物	zhíwù	n	plant	17
只	只	zhǐ	adv	only	4
纸	紙	zhǐ	n	paper	7
中	中	zhōng	adj	medium; middle	9
中国	中國	Zhōngguó	pn	China	1
中国城	中國城	Zhōngguóchéng	n	Chinatown	13
中国国际航空公司	中國國際航空公司	Zhōngguó Guójì Hángkōng Gōngsī	pn	Air China	19
中间	中間	zhōngjiān	n	middle	13
中文	中文	Zhōngwén	pn	Chinese (language)	6
中午	中午	zhōngwǔ	n	noon	8
中心	中心	zhōngxīn	n	center	13
中学	中學	zhōngxué	n	middle school ; secondary school	14
钟头	鐘頭	zhōngtóu	n	hour	14
种	種	zhǒng	m	(measure word for kinds, sorts, types)	9
重	重	zhòng	adj	heavy; serious	14
周末	週末	zhōumò	n	weekend	4
猪肉	豬肉	zhūròu	n	pork	12
住	住	zhù	v	to live (in a certain place)	14
祝	祝	zhù	v	to wish (well)	8
专业	專業	zhuānyè	n	major (in college); specialty	8
转机	轉機	zhuǎn jī	vo	change planes	19
准	准	zhǔn	v	to allow; to be allowed	17
准备	準備	zhǔnbèi	v	to prepare	6
桌子	桌子	zhuōzi	n	table	12
紫色	紫色	zǐsè	n	purple	9
字	字	zì	n	character	7
字典	字典	zìdiǎn	n	dictionary	7
自己	自己	zìjǐ	pr	oneself	10
走	走	zǒu	v	to go by way of; to walk	10
走道	走道	zǒudào	n	aisle	19
走路	走路	zǒu lù	vo	to walk	10, 17
租	租	zū	v	to rent	19

Simplified	Traditional	Pinyin	Part of Speech	English	Lesson
足球	足球	zúqiú	n	soccer; football	18
嘴	嘴	zuǐ	n	mouth	14
最	最	zuì	adv	most, (of superlative degree) -est	14
最好	最好	zuìhǎo	adv	had better	15
最后	最後	zuìhòu		final; last	10
最近	最近	zuìjìn	t	recently	8
昨天	昨天	zuótiān	t	yesterday	4
左	左	zuǒ	n	left	13
做	做	zuò	v	to do	2
做饭	做飯	zuò fàn	vo	to cook; to prepare a meal	17
做瑜伽	做瑜伽	zuò yújiā	vo	to do yoga	18
坐	坐	zuò	v	to sit	5
坐	坐	zuò	v	to travel by	10
坐船	坐船	zuò chuán	vo	to travel by ship; to take a boat	10
坐电车	坐電車	zuò diànchē	vo	to take a cable car, trolley bus, or tram	10
坐火车	坐火車	zuò huǒchē	vo	to travel by train	10
坐计程车	坐計程車	zuò jìchéngchē	vo	to take a taxi (in Taiwan)	10

Vocabulary Index (English-Chinese)

Proper nouns from the dialogues and readings are shown in green. Supplementary vocabulary from the "How About You?" section is shown in blue.

English	Characters	Pinyin	Part of Speech	Lesson
A				
a little, a bit; some	点(儿)	diǎn(r)	m	5
a long time	好久	hǎo jiǔ		4
activity	活动	huódòng	n	13
advertisement	广告	guǎnggào	n	17
after	以后	yǐhòu	t	6
afternoon	下午	xiàwǔ	t	6
again	再	zài	adv	9
again	又	yòu	adv	11
ahead; in front of	前面	qiánmian	n	13
Air China	中国国际航空公司	Zhōngguó Guójì Hángkōng Gōngsī	pn	19
airplane	飞机	fēijī	n	10
airport	(飞)机场	(fēi)jīchǎng	n	10
aisle	走道	zǒudào	n	19
all right; O.K.	行	xíng	v	6
allow; be allowed	准	zhǔn	v	17
allow or cause (somebody to do something)	让	ràng	v	10
almost; nearly; similar	差不多	chàbuduō	adv/adj	17
already	已经	yǐjīng	adv	8
also; too; as well	还	hái	adv	3
although	虽然	suīrán	conj	9
altogether	一共	yígòng	adv	9
America	美国	Měiguó	pn	1
American-style	美式	Měishì	adj	18
and	和	hé	conj	2
apartment	公寓	gōngyù	n	17
apple	苹果	píngguǒ	n	14

English	Characters	Pinyin	Part of Speech	Lesson
Asian studies	亚洲研究	Yàzhōu yánjiū	n	8
ask (a question)	问	wèn	v	1
aspirin	阿司匹林	āsīpǐlín	n	19
assume erroneously	以为	yǐwéi	v	14
at; in; on	在	zài	prep	5
at night	夜里	yèli	n	15
aunt	阿姨	āyí	n	20
autumn; fall	秋天	qiūtiān	n	11
aviation	航空	hángkōng	n	19
away from	离	lí	prep	13

B

English	Characters	Pinyin	Part of Speech	Lesson
bag; sack; bundle; package	包	bāo	n	20
Bai Ying'ai	白英爱	Bái Yīng'ài (a personal name)	pn	2
balloons	气球	qìqiú	n	14
ballpoint pen	圆珠笔	yuánzhūbǐ	n	7
banana	香蕉	xiāngjiāo	n	14
basketball	篮球	lánqiú	n	18
bathroom	卫生间	wèishēngjiān	n	17
be	是	shì	v	1
be acquainted with; recognize	认识	rènshi	v	3
be allergic to	过敏	guòmǐn	v	15
be called; call	叫	jiào	v	1
be careful	小心	xiǎoxīn	v	20
be like; look like; take after	像	xiàng	v	14
be overweight (of luggage, freight, etc.)	超重	chāozhòng	v	20
be present; be at (a place)	在	zài	v	6
be sold out	卖完	mài wán	vc	12
be told; hear of	听说	tīngshuō	v	13
be willing	愿意	yuànyì	av	18
because	因为	yīnwèi	conj	3
become	成	chéng	v	16
bedroom	卧室	wòshì	n	17

English	Characters	Pinyin	Part of Speech	Lesson
beef	牛肉	niúròu	n	12
before	以前	yǐqián	t	8
begin, start; beginning	开始	kāishǐ	v/n	7
beginning	初	chū	n	19
Beijing	北京	Běijīng	pn	1
belly; abdomen	肚子	dùzi	n	15
belong to	属	shǔ	v	14
beverage	饮料	yǐnliào	n	14
big; old	大	dà	adj	3
birthday	生日	shēngrì	n	3
black	黑	hēi	adj	9
blanket	毯子	tǎnzi	n	19
blue	蓝	lán	adj	10
boarding gate	登机口	dēngjīkǒu	n	20
boarding pass	登机牌	dēngjīpái	n	20
body; health	身体	shēntǐ	n	15
bok choy	白菜	báicài	n	12
book	书	shū	n	4
bookcase; bookshelf	书架	shūjià	n	17
bookstore	书店	shūdiàn	n	13
both; all	都	dōu	adv	2
bowl	碗	wǎn	n	12
braise in soy sauce	红烧	hóngshāo	v	12
breakfast	早饭	zǎofàn	n	8
bring; take; carry; come with	带	dài	v	12
Britain; England	英国	Yīngguó	pn	3
brown; coffee colored	咖啡色	kāfēisè	n	9
bus	公共汽车	gōnggòng qìchē	n	10
business class	商务舱	shāngwùcāng	n	19
business management	工商管理	gōngshāng guǎnlǐ	n	8
busy	忙	máng	adj	3
but	但是	dànshì	conj	6
but	可是	kěshì	conj	3
buy	买	mǎi	v	9
by	被	bèi	prep	18

English	Characters	Pinyin	Part of Speech	Lesson
C				
cabinet; cupboard	柜子	guìzi	n	17
cake	蛋糕	dàngāo	n	14
California	加州	Jiāzhōu	pn	1, 11
camera	照相机	zhàoxiàngjī	n	19
can; able to	能	néng	mv	8
can; know how to	会	huì	mv	8
can; may	可以	kěyǐ	mv	5
Canada	加拿大	Jiā'nádà	pn	1
candy	糖（果）	táng (guǒ)	n	14
Capital Airport (in Beijing)	首都机场	Shǒudū Jīchǎng	pn	20
capital city	首都	shǒudū	n	19
card	卡片	kǎpiàn	n	14
carrot	胡萝卜	húluóbo	n	12
cash	现金	xiànjīn	n	19
catch; meet; welcome	接	jiē	v	14
cats	猫	māo	n	15
cell phone	手机	shǒujī	n	10
center	中心	zhōngxīn	n	13
certain(ly); definite(ly)	一定	yídìng	adj/adv	14
chair	椅子	yǐzi	n	17
change planes	转机	zhuǎn jī	vo	19
character	字	zì	n	7
chat	聊天(儿)	liáo tiān(r)	vo	5
cheap; inexpensive	便宜	piányi	adj	9
check; look into	查	chá	v	19
check (luggage)	托运	tuōyùn	v	20
chemistry	化学	huàxué	n	8
chicken	鸡	jī	n	12
child	孩子	háizi	n	2
China	中国	Zhōngguó	pn	1
Chinatown	中国城	Zhōngguóchéng	n	13
Chinese characters	汉字	Hànzì	n	7
Chinese (language)	中文	Zhōngwén	pn	6

English	Characters	Pinyin	Part of Speech	Lesson
city	城市	chéngshì	n	10
class	班	bān	n	14
class; course; lesson	课	kè	n	6
classmate	同学	tóngxué	n	3
classroom	教室	jiàoshì	n	8
clean	干净	gānjìng	adj	17
clean up (a room, apartment or house)	打扫	dǎsǎo	v	16
clear	清楚	qīngchu	adj	12
clothes	衣服	yīfu	n	9
Coca-Cola	可口可乐	Kěkǒukělè	pn	5
coffee	咖啡	kāfēi	n	5
[Coke or Pepsi] cola	可乐	kělè	n	5
cold	冷	lěng	adj	11
(of food) cold "blended"; cold tossed	凉拌	liángbàn	v	12
college student	大学生	dàxuéshēng	n	2
color	颜色	yánsè	n	9
come	来	lái	v	5
come back	回来	huí lai	vc	6
come in	进来	jìn lai	vc	5
comfortable	舒服	shūfu	adj	11
company	公司	gōngsī	n	19
(comparison marker); compare	比	bǐ	prep/v	11
computer	电脑	diànnǎo	n	8
concert	音乐会	yīnyuèhuì	n	8
concourse (of airport)	航站楼	hángzhànlóu	n	20
convenient	方便	fāngbiàn	adj	6
cook; prepare a meal	做饭	zuò fàn	vo	17
cooked rice	米饭	mǐfàn	n	12
cookies; crackers	饼干	bǐnggān	n	14
cool	酷	kù	adj	7
cough	咳嗽	késòu	v	15
credit card	信用卡	xìnyòngkǎ	n	9
cry; weep	哭	kū	v	20

English	Characters	Pinyin	Part of Speech	Lesson
cucumber	黄瓜	huánggua	n	12
culture	文化	wénhuà	n	19
customs	海关	hǎiguān	n	20
cute; lovable	可爱	kě'ài	adj	14

D

English	Characters	Pinyin	Part of Speech	Lesson
dance	跳舞	tiào wǔ	vo	4
dance party; ball	舞会	wǔhuì	n	14
dangerous	危险	wēixiǎn	adj	18
daughter	女儿	nǚ'ér	n	2
day	天	tiān	n	3
day after tomorrow	后天	hòutiān	t	16
delicious	好吃	hǎochī	adj	12
desk	书桌	shūzhuō	n	17
diary	日记	rìjì	n	8
dictionary	字典	zìdiǎn	n	7
difficult	难	nán	adj	7
dining room, cafeteria	餐厅	cāntīng	n	8
dining table	饭桌	fànzhuō	n	17
dinner; supper	晚饭	wǎnfàn	n	3
disc; small plate, dish, saucer	碟	dié	n	11
dishes, cuisine	菜	cài	n	3
do	做	zuò	v	2
do Tai Chi (a kind of traditional Chinese shadow boxing)	打太极拳	dǎ tàijíquán	vo	18
do yoga	做瑜伽	zuò yújiā	vo	18
doctor; physician	医生	yīshēng	n	2
dog	狗	gǒu	n	14
don't	别	bié	adv	6
dormitory	宿舍	sùshè	n	8
draw; paint	画画儿	huà huàr	vo	4
drink	喝	hē	v	5
drive a car	开车	kāi chē	vo	10
drown	淹死	yān sǐ	vc	18

English	Characters	Pinyin	Part of Speech	Lesson
dumplings (with vegetable and/or meat filling)	饺子	jiǎozi	n	12
dust	灰尘	huīchén	n	15
duty-free shop	免税商店	miǎn shuì shāngdiàn	n	20
(dynamic particle)	了	le	p	5

E

English	Characters	Pinyin	Part of Speech	Lesson
early	早	zǎo	adj	7
easy	容易	róngyì	adj	7
east	东	dōng	n	13
eat	吃	chī	v	3
economics	经济	jīngjì	n	8
egg	蛋	dàn	n	12
egg drop soup	蛋花汤	dànhuātāng	n	12
eighteen	十八	shíbā	nu	3
eldest brother	大哥	dàgē	n	2
eldest sister	大姐	dàjiě	n	2
electricity	电	diàn	n	16
email	电子邮件	diànzǐ yóujiàn	n	10
engineer	工程师	gōngchéngshī	n	2
England; Britain	英国	Yīngguó	pn	3
English (language)	英文	Yīngwén	pn	2
enough	够	gòu	adj	12
enter	进	jìn	v	5
especially	特别	tèbié	adv	10
even	连	lián	prep	17
even more	更	gèng	adv	11
evening; night	晚上	wǎnshang	t/n	3
every; each	每	měi	pr	10
everybody	大家	dàjiā	pr	7
examine	检查	jiǎnchá	v	15
exchange; change	换	huàn	v	9
(exclamatory particle to express surprise or dissatisfaction)	哎	āi	excl	13

English	Characters	Pinyin	Part of Speech	Lesson
exercise book	练习本	liànxíběn	n	7
extremely	极	jí	adv	12
eye	眼睛	yǎnjing	n	14

F

English	Characters	Pinyin	Part of Speech	Lesson
face	脸	liǎn	n	14
family; home	家	jiā	n	2
famous; well-known	有名	yǒumíng	adj	19
famous scenic spots and historic sites	名胜古迹	míngshèng gǔjì		19
fantastic; super [colloq.]	棒	bàng	adj	18
far	远	yuǎn	adj	13
farmer; peasant	农民	nóngmín	n	2
fat	胖	pàng	adj	18
father, dad	爸爸	bàba	n	2
Father's Day	父亲节	Fùqīnjié	pn	3
fear; be afraid of	怕	pà	v	18
fee; expenses	费	fèi	n	17
feel; think	觉得	juéde	v	4
feel embarrassed	不好意思	bù hǎoyìsi		10
female	女	nǚ	adj	2
field	场	chǎng	n	13
final; last	最后	zuìhòu		10
fine; good; nice; O.K.; it's settled	好	hǎo	adj	1
first	先	xiān	adv	10
first class	头等舱	tóuděngcāng	n	19
fish	鱼	yú	n	12
fish in sweet and sour sauce	糖醋鱼	tángcùyú	n	12
flower	花	huā	n	14
fly directly	直飞	zhí fēi		19
foot	脚	jiǎo	n	18
for the sake of	为了	wèile	prep	18
forecast	预报	yùbào	v	11
foreign country	外国	wàiguó	n	4

English	Characters	Pinyin	Part of Speech	Lesson
forget	忘	wàng	v	12
forget it; never mind	算了	suàn le		4
forward; ahead	前	qián	n	13
fountain pen	钢笔	gāngbǐ	n	7
France	法国	Fǎguó	pn	1
free time	空(儿)	kòng(r)	n	6
French language	法文	Fǎwén	n	6
friend	朋友	péngyou	n	3
from	从	cóng	prep	13
fruit	水果	shuǐguǒ	n	14
fruit juice	果汁	guǒzhī	n	5
fun, amusing, interesting	好玩儿	hǎowánr	adj	11
furniture	家具	jiājù	n	17
furthermore; in addition	另外	lìngwài	conj	17

G

English	Characters	Pinyin	Part of Speech	Lesson
game; match; competition; to compete	比赛	bǐsài	n/v	18
Gao Wenzhong	高文中	Gāo Wénzhōng	pn	2
Gao Xiaoyin	高小音	Gāo Xiǎoyīn	pn	5
Germany	德国	Déguó	pn	1
German language	德文	Déwén	pn	6
get an injection	打针	dǎ zhēn	vo	15
get off (a bus, train, etc.)	下车	xià chē	vo	10
get sick	生病	shēng bìng	vo	15
get sick because of bad food	吃坏	chī huài	vc	15
get up	起床	qǐ chuáng	vo	8
gift; present	礼物	lǐwù	n	14
give	给	gěi	v	5
give as a gift	送	sòng	v	14
give change	找(钱)	zhǎo (qián)	v(o)	9
give or take a test; test	考试	kǎo shì	vo/n	6
go	去	qù	v	4
go [colloq.]	上	shàng	v	13
go back; return	回去	huí qu	vc	11

English	Characters	Pinyin	Part of Speech	Lesson
go by way of; walk	走	zǒu	v	10
go for a drive	兜风	dōu fēng	vo	16
go home	回家	huí jiā	vo	5
go on vacation; have time off	放假	fàng jià	vo	19
go online; surf the internet	上网	shàng wǎng	vo	8
go out	出去	chū qu	vc	11
go to; arrive	到	dào	v	6
go to a class; start a class; be in class	上课	shàng kè	vo	7
go to a concert	听音乐会	tīng yīnyuèhuì	vo	16
goodbye; see you again	再见	zàijiàn	v	3
grade in school	年级	niánjí	n	6
grammar	语法	yǔfǎ	n	7
grape	葡萄	pútao	n	14
gray	灰色	huīsè	n	9
Great Wall	长城	Chángchéng	pn	19
Greek language	希腊文	Xīlàwén	pn	6
green	绿	lǜ	adj	10
green/leafy vegetable	青菜	qīngcài	n	12
grow; appear	长	zhǎng	v	14
grow up	长大	zhǎng dà	vc	14

H

had better	最好	zuìhǎo	adv	15
half; half an hour	半	bàn	nu	3
half a day; a long time	半天	bàntiān		18
hand	手	shǒu	n	18
handle; do	办	bàn	v	11
handsome	帅	shuài	adj	7
happy	快乐	kuàilè	adj	10
happy, pleased	高兴	gāoxìng	adj	5
hard to bear; uncomfortable	难受	nánshòu	adj	18
hard-working; diligent; studious	用功	yònggōng	adj	14
hat; cap	帽子	màozi	n	9
have; exist	有	yǒu	v	2

English	Characters	Pinyin	Part of Speech	Lesson
have a cold	感冒	gǎnmào	v	15
have a fever	发烧	fā shāo	vo	15
have a good trip; bon voyage	一路平安	yí lù píng'ān		20
have a headache	头疼	tóu téng		15
have a meeting	开会	kāi huì	vo	6
have a runny nose	流鼻涕	liú bítì	vo	15
have fun; play	玩(儿)	wán(r)	v	5
Hawaii	夏威夷	Xiàwēiyí	pn	1
he; him	他	tā	pr	2
healthy; health	健康	jiànkāng	adj/n	15
heavy; serious	重	zhòng	adj	14
Helen	海伦	Hǎilún	pn	14
Hello!; Hey! (on telephone)	喂	wéi/wèi	interj	6
help	帮	bāng	v	6
here	这儿	zhèr	pr	9
highway	高速公路	gāosù gōnglù	n	10
history	历史	lìshǐ	n	8
hold or carry in the arms	抱	bào	v	18
home-style	家常	jiācháng	n	12
homework; schoolwork	功课	gōngkè	n	7
Hong Kong	香港	Xiānggǎng	pn	19
honorable; expensive	贵	guì	adj	1
hope; hope	希望	xīwàng	v/n	8
hospital	医院	yīyuàn	n	15
hot	热	rè	adj	11
hot and sour soup	酸辣汤	suānlàtāng	n	12
hot and stifling	闷热	mēnrè	adj	11
hotel	旅馆	lǚguǎn	n	19
hour	小时	xiǎoshí	n	15
hour	钟头	zhōngtóu	n	14
how; how come	怎么	zěnme	qpr	7
how many; some; a few	几	jǐ	nu	2
how many/much; to what extent	多	duō	adv	3
how much/many	多少	duōshao	qpr	9

English	Characters	Pinyin	Part of Speech	Lesson
however; but	不过	búguò	conj	9
hundred	百	bǎi	nu	9
hungry	饿	è	adj	12

I

English	Characters	Pinyin	Part of Speech	Lesson
I; me	我	wǒ	pr	1
ice skate	滑冰	huá bīng	vo	11
iced tea	冰茶	bīngchá	n	12
ID; document	证件	zhèngjiàn	n	19
if	要是	yàoshi	conj	6
if	如果⋯的话	rúguǒ… de huà	conj	9
immediately; right away	马上	mǎshàng	adv	19
impression	印象	yìnxiàng	n	16
improve; raise; heighten;	提高	tígāo	v	18
in a terrible mess; how terrible	糟糕	zāogāo	adj	11
in addition to; besides	除了⋯以外	chúle…yǐwài	conj	8
in that case; then	那	nà	conj	4
in the middle of (doing something)	正在	zhèngzài	adv	8
India	印度	Yìndù	pn	1
(indicating a thing is disposed of)	把	bǎ	prep	15
inside	里边	lǐbian	n	13
insurance	保险	bǎoxiǎn	n	15
interest	兴趣	xìngqù	n	17
interesting	有意思	yǒu yìsi	adj	4
(interjectory particle used to soften a question)	呀	ya	p	5
intern	实习	shíxí	v	19
international	国际	guójì	adj	18
intersection	路口	lùkǒu	n	13
interview	面试	miànshì	v/n	11
introduce	介绍	jièshào	v	5
invite someone (to dinner, coffee, etc.); play the host	请客	qǐng kè	vo	4
Is it O.K.? How is that? How does that sound?	怎么样	zěnmeyàng	qpr	3
it	它	tā	pr	9

English	Characters	Pinyin	Part of Speech	Lesson
it doesn't matter	没关系	méi guānxi		12
it's a deal, that settles it; it's decided	一言为定	yì yán wéi dìng		16
Italian language	意大利文	Yìdàlìwén	pn	6
itchy	痒	yǎng	adj	15
J				
jacket	夹克	jiákè	n	9
Japan	日本	Rìběn	pn	1, 13
Japanese (language)	日文	Rìwén	pn	6, 13
job; work	工作	gōngzuò	n/v	2
jog	跑步	pǎo bù	vo	18
jog; jogging	慢跑	mànpǎo	v/n	18
just	刚	gāng	adv	12
just; only (indicating a small number)	就	jiù	adv	16
just now; a moment ago	刚才	gāngcái	t	11
K				
kick	踢	tī	v	18
kitchen	厨房	chúfáng	n	17
know	知道	zhīdào	v	8
Korea (South)	韩国	Hánguó	pn	1
Korean language	韩文	Hánwén	pn	6
Kung Pao chicken	宫保鸡丁	gōngbǎo jīdīng	n	12
L				
lamb; mutton	羊肉	yángròu	n	12
lamp; light	灯	dēng	n	17
last time	上次	shàng cì		15
last year	去年	qùnián	t	14
late	晚	wǎn	adj	7
later	后来	hòulái	t	8
Latin language	拉丁文	Lādīngwén	pn	6
laugh at; laugh; smile	笑	xiào	v	8

English	Characters	Pinyin	Part of Speech	Lesson
lawyer	律师	lǜshī	n	2
lazy	懒	lǎn	adj	15
lean on; lean against; be next to	靠	kào	v	19
left	左	zuǒ	n	13
length	长短	chángduǎn	n	9
letter (correspondence)	信	xìn	n	8
level; standard	水平	shuǐpíng	n	18
Li You	李友	Lǐ Yǒu	pn	1
library	图书馆	túshūguǎn	n	5
lie down	躺下	tǎng xia	vc	15
like	喜欢	xǐhuan	v	3
line	线	xiàn	n	10
linguistics	语言学	yǔyánxué	n	8
listen	听	tīng	v	4
live (in a certain place)	住	zhù	v	14
living room	客厅	kètīng	n	17
look after; care for; attend to	照顾	zhàogu	v	20
look for	找	zhǎo	v	4
love; like; be fond of	爱	ài	v	14
luggage	行李	xíngli	n	20
lunch, midday meal	午饭	wǔfàn	n	8

M

English	Characters	Pinyin	Part of Speech	Lesson
major (in college); specialty	专业	zhuānyè	n	8
make a phone call	打电话	dǎ diànhuà	vo	6
make a round trip; go there and back	往返	wǎngfǎn	v	19
make an appointment	约	yuē	v	11
male	男	nán	adj	2
manager	经理	jīnglǐ	n	2
many; much	多	duō	adj	7
map	地图	dìtú	n	13
mapo tofu	麻婆豆腐	mápó dòufu	n	12

English	Characters	Pinyin	Part of Speech	Lesson
master worker	师傅	shīfu	n	12
mathematics	数学	shùxué	n	8
matter; affair; event	事（儿）	shì(r)	n	3
maybe; possible	可能	kěnéng	mv/adj	17
meal; (cooked) rice	饭	fàn	n	3
meal card	饭卡	fànkǎ	n	12
(measure word for a pair)	双	shuāng	m	9
(measure word for an indefinite amount); some	些	xiē	m	12
(measure word for books)	本	běn	m	14
(measure word for bottles); bottle	瓶	píng	m/n	5
(measure word for bunches of things, and chairs)	把	bǎ	m	14
(measure word for class periods)	节	jié	m	6
(measure word for complete courses of an action or instances of an action)	遍	biàn	m	15
(measure word for cup and glass)	杯	bēi	m	5
(measure word for essays, articles, etc.)	篇	piān	m	8
(measure word for flat objects, paper, pictures, etc.)	张	zhāng	m	7
(measure word for frequency)	次	cì	m	13
(measure word for kinds, sorts, types)	种	zhǒng	m	9
(measure word for letters)	封	fēng	m	8
(measure word for long, thin, inflexible objects, pens, rifles, etc.)	枝	zhī	m	7
(measure word for many common everyday objects)	个	gè/ge	m	2
(measure word for meal order, job)	份	fèn	m	19
(measure word for number in a series; day of the month)	号	hào	m	3
(measure word for number of family members)	口	kǒu	m	2
(measure word for 1/100 of a kuai, cent)	分	fēn	m	9

English	Characters	Pinyin	Part of Speech	Lesson
(measure word for 1/10 of a kuai, dime (for US money))	毛	máo	m	9
(measure word for pants and long, thin objects)	条	tiáo	m	9
(measure word for people (polite))	位	wèi	m	6
(measure word for quarter (of an hour))	刻	kè	m	3
(measure word for shirts, dresses, jackets, coats, etc.)	件	jiàn	m	9
(measure word for stops of a bus, train, etc.)	站	zhàn	m	10
(measure word for suite or set)	套	tào	m	17
(measure word for tablet; slice)	片	piàn	m	15
(measure word for the basic Chinese monetary unit)	块	kuài	m	9
(measure word for the basic Chinese monetary unit); *yuan*	元	yuán	m	17
meat	肉	ròu	n	12
medicine	药	yào	n	15
medium; middle	中	zhōng	adj	9
meet up; meet with	见面	jiàn miàn	vo	6
merchant; businessperson	商人	shāngrén	n	2
method; way (of doing something)	办法	bànfǎ	n	15
Mexico	墨西哥	Mòxīgē	pn	1
middle	中间	zhōngjiān	n	13
middle school; secondary school	中学	zhōngxué	n	14
mineral water	矿泉水	kuàngquánshuǐ	n	5
minute	分钟	fēnzhōng	n	17
Miss; young lady	小姐	xiǎojiě	n	1
money	钱	qián	n	9
monosodium glutamate (MSG)	味精	wèijīng	n	12
month	月	yuè	n	3
more and more	越来越	yuè lái yuè	adv	15
moreover	再说	zàishuō	conj	15
morning	上午	shàngwǔ	t	6

English	Characters	Pinyin	Part of Speech	Lesson
morning	早上	zǎoshang	t	7
most, (of superlative degree) -est	最	zuì	adv	14
mother, mom	妈妈	māma	n	2
Mother's Day	母亲节	Mǔqīnjié	pn	3
mouth	嘴	zuǐ	n	14
move	搬	bān	v	16
movie	电影	diànyǐng	n	4
Mr.; husband; teacher	先生	xiānsheng	n	1
multi-storied building; floor (of a multi-level building)	楼	lóu	n	14
music	音乐	yīnyuè	n	4
must; have to	得	děi	mv	6

N

English	Characters	Pinyin	Part of Speech	Lesson
name	名字	míngzi	n	1
near	近	jìn	adj	13
need not	不用	búyòng		9
nervous, anxious	紧张	jǐnzhāng	adj	10
new	新	xīn	adj	8
new words; vocabulary	生词	shēngcí	n	7
new year	新年	xīnnián	n	10
New York	纽约	Niǔyuē	pn	1
newspaper	报纸	bàozhǐ	n	17
next one	下个	xià ge		6
noon	中午	zhōngwǔ	n	8
north	北	běi	n	13
Northwest Airlines	西北航空公司	Xīběi Hángkōng Gōngsī	pn	19
nose	鼻子	bízi	n	14
not	没	méi	adv	2
not; no	不	bù	adv	1
not only..., but also...	不但…而且…	búdàn..., érqiě...	conj	11
not until, only then	才	cái	adv	5
notebook	本子	běnzi	n	7

English	Characters	Pinyin	Part of Speech	Lesson
now	现在	xiànzài	t	3
number	号码	hàomǎ	n	16
nurse	护士	hùshi	n	2

O

English	Characters	Pinyin	Part of Speech	Lesson
o'clock (lit. dot, point, thus "points on the clock")	点	diǎn	m	3
of course	当然	dāngrán	adv	18
office	办公室	bàngōngshì	n	6
often	常常	chángcháng	adv	4
older brother	哥哥	gēge	n	2
older female cousin	表姐	biǎojiě	n	14
older sister	姐姐	jiějie	n	2
on the internet	网上	wǎng shang		11
once; a bit	一下	yí xià	n+m	5
one bedroom and one living room	一房一厅	yì fáng yì tīng		17
one-way street	单行道	dānxíngdào	n	13
one-way trip	单程	dānchéng	n	19
oneself	自己	zìjǐ	pr	10
onion	洋葱	yángcōng	n	12
only	只	zhǐ	adv	4
or	还是	háishi	conj	3
or	或者	huòzhě	conj	10
orange (color)	橘红色	júhóngsè	n	9
order food	点菜	diǎn cài	vo	12
other people; another person	别人	biérén	n	4
otherwise	要不然	yàobùrán	conj	15
outer garment; coat; jacket	外套	wàitào	n	9
overcast day	阴天	yīntiān	n	11
overcoat	大衣	dàyī	n	9

P

English	Characters	Pinyin	Part of Speech	Lesson
pants	裤子	kùzi	n	9
paper	纸	zhǐ	n	7
parents; father and mother	父母	fùmǔ	n	19

English	Characters	Pinyin	Part of Speech	Lesson
park	公园	gōngyuán	n	11
(particle to link adverbial and verb)	地	de	p	20
(particle used after a verb to indicate a past experience)	过	guo	p	13
pass	过	guò	v	13
passport	护照	hùzhào	n	19
paternal grandfather	爷爷	yéye	n	20
paternal grandmother	奶奶	nǎinai	n	20
patient	病人	bìngrén	n	15
pay money	付钱	fù qián	vo	9
pay with a credit card	刷卡	shuā kǎ	vo	9
peach	桃儿	táor	n	14
peanuts	花生	huāshēng	n	15
pear	梨	lí	n	14
pedestrian overpass	天桥	tiānqiáo	n	13
pedestrian underpass	地下(通)道	dìxià (tōng)dào	n	13
pen	笔	bǐ	n	7
pencil	铅笔	qiānbǐ	n	7
people; person	人	rén	n	1
Pepsi-Cola	百事可乐	Bǎishìkělè	pn	5
pet	宠物	chǒngwù	n	17
pharmacy	药店	yàodiàn	n	15
physics	物理	wùlǐ	n	8
picnic	野餐	yěcān	v	16
picture; photo	照片	zhàopiàn	n	2
pillow	枕头	zhěntou	n	19
pink	粉红色	fěnhóngsè	n	9
place	地方	dìfang	n	13
plan; plan	打算	dǎsuàn	v/n	19
plan; plan	计划	jìhuà	n/v	19
plant	植物	zhíwù	n	17
plate; dish	盘	pán	n	12
play ball	打球	dǎ qiú	vo	4
play baseball	打棒球	dǎ bàngqiú	vo	18

English	Characters	Pinyin	Part of Speech	Lesson
play chess	下棋	xià qí	vo	4
play table tennis	打乒乓球	dǎ pīngpāngqiú	vo	18
play videogames	玩游戏机	wán yóuxìjī	vo	4
pleasantly cool	凉快	liángkuai	adj	11
please (polite form of request); treat or invite (somebody)	请	qǐng	v	1
polite	客气	kèqi	adj	6
politics	政治	zhèngzhì	n	19
pollen	花粉	huāfěn	n	15
pork	猪肉	zhūròu	n	12
Portuguese language	葡萄牙文	Pútáoyáwén	pn	6
(possessive or descriptive particle)	的	de	p	2
poster	海报	hǎibào	n	17
practice	练习	liànxí	v	6
precisely; exactly	就	jiù	adv	6
(prefix for ordinal numbers)	第	dì	prefix	7
prepare	准备	zhǔnbèi	v	6
press; hold down; weigh down	压	yā	v	18
pretty	漂亮	piàoliang	adj	5
pretty good	不错	búcuò	adj	4
preview	预习	yùxí	v	7
previous one	上个	shàng ge		7
professor	教授	jiàoshòu	n	2
pronunciation	发音	fāyīn	n	8
purple	紫色	zǐsè	n	9
put; place	放	fàng	v	12
put in order	整理	zhěnglǐ	v	16

Q

English	Characters	Pinyin	Part of Speech	Lesson
quarrel; noisy	吵	chǎo	v/adj	17
quarter (of an hour)	刻	kè	m	4
question; problem	问题	wèntí	n	6
(question particle)	吗	ma	qp	1
(question particle)	呢	ne	qp	1
quickly, fast, quick	快	kuài	adv/adj	5

English	Characters	Pinyin	Part of Speech	Lesson
quiet	安静	ānjìng	adj	17
quite a few	好几	hǎo jǐ		15
R				
racket	拍	pāi	n	18
rain	下雨	xià yǔ	vo	11
raise	养	yǎng	v	17
randomly; arbitrarily; messily	乱	luàn	adv	15
read aloud	念	niàn	v	7
really	真	zhēn	adv	7
really painful	疼死	téng sǐ	adj+c	15
receive; accept	收	shu	v	9
recently	最近	zuìjìn	t	8
red	红	hóng	adj	9
refrigerator	冰箱	bīngxiāng	n	15
remember	记得	jìde	v	16
remember; recall	想起来	xiǎng qi lai	vc	16
renminbi (RMB, Chinese currency)	人民币	rénmínbì	n	17
rent	房租	fángzū	n	17
rent	租	zū	v	19
rent out	出租	chūzū	v	17
reserve; book (a ticket, a hotel room, etc.)	订	dìng	v	19
restaurant	饭馆(儿)	fànguǎn(r)	n	12
restroom, toilet	厕所	cèsuǒ	n	15
return (something)	还	huán	v	17
review	复习	fùxí	v	7
ride a bicycle	骑自行车	qí zìxíngchē	vo	10
ride a motorcycle	骑摩托车	qí mótuōchē	vo	10
right	右	yòu	n	13
right; correct	对	duì	adj	4
right away; quickly; in a hurry	赶快	gǎnkuài	adv	15
roast duck	烤鸭	kǎoyā	n	20
room	房间	fángjiān	n	16
round	圆	yuán	adj	14
Russian language	俄文	Éwén	pn	6

S

English	Characters	Pinyin	Part of Speech	Lesson
salt	盐	yán	n	12
same; alike	同	tóng	adj	16
same; alike	一样	yíyàng	adj	9
say; speak	说	shuō	v	6
scheduled flight	航班	hángbān	n	19
school	学校	xuéxiào	n	5
school term; semester/quarter	学期	xuéqī	n	8
seat	位子	wèizi	n	12
second oldest sister	二姐	èrjiě	n	2
security deposit	押金	yājīn	n	17
see	见	jiàn	v	3
see a doctor; (of a doctor) to see a patient	看病	kàn bìng	vo	15
see off or out; take (someone somewhere)	送	sòng	v	10
seem; be like	好像	hǎoxiàng	v	12
sell at a discount; give a discount	打折	dǎ zhé	vo	19
send a text message; (lit.) send a short message	发短信	fā duǎnxìn	vo	10
(sentence-final particle)	啊	a	p	6
(sentence-final particle)	吧	ba	p	5
September	九月	jiǔyuè	n	3
serve as; to be	当	dāng	v	17
serve food	上菜	shàng cài	vo	12
Shanghai	上海	Shànghǎi	pn	1, 12
she; her	她	tā	pr	2
shirt	衬衫	chènshān	n	9
shoes	鞋	xié	n	9
shop assistant; salesclerk	售货员	shòuhuòyuán	n	9
should; ought to	应该	yīnggāi	mv	18
show (a film); perform	演	yǎn	v	16
shrimp	虾	xiā	n	12
side	旁边	pángbiān	n	13
simple	简单	jiǎndān	adj	18

English	Characters	Pinyin	Part of Speech	Lesson
simultaneously; at the same time	一边	yìbiān	adv	8
sing (a song)	唱歌(儿)	chàng gē(r)	vo	4
sing karaoke	唱卡拉OK	chàng kǎlā'ōukēi	vo	16
sit	坐	zuò	v	5
size	大小	dàxiǎo	n	9
size	号	hào	n	9
skirt	裙子	qúnzi	n	9
sleep	睡觉	shuì jiào	vo	4
slow	慢	màn	adj	7
small; little	小	xiǎo	adj	4
smart; bright; clever	聪明	cōngming	adj	14
snacks	零食	língshí	n	14
sneeze	打喷嚏	dǎpēnti	vo	15
snow	下雪	xià xuě	vo	11
so	所以	suǒyǐ	conj	4
so; such	这么	zhème	pr	7
(indicating degree) so, such	那么	nàme	pr	11
soccer; football	足球	zúqiú	n	18
socks	袜子	wàzi	n	9
sofa	沙发	shāfā	n	17
soft drink; soda pop	汽水（儿）	qìshuǐ(r)	n	5, 14
soldier; military officer	军人	jūnrén	n	2
some	有的	yǒude	pr	4
son	儿子	érzi	n	2
sorry	对不起	duìbuqǐ	v	5
sound recording; record	录音	lùyīn	n/vo	7
sour	酸	suān	adj	12
south	南	nán	n	13
Spanish language	西班牙文	Xībānyáwén	pn	6
spend	花	huā	v	10
spend; take (effort)	费	fèi	v	16
sports	运动	yùndòng	n	13
sportswear; athletic clothing	运动服	yùndòngfú	n	18
spring	春天	chūntiān	n	11

English	Characters	Pinyin	Part of Speech	Lesson
Sprite	雪碧	Xuěbì	pn	5
stereo system	音响	yīnxiǎng	n	17
stir-fried noodles	炒面	chǎomiàn	n	12
store; shop	商店	shāngdiàn	n	9
straight; continuously	一直	yìzhí	adv	13
strawberry	草莓	cǎoméi	n	14
strength; effort	力气	lìqi	n	16
(structural particle)	得	de	p	7
student	学生	xuésheng	n	1
study; learn	学	xué	v	7
study; learn	学习	xuéxí	v	7
style	样子	yàngzi	n	9
subway	地铁	dìtiě	n	10
suit (western-style)	西装	xīzhuāng	n	9
suitable	合适	héshì	adj	9
suitcase; box	箱子	xiāngzi	n	20
summer	夏天	xiàtiān	n	11
summer term	暑期	shǔqī	n	14
summer vacation	暑假	shǔjià	n	19
(one's) surname is...; be surnamed; surname	姓	xìng	v/n	1
sunny day	晴天	qíngtiān	n	11
sweater (woolen)	毛衣	máoyī	n	9
sweet	甜	tián	adj	12
swim	游泳	yóu yǒng	vo	18

T

English	Characters	Pinyin	Part of Speech	Lesson
T-shirt	T恤衫	T-xùshān	n	9
table	桌子	zhuōzi	n	12
Taipei	台北	Táiběi	pn	19
take; get	拿	ná	v	13
take a bath/shower	洗澡	xǐ zǎo	vo	8
take a break; to rest	休息	xiūxi	v	15
take a cable car, trolley bus, or tram	坐电车	zuò diànchē	vo	10

English	Characters	Pinyin	Part of Speech	Lesson
take a taxi	打车	dǎ chē	vo	10
take a taxi (in Taiwan)	坐计程车	zuò jìchéngchē	vo	10
(of airplanes) take off	起飞	qǐfēi	v	20
talk	说话	shuō huà	vo	7
tangerine	橘子	júzi	n	14
taxi	出租汽車	chūzū qìchē	n	10
tea	茶	chá	n	5
teach	教	jiāo	v	7
teacher	老师	lǎoshī	n	1
Teacher Chang	常老师	Cháng lǎoshī	pn	6
television	电视	diànshì	n	4
tell	告诉	gàosu	v	8
tennis	网球	wǎngqiú	n	18
textbook	课本	kèběn	n	7
text of a lesson	课文	kèwén	n	7
thank	谢谢	xièxie	v	3
Thanksgiving	感恩节	Gǎn'ēnjié	pn	3
that	那	nà	pr	2
then	然后	ránhòu	adv	10
there	那里	nàli	pr	17
there	那儿	nàr	pr	8
thin, slim (usually of a person or animal); lean	瘦	shòu	adj	20
things; objects	东西	dōngxi	n	9
thirsty	渴	kě	adj	12
this	这	zhè	pr	2
this year	今年	jīnnián	t	3
thousand	千	qiān	nu	19
Thursday	星期四	xīngqīsì	n	3
ticket	票	piào	n	10
time	时间	shíjiān	n	6
time (a point in); moment; time (a duration of)	时候	shíhou	n	4
tired	累	lèi	adj	8
to; for	给	gěi	prep	6

English	Characters	Pinyin	Part of Speech	Lesson
today	今天	jīntiān	t	3
tofu; bean curd	豆腐	dòufu	n	12
together	一起	yìqǐ	adv	5
Tokyo	东京	Dōngjīng	pn	13
Tom	汤姆	Tāngmǔ	pn	14
tomorrow	明天	míngtiān	t	3
too; also	也	yě	adv	1
too; extremely	太…了	tài…le		3
tour guide	导游	dǎoyóu	n	19
towards	往	wǎng	prep	13
traffic light	红绿灯	hónglǜdēng	n	13
travel	旅行	lǚxíng	v	16
travel agency	旅行社	lǚxíngshè	n	19
travel by	坐	zuò	v	10
travel by train	坐火车	zuò huǒchē	vo	10
travel by ship; take a boat	坐船	zuò chuán	vo	10
troublesome	麻烦	máfan	adj	10
try	试	shì	v	9
turn	拐	guǎi	v	13
twelve	十二	shí'èr	nu	3
(coll.) two	俩	liǎ	nu+m	16
two; a couple of	两	liǎng	nu	2

U

English	Characters	Pinyin	Part of Speech	Lesson
uncle	叔叔	shūshu	n	20
understand	懂	dǒng	v	7
upper garment	上衣	shàngyī	n	9
U.S. currency	美元	Měiyuán	n	17
use	用	yòng	v	8
usually	平常	píngcháng	adv	7

V

English	Characters	Pinyin	Part of Speech	Lesson
Valentine's Day	情人节	Qíngrénjié	pn	3
vegetarian; made from vegetables	素	sù	adj	12
vegetarian meal	素餐	sùcān	n	19

English	Characters	Pinyin	Part of Speech	Lesson
very	很	hěn	adv	3
very, extremely, exceedingly	非常	fēicháng	adv	11
very; rather	挺	tǐng	adv	9
vicinity; neighborhood; nearby area	附近	fùjìn	n	17
Vietnam	越南	Yuènán	pn	1
visa	签证	qiānzhèng	n	19
visit a museum	参观博物馆	cānguān bówùguǎn	vo	16

W

English	Characters	Pinyin	Part of Speech	Lesson
wait; wait for	等	děng	v	6
waiter; attendant	服务员	fúwùyuán	n	12
walk	走路	zǒu lù	vo	10, 17
Wang Hong	王红	Wáng Hóng	pn	14
Wang Peng	王朋	Wáng Péng	pn	1
want	要	yào	v	5
want to; would like to; think	想	xiǎng	mv	4
warm	暖和	nuǎnhuo	adj	11
watch; look; read	看	kàn	v	4
water	水	shuǐ	n	5
water dispenser	饮水器	yǐnshuǐqì	n	20
watermelon	西瓜	xīgua	n	14
we	我们	wǒmen	pr	3
wear; put on	穿	chuān	v	9
weather	天气	tiānqì	n	11
week	星期	xīngqī	n	3
weekend	周末	zhōumò	n	4
welcome	欢迎	huānyíng	v	20
west	西	xī	n	13
wet; humid	潮湿	cháoshī	adj	11
what	什么	shénme	qpr	1
where	哪里	nǎli	pr	7
where	哪儿	nǎr	qpr	5
which	哪	nǎ/něi	qpr	6

English	Characters	Pinyin	Part of Speech	Lesson
who	谁	shéi	qpr	2
why	为什么	wèishénme	qpr	3
will	会	huì	mv	11
will; be going to; want to, have a desire to	要	yào	mv	6
wind	风	fēng	n	11
window	窗户	chuānghu	n	19
windowshop	逛街	guàng jiē	vo	4
winter	冬天	dōngtiān	n	11
winter vacation	寒假	hánjià	n	10
wish (well)	祝	zhù	v	8
with	跟	gēn	prep	6
work at a temporary job (often part time)	打工	dǎ gōng	vo	19
worker	工人	gōngrén	n	2
worry	担心	dān xīn	vo	18
write	写	xiě	v	7
writing brush	毛笔	máobǐ	n	7
wrong	错	cuò	adj	12

Y

English	Characters	Pinyin	Part of Speech	Lesson
year (of age)	岁	suì	n	3
yellow	黄	huáng	adj	9
yesterday	昨天	zuótiān	t	4
you	你	nǐ	pr	1
you (honorific for 你)	您	nín	pr	6
younger brother	弟弟	dìdi	n	2
younger sister	妹妹	mèimei	n	2

Z

English	Characters	Pinyin	Part of Speech	Lesson
zebra crossing; pedestrian crosswalk	斑马线	bānmǎxiàn	n	13

Vocabulary by Grammar Category and by Lesson

Lesson & Section	noun	measure word	pronoun	numeral	verb	modal verb
L11-1	天气 公园 碟				下雪 约 滑冰 预报 办	会
L11-2	冬天 夏天 春天 秋天		那么		出去 下雨 面试 回去	
L12-1	饭馆(儿) 位子 服务员 桌子 盘子 饺子 家常豆腐 肉 碗 酸辣汤 味精 盐 白菜 青菜 冰茶	些			好像 服务 点菜 放 卖完 上菜	
L12-2	师傅 糖醋鱼 牛肉 鱼 黄瓜 米饭 饭卡				红烧 凉拌 忘 带	

	adjective	adverb	preposition	conjunction	time word	particle	others	proper noun
	暖和 冷	更	比	不但…， 而且…	刚才		网上	
	好玩儿 糟糕 热 舒服	非常 又						加州
	素 渴 够 饿	刚						
	好吃 甜 酸 错 清楚	极					没关系	

Lesson & Section	noun	measure word	pronoun	numeral	verb	modal verb
L13-1	中心 运动场 旁边 活动 中间 书店 地方 里边				上 听说	
L13-2	中国城 地图 南 路口 西 东 北 前 红绿灯 右 左 前面	次			拿 过 拐	
L14-1	舞会 表姐 中学 礼物 饮料 水果 花 苹果 梨 西瓜 楼	本 把			送 爱 住 接	
L14-2	钟头 暑期 班 去年 狗 脸 眼睛 嘴 蛋糕				以为 长 属 像 长大	

adjective	adverb	preposition	conjunction	time word	particle	others	proper noun
远 近		离					
	一直	从 往			过	哎	文京 东京 日本 日文
重							王红
聪明 用功 可爱 圆	一定 最						海伦 汤姆

Lesson & Section	noun	measure word	pronoun	numeral	verb	modal verb
L15-1	医院 病人 肚子 夜里 厕所 冰箱 药 小时 办法	片 遍			看病 发烧 躺下 检查 吃坏 打针	
L15-2	身体 药店 保险				感冒 生病 过敏 休息	
L16-1	印象 力气				成 演 费	
L16-2	号码 房间 电				记得 想起来 搬 打扫 整理 旅行	
L17-1	报纸 广告 附近 公寓 分钟 卧室 厨房 卫生间 客厅 家具	套			吵 做饭 出租 走路	
L17-2	沙发 饭桌 椅子 书桌 书架 房租 美元 人民币 费 押金 宠物 兴趣	元	那里		还 准 养	

adjective	adverb	preposition	conjunction	time word	particle	others	proper noun
疼死	最好	把				好几	
痒 健康 懒 乱	赶快 越来越		要不然 再说	后天		上次 一言为定	
同	就					俩	
	可能	连					
干净 安静	差不多		另外			一房一厅	

Lesson & Section	noun	measure word	pronoun	numeral	verb	modal verb
L18-1	网球 球拍 篮球				怕 跑步 游泳 淹死	愿意
L18-2	水平 足球 比赛 脚 手 运动服				上大学 提高 踢 抱 压 担心	应该
L19-1	公司 计划 暑假 父母 首都 政治 文化 导游 护照 签证 旅行社				放假 实习 打工 打算 订	
L19-2	初 单程 航空 航班 窗户 走道 素餐 旅馆	份		千	往返 查 打折 转机 靠 租	
L20-1	行李 包 箱子 登机牌 登机口				托运 重 超 哭 照顾 起飞 小心	
L20-2	叔叔 阿姨 爷爷 奶奶 烤鸭				欢迎	

adjective	adverb	preposition	conjunction	time word	particle	others	proper noun
胖 简单 难受 危险	当然						
国际 美式 棒		为了 被				半天	
有名	马上					名胜古迹	长城 香港 台北
						直飞	中国国际 航空公司 西北航空 公司
					地	一路平安	
瘦							首都机场

Alternate Characters (Texts in Traditional Form)

Lesson 11

Dialogue I: Tomorrow's Weather Will Be Even Better!

(Gao Xiaoyin is looking out the window.)

 今天天氣比①昨天好，不下雪了②。

我約了朋友明天去公園滑冰，不知道天氣會③怎麼樣？

我剛才看了網上的天氣預報，明天天氣比今天更好。不但不會下雪，而且❶會暖和一點兒④。

是嗎？太好了！

你約了誰去滑冰？

白英愛。

你約了白英愛？可是她今天早上坐飛機去紐約了。

真的啊？那我明天怎麼辦？

 你還是在家看碟❷吧！

Dialogue II: The Weather Here Is Awful!

（高文中在網上找白英愛聊天兒。）

 英愛，紐約那麼好玩兒，你怎麼在網上，沒出去？

這兒的天氣非常糟糕。

怎麼了？❶

昨天下大雨，今天又⑤下雨了。

這個週末這兒天氣很好，你快一點兒回來吧。

這個週末紐約也會暖和一點兒。我下個星期有一個面試，還不能回去。

我在加州找了一個工作，你也去吧。加州冬天不冷，夏天不熱，春天和秋天更舒服。

加州好是好⑥，可是我更喜歡紐約。

Lesson 12

Dialogue I: Dining Out

（在飯館兒）

 請進，請進。

 人怎麼這麼❶多？好像一個位子都①沒有了。

 服務員②，請問，還有沒有位子？

有，有，有。那張桌子沒有人。

＊　＊　＊

 兩位想吃點兒什麼？

 王朋，你點菜吧。

 好。先給我們兩盤餃子，要素的。

 除了餃子以外，還要什麼？

 李友，你說呢？

 還要一盤家常豆腐，不要放肉，我吃素。

 我們的家常豆腐沒有肉。

 還要兩碗酸辣湯❸，請別放味精，少②放點兒鹽。有小白菜嗎？

 對不起，小白菜剛③賣完④。

 那就不要青菜了。

 那喝點兒❹什麼呢？

 我要一杯冰茶。李友，你喝什麼？

 我很渴，請給我一杯可樂，多放點兒冰。

 好，兩盤餃子，一盤家常豆腐，兩碗酸辣湯，一杯冰茶，一杯可樂，多放冰。還要別的嗎？

 不要別的了，這些夠❺了。服務員，我們都餓了，請上菜快一點兒。

 沒問題，菜很快就能做好⑤。

Dialogue II: Eating in a Cafeteria

（今天是星期四，學生餐廳有中國菜，師傅是
上海人。）

 師傅❶，請問今天晚飯有什麼好吃的？

我們今天有糖醋魚，甜甜的⑥、酸酸的，好吃
極了❷，你買一個吧。

好。今天有没有紅燒牛肉？

没有。你已經要魚了，別吃肉了。來⑦個涼拌
黃瓜吧？

好。再來一碗米飯。一共多少錢？

糖醋魚，四塊五，涼拌黃瓜，一塊七；一碗
米飯，五毛錢。一共六塊七。

師傅，糟糕，我忘了帶飯卡了。這是十塊
錢。

找你三塊三。

師傅，錢你找錯了，多找了我一塊錢。

對不起，我没有看清楚。

没關係❸。

下個星期四再來。

好，再見。

Lesson 13

Dialogue I: Where Are You Off To?

小白，下課了？上哪兒去❶？

您好，常老師。我想去學校的電腦中心，不知道怎麼走，聽說就在運動場旁邊①。

電腦中心沒有②運動場那麼③遠。你知道學校圖書館在哪裏②嗎？

知道，離王朋的宿舍不遠。

電腦中心離圖書館很近，就在圖書館和學生活動中心中間。

常老師，您去哪兒呢？

我想到學校書店去買書④。

書店在什麼地方❸？

就在學生活動中心裏邊。我們一起走吧。

好。

Dialogue II: Going to Chinatown

我們去中國城吃中國飯吧！

我沒去過⑤中國城，不知道中國城在哪兒。

沒問題❶，你開車，我告訴你怎麼走。

你有地圖嗎？給我看看⑥。

地圖在宿舍裏，我忘了拿來了。

沒有地圖，走錯了怎麼辦？

沒有地圖沒關係，中國城我去過很多次，不用地圖也能找到⑦。你從這兒一直往南開，過三個路口，往西一拐❷就⑧到了。

哎，我不知道東南西北❸。

那你一直往前開，過三個紅綠燈，往右一拐就到了。

（過了三個路口）

不對，不對。你看，這個路口只能往左拐，不能往右拐。

那就是下一個路口。往右拐，再往前開。到了，到了，你看見了嗎？前面有很多中國字。

那不是中文，那是日文，我們到了小東京了。

是嗎？那我們不吃中國飯了，吃日本飯吧！

Lesson 14

Dialogue I: Let's Go to a Party!

（李友給王朋打電話。）

 王朋，你做什麼呢^①？

我看書呢。

今天高小音過生日❶，晚上我們在她家開舞會，你能去嗎？

能去。幾點？

七點。我們先吃飯，吃完飯再唱歌跳舞。

有哪些人？

小音和她的男朋友，小音的表姐❷，白英愛，你妹妹王紅，聽說還有小音的中學同學。

你要送給小音什麼生日禮物？

我買了一本書送給她。

那我帶什麼東西？

飲料或者水果都可以。

那我帶一些飲料，再買一把花兒。

小音愛吃水果，我再買一些蘋果、梨和西瓜吧。

你住的地方②離小音家很遠，水果很重，我開車來接你，我們一起去吧。

好，我六點半在樓下等你。

Dialogue II: Attending a Birthday Party

（在高小音家）

王朋，李友，快進來。

小音，祝你生日快樂！這是送給你的生日禮物。

謝謝！(She opens the gift.) 太好了！我一直想買這本書。帶這麼多東西，你們太客氣了。

哥哥，李友，你們來了❶。

啊。小紅，你怎麼樣？

我很好。每天都在學英文。

小紅，你每天練習英文練習多長時間③？

三個半鐘頭❷。還看兩個鐘頭的英文電視。

哎，你們兩個是什麼時候到的④？

剛到。

白英愛沒跟你們一起來嗎？

她還⑤沒來？我以為❸她已經來了。

王朋，李友，來，我給你們介紹一下，這是我表姐海倫，這是她的兒子湯姆。

你好，海倫。

你好，王朋。文中和小音都說你又聰明④又用功⑥。

哪裏，哪裏。你的中文說得真好，是在哪兒學的？

在暑期班⑤學的。

哎，湯姆長⑥得真可愛！你們看，他笑了。他幾歲了？

剛一歲，是去年生的，屬狗。

你們看，他的臉圓圓的，眼睛大大的，鼻子高高的，嘴不大也不小，長得很像海倫。

媽媽這麼漂亮，兒子長大一定也很帥。

來，來，來，我們吃蛋糕吧。

等等白英愛吧。她最愛吃蛋糕。

Lesson 15

Dialogue I: My Stomachache Is Killing Me!

（病人去醫院看病）

醫生，我肚子疼死①了。

你昨天吃什麼東西了？

我姐姐上個星期過生日，蛋糕沒吃完。昨天晚上我吃了幾口②，夜裏肚子就疼起來了③，今天早上上了好幾次②廁所。

你把④蛋糕放在哪兒了？

放在冰箱裏了。

放了幾天了？

五、六❶天了。

發燒嗎？

不發燒。

你躺下。先檢查一下。

＊　＊　＊

你吃蛋糕把肚子吃壞了。

要不要打針？

不用打針，吃這種藥❷就可以。一天三次，一次兩片。

醫生，一天吃幾次？請您再說一遍。

 一天三次，一次兩片。

 好！飯前❸吃還是飯後吃？

 飯前飯後都可以。不過，你最好二十四小時不吃飯。

 那我要餓死了。不行，這個辦法不好！

Dialogue II: Allergies

 王朋，你怎麼了？眼睛怎麼紅紅的，感冒了嗎？

 沒感冒。我也不知道怎麼了，最近這幾天身體很不舒服。眼睛又紅又癢。

 你一定是對❺什麼過敏了。

 我想也是，所以去藥店買了一些藥。已經吃了四、五種了，花了不少錢，都沒有用。

把你買的藥拿出來給我看看。

這些就是。

這些藥沒有用。為什麼不去看醫生？你沒有健康保險嗎？

我有保險。可是我這個學期功課很多，看醫生太花時間。

那你也得趕快去看醫生❶。要不然病會越來越⑥重。

我想再吃點兒別的藥試試❷。我上次生病，没去看醫生，休息兩天，最後也好了。

不行，不行，你太懶了。再説⑦，你不能自己亂吃藥。走，我跟你看病去。

Lesson 16

Dialogue I: Seeing a Movie

王朋跟李友在同一個學校學習，他們認識已經快半年了。王朋常常幫李友練習説中文。他們也常常一起出去玩兒，每次都玩兒得①很高興。李友對王朋的印象❶很好，王朋也很喜歡李友，他們成了好朋友。

* * *

這個週末學校演❷一個中國電影，我們一起去看，好嗎？

好啊！不過，聽説看電影的人很多，買得到②票嗎？

票已經買好了，我費了很大的力氣才買到。

好極了！我早③就想看中國電影了。還有別人跟我們一起去嗎？

沒有，就③我們倆④。

 好。什麼時候？

 後天晚上八點。

 看電影以前，我請你吃晚飯。

 太好了！一言為定⑤。

Dialogue II: Turning Down an Invitation

 喂，請問李友小姐在嗎？

 我就是。請問你是哪一位？

 我姓費，你還記得❶我嗎？

 姓費？

你還記得上個月高小音的生日舞會嗎？我就是最後請你跳舞的那個人。你再想想。想起來了嗎？

對不起，我想不起來。

我是高小音的中學同學。

是嗎？你是怎麼知道我的電話號碼的？

是小音告訴我的。

費先生，你有事嗎？

這個週末你有空兒嗎？我想請你去跳舞。

這個週末不行，下個星期我有三個考試。

没關係，下個週末怎麼樣？你考完試，我們好好兒❷玩兒玩兒。

下個週末也不行，我要從宿舍搬出去④，得打掃、整理房間。

你看下下個週末，好不好？

對不起，下下個週末更不行了，我要跟我的男朋友去紐約旅行。

…那…

費先生，對不起，我的手機沒電了。再見！

喂…喂…

Lesson 17

Narrative: Finding a Better Place

王朋在學校的宿舍住了兩個學期了①。他覺得宿舍太吵，睡不好覺，房間太小，連電腦都②放不下③，再說也沒有地方可以做飯，很不方便，所以準備下個學期搬出去住。他找房子找了一個多④月了，可是還沒有找到合適的。剛才他在報紙上看到了一個廣告，說學校附近有一套公寓出租，離學校很近，走路只要五分鐘，很方便。公寓有一個臥室，一個廚房，一個衛生間❶，一個客廳，還帶傢具。王朋覺得這套公寓可能對他很合適。

Dialogue: Calling about an Apartment for Rent

喂，請問你們是不是有公寓出租？

有啊，一房一廳❶，非常乾淨，還帶傢具。

有什麼傢具？

客廳裏有一套沙發、一張飯桌跟四把椅子。臥室裏有一張床、一張書桌和一個書架。

你們那裏安靜不安靜？

非常安靜。

每個月房租多少錢？

八百五十元。

八百五十美元？人民幣差不多是…有一點兒貴，能不能便宜點兒？

那你不用付水電費。

要不要付押金？

要多付一個月的房租當押金，搬出去的時候還給你。另外，我們公寓不准養寵物。

没關係，我對養寵物沒有興趣❷，什麼寵物都⑤不養。

那太好了。你今天下午來看看吧。

好。

Lesson 18

Dialogue I: My Gut Keeps Getting Bigger and Bigger!

你看，我的肚子越來越大了。

你平常吃得那麼多，又❶不運動，當然越來越胖了。

那怎麼辦呢？

如果怕胖，你一個星期運動兩、三次，每次半個小時，肚子就會小了。

我兩年沒運動了①，做什麼運動呢？

最簡單的運動是跑步。

冬天那麼冷，夏天那麼熱，跑步太難受②了。

你打網球吧。

打網球得買網球拍、網球鞋，你知道，網球拍、網球鞋貴極了！

找幾個人打籃球吧。買個籃球很便宜。

那每次都得打電話約人，麻煩死了。

你去游泳吧。不用找人，也不用花很多錢，什麼時候去都可以。

游泳？我怕水，太危險了，淹死了怎麼辦？

我也沒辦法了。你不願意運動，那就胖下去③吧。

Dialogue II: Watching American Football

王朋的妹妹王紅剛從北京來，要在美國上大學❶，現在住在高小音家裏學英文。為了❷提高英文水平，她每天都看兩個小時的電視④。

* * *

 快把電視打開，足球比賽開始了。

 是嗎？我也喜歡看足球賽❸。…這是什麼足球④啊？怎麼不是圓的？

這不是國際足球，這是美式足球。

足球應該用腳踢，為什麼那個人用手抱著③跑呢？

 美式足球可以用手。

你看，你看，那麼多人都壓在一起，下面的人不是要被⑥壓壞了嗎？

別擔心，他們的身體都很棒，而且還穿特別的運動服，沒問題。

我看了半天⑤也看不懂。還是看別的吧。

 你在美國住半年就會喜歡了。我男朋友看美式足球的時候，常常連飯都忘了吃。

Lesson 19

Dialogue I: Traveling to Beijing

李友，時間過得真快，馬上就要放假了，我們的同學，有的去暑期班學習，有的去公司實習，有的回家打工，你有什麼計劃？

我還沒有想好。你呢，王朋？

我暑假打算❶回北京去看父母。

是嗎？我聽說北京這個城市很有意思。

當然。北京是中國的首都，也是中國的政治、文化中心，有很多名勝古蹟。

對啊，長城很有名。

還有，北京的好飯館多得不得了①。

真的？我去過香港、台北，還沒去過北京，要是能去北京就好了。

那你跟我一起回去吧，我當你的導遊。

真的嗎？那太好了！護照我已經有了，我得趕快辦簽證❷。

那我馬上給旅行社打電話訂飛機票。

Dialogue II: Planning an Itinerary

 天一旅行社，你好。

 你好。請問六月初❶到北京的機票多少錢？

 您要買單程票還是往返票？

 我要買兩張往返票。

 你想買哪家航空公司的？

 哪家的便宜，就買哪②家的。

 請等等，我查一下…好幾家航空公司都有航班❷。中國國際航空公司，一千五③，直飛。西北航空公司正在打折③，差不多一千四百六十，可是要轉機。

 西北只比國航❹便宜四十幾塊錢④，我還是買國航吧。

 哪一天走❺？哪一天回來？

 六月十號走，七月十五號回來。現在可以訂位子嗎？

 可以。你們喜歡靠窗戶的還是靠走道的？

 靠走道的。對了❻，我朋友吃素，麻煩幫她訂一份素餐。

 沒問題…您在北京要訂旅館、租車嗎？

 不用，謝謝！

Lesson 20

Dialogue I: Checking In at the Airport

（在國航的服務台）

 小姐，這是我們的①機票。

請把護照給我看看。你們有幾件行李要托運？

兩件。這個包不托運，我們帶上飛機。

麻煩❶您把箱子拿上來。

小姐，沒超重吧？

沒有。這是你們的護照、機票，這是登機牌❷。請到五號登機口❸上飛機。

謝謝。

*　　*　　*

哥哥，你們去北京了，就我一個人在這兒。

小紅，別哭，我們幾個星期就回來，你好好兒地①學英文，別亂跑。

不是幾個星期就回來，是幾個星期以後才回來。

別擔心，我姐姐小音會照顧你。

對，別擔心。

飛機幾點起飛？

 中午十二點，還有兩個多小時。

 白英愛，你什麼時候去紐約實習？

 我不去紐約了。文中幫我在加州找了一份實習工作。

 對，我們下個星期開車去加州。

 是嗎？一邊兒開車，一邊兒玩兒，太好了。

 開車小心。祝你們玩兒得①高興。

 祝你們一路平安。到了北京以後②，別忘了給我們發個電子郵件。

 好，那我們秋天見。

 下個學期見。

 再見！

Dialogue II: Arriving in Beijing

（在北京首都機場）

 小朋！

 爸，媽！

 累壞了吧？

 還好③。爸，媽，我給你們介紹一下，這是我的同學李友。

叔叔，阿姨④❶，你們好。

歡迎你來北京。

李友，你的中文説得真好。

謝謝。是因為王朋教得好。

哪裏，是因為你聰明。

哎，你們倆都聰明。

小朋，你好像瘦了點兒。是不是打工太忙，
沒有時間吃飯？

我没瘦。我常常運動，身體比以前棒多了。

小紅怎麽樣？

她很好，英文水平提高了很多。

走吧，我們上車以後，再慢慢兒地聊吧。
爺爺、奶奶在烤鴨店等我們呢！

烤鴨店？